14th Workshop on Graph-Based Methods for Natural Language Processing (TextGraphs-14)

Held online due to COVID-19

Barcelona, Spain
13 December 2020

ISBN: 978-1-7138-2840-2

Printed from e-media with permission by:

Curran Associates, Inc.
57 Morehouse Lane
Red Hook, NY 12571

Some format issues inherent in the e-media version may also appear in this print version.

Copyright© (2020) by the Association for Computational Linguistics
All rights reserved.
Copyright for individual papers remains with the authors and are licensed under a Creative Commons 4.0
license, CC-BY. (https://creativecommons.org/licenses/by/4.0/)

Printed with permission by Curran Associates, Inc. (2021)

For permission requests, please contact the Association for Computational Linguistics
at the address below.

Association for Computational Linguistics
209 N. Eighth Street
Stroudsburg, Pennsylvania 18360

Phone: 1-570-476-8006
Fax: 1-570-476-0860

acl@aclweb.org

Additional copies of this publication are available from:

Curran Associates, Inc.
57 Morehouse Lane
Red Hook, NY 12571 USA
Phone: 845-758-0400
Fax: 845-758-2633
Email: curran@proceedings.com
Web: www.proceedings.com

COLING 2020

Graph-based Methods for Natural Language Processing

Proceedings of the Fourteenth Workshop (TextGraphs-14)

December 13, 2020
Barcelona, Spain (Online)

Copyright of each paper stays with the respective authors (or their employers).

Introduction

Welcome to TextGraphs, the Workshop on Graph-Based Methods for Natural Language Processing. The fourteenth edition of our workshop is being organized online on December 13, 2020, in conjunction with the 28th International Conference on Computational Linguistics (COLING).

The workshops in the TextGraphs series have published and promoted the synergy between the field of Graph Theory (GT) and Natural Language Processing (NLP) for over a decade. The target audience of our workshop comprises of researchers working on problems related to either Graph Theory or graph-based algorithms applied to Natural Language Processing, Social Media, and the Semantic Web.

TextGraphs addresses a broad spectrum of research areas within NLP. This is because, besides traditional NLP applications like parsing, word sense disambiguation, semantic role labeling, and information extraction, graph-based solutions also target web-scale applications like information propagation in social networks, rumor proliferation, e-reputation, language dynamics learning, and future events prediction.

The selection process was competitive: we received 17 submissions and accepted 10 of them for oral presentation (6 long papers, 3 short papers, and 1 non-archival paper). This resulted in the overall acceptance rate of 59%.

Similarly to the last year, we organized a shared task on Multi-Hop Inference for Explanation Regeneration. The goal of the task was to provide detailed gold explanations for standardized elementary science exam questions by selecting facts from a knowledge base. This year's shared task on multi-hop explanation regeneration attracted ten teams around the world, substantially advancing the state-of-the-art in this challenging problem. Four participants' reports and one non-archival report along with the shared task overview by its organizers are also presented at the workshop.

We thank Danai Koutra, Sujith Ravi, and Yizhou Sun for their invited talks.

Finally, we are thankful to the members of the program committee for their valuable and high quality reviews. All submissions have benefited from their expert feedback. Their timely contribution was the basis for accepting an excellent list of papers and making the fourteenth edition of TextGraphs a success.

Dmitry Ustalov, Swapna Somasundaran, Alexander Panchenko, Fragkiskos D. Malliaros,
Ioana Hulpuş, Peter Jansen, and Abhik Jana
TextGraphs-14 Organizers
December 2020

Organizers:

Dmitry Ustalov, Yandex, Russian Federation
Swapna Somasundaran, Educational Testing Service, USA
Alexander Panchenko, Skolkovo Institute of Science and Technology, Russian Federation
Fragkiskos D. Malliaros, Paris-Saclay University, France
Ioana Hulpuş, University of Mannheim, Germany
Peter Jansen, University of Arizona, USA
Abhik Jana, University of Hamburg, Germany

Program Committee:

Željko Agić, Unity Technologies, Denmark
Ilseyar Alimova, Kazan Federal University, Russian Federation
Prithviraj Ammanabrolu, Georgia Institute of Technology, USA
Martin Andrews, Red Dragon AI, Singapore
Amir Bakarov, Higher School of Economics, Russian Federation
Tomáš Brychcín, University of West Bohemia, Czech Republic
Ruben Cartuyvels, Catholic University of Leuven, Belgium
Flavio Massimiliano Cecchini, Università Cattolica del Sacro Cuore, Italy
Tanmoy Chakraborty, Indraprastha Institute of Information Technology Delhi (IIIT-D), India
Chen Chen, Magagon Labs, USA
Monojit Choudhury, Microsoft Research, India
Alexandre Duval, Paris-Saclay University, France
Jennifer D'Souza, TIB Leibniz Information Centre for Science and Technology, Germany
Stefano Faralli, University of Rome Unitelma Sapienza, Italy
Goran Glavaš, University of Mannheim, Germany
Natalia Grabar, Université de Lille, France
Aayushee Gupta, IIIT Bangalore, India
Binod Gyawali, Educational Testing Service, USA
Carlos Gómez-Rodríguez, Universidade da Coruña, Spain
Tomáš Hercig, University of West Bohemia, Czech Republic
Dmitry Ilvovsky, Higher School of Economics, Russian Federation
Ming Jiang, University of Illinois at Urbana-Champaign, USA
Sammy Khalife, École Polytechnique, France
Andrey Kutuzov, University of Oslo, Norway
Anne Lauscher, University of Mannheim, Germany
Weibin Li, Baidu, China
Valentin Malykh, Huawei Noah's Ark Lab / Kazan Federal University, Russian Federation
Gabor Melli, OpenGov, USA
Clayton Morrison, University of Arizona, USA
Animesh Mukherjee, IIT Kharagpur, India
Matthew Mulholland, Educational Testing Service, USA
Giannis Nikolentzos, École Polytechnique, France
Enrique Noriega-Atala, University of Arizona, USA
Damien Nouvel, Inalco ERTIM, France
Aditya Girish Pawate, IIT Kharagpur, India
Jan Wira Gotama Putra, Tokyo Institute of Technology, Japan

Zimeng Qiu, Amazon Alexa AI, USA
Steffen Remus, University of Hamburg, Germany
Leonardo F. R. Ribeiro, TU Darmstadt, Germany
Brian Riordan, Educational Testing Service, USA
Viktor Schlegel, University of Manchester, UK
Natalie Schluter, IT University of Copenhagen, Denmark
Robert Schwarzenberg, German Research Center For Artificial Intelligence (DFKI), Germany
Rebecca Sharp, University of Arizona, USA
Artem Shelmanov, Skolkovo Institute of Science and Technology, Russian Federation
Khalil Simaan, University of Amsterdam, The Netherlands
Konstantinos Skianis, BLUAI, Greece
Saatviga Sudhahar, Healx, UK
Mihai Surdeanu, University of Arizona, USA
Yuki Tagawa, Fuji Xerox Co., Ltd., Japan
Mokanarangan Thayaparan, University of Manchester, UK
Antoine Tixier, École Polytechnique, France
Nicolas Turenne, BNU HKBU United International College (UIC), China
Elena Tutubalina, Insilico Medicine, Russian Federation
Vaibhav Vaibhav, Apple, USA
Serena Villata, Université Côte d'Azur, CNRS, Inria, I3S, France
Xiang Zhao, National University of Defense Technology, China

Invited Speakers:

Danai Koutra, University of Michigan, Ann Arbor, USA
Sujith Ravi, Amazon, USA
Yizhou Sun, UCLA, USA

Table of Contents

Workshop Program

Sunday, December 13, 2020

14:00–14:10   **Opening Session**

14:10–15:00   **Invited Talk by Sujith Ravi (Amazon Alexa AI, USA)**

15:00–15:10   *Break*

15:10–16:00   **Invited Talk by Danai Koutra (University of Michigan, Ann Arbor, USA)**

16:00–16:30   **Oral Presentations Session 1**

16:00–16:30   *A survey of embedding models of entities and relationships for knowledge graph completion*
Dat Quoc Nguyen

16:00–16:30   *Graph-based Aspect Representation Learning for Entity Resolution*
Zhenqi Zhao, Yuchen Guo, Dingxian Wang, Yufan Huang, Xiangnan He and Bin Gu

16:00–16:30   *Merge and Recognize: A Geometry and 2D Context Aware Graph Model for Named Entity Recognition from Visual Documents*
Chuwei Luo, Yongpan Wang, Qi Zheng, Liangchen Li, Feiyu Gao and Shiyu Zhang

16:00–16:30   *Joint Learning of the Graph and the Data Representation for Graph-Based Semi-Supervised Learning*
Mariana Vargas-Vieyra, Aurélien Bellet and Pascal Denis

16:00–16:30   *Contextual BERT: Conditioning the Language Model Using a Global State*
Timo I. Denk and Ana Peleteiro Ramallo

16:00–16:30   *Graph-to-Graph Transformer for Transition-based Dependency Parsing*
Alireza Mohammadshahi and James Henderson

16:30–16:40   *Break*

16:40–17:30   Invited Talk by Yizhou Sun (University of California, Los Angeles, USA)

17:30–18:00   Oral Presentations Session 2

17:30–18:00   *Semi-supervised Word Sense Disambiguation Using Example Similarity Graph*
Rie Yatabe and Minoru Sasaki

17:30–18:00   *Incorporating Temporal Information in Entailment Graph Mining*
Liane Guillou, Sander Bijl de Vroe, Mohammad Javad Hosseini, Mark Johnson and
Mark Steedman

17:30–18:00   *Graph-based Syntactic Word Embeddings*
Ragheb Al-Ghezi and Mikko Kurimo

17:30–18:00   *Relation Specific Transformations for Open World Knowledge Graph Completion*
Haseeb Shah, Johannes Villmow and Adrian Ulges

17:30–18:00   *TextGraphs 2020 Shared Task on Multi-Hop Inference for Explanation Regeneration*
Peter Jansen and Dmitry Ustalov

18:00–18:10   *Break*

18:10–18:50   Poster Session

18:10–18:50   *PGL at TextGraphs 2020 Shared Task: Explanation Regeneration using Language
and Graph Learning Methods*
Weibin Li, Yuxiang Lu, Zhengjie Huang, Weiyue Su, Jiaxiang Liu, Shikun Feng
and Yu Sun

18:10–18:50   *ChiSquareX at TextGraphs 2020 Shared Task: Leveraging Pretrained Language
Models for Explanation Regeneration*
Aditya Girish Pawate, Varun Madhavan and Devansh Chandak

18:10–18:50   *Explanation Regeneration via Multi-Hop ILP Inference over Knowledge Base*
Aayushee Gupta and Gopalakrishnan Srinivasaraghavan

A survey of embedding models of entities and relationships for knowledge graph completion

Dat Quoc Nguyen
VinAI Research, Vietnam
`v.datnq9@vinai.io`

Abstract

Knowledge graphs (KGs) of real-world facts about entities and their relationships are useful resources for a variety of natural language processing tasks. However, because knowledge graphs are typically incomplete, it is useful to perform *knowledge graph completion* or *link prediction*, i.e. predict whether a relationship not in the knowledge graph is likely to be true. This paper serves as a comprehensive survey of embedding models of entities and relationships for knowledge graph completion, summarizing up-to-date experimental results on standard benchmark datasets and pointing out potential future research directions.

1 Introduction

Let us revisit the classic Word2Vec example of a "royal" relationship between "king" and "man", and between "queen" and "woman". As illustrated in this example: $v_{king} - v_{man} \approx v_{queen} - v_{woman}$, word vectors learned from a large corpus can model relational similarities or linguistic regularities between pairs of words as translations in the projected vector space (Mikolov et al., 2013; Pennington et al., 2014). Figure 1 shows another example of a relational similarity between word pairs of countries and capital cities:

$$v_{Japan} - v_{Tokyo} \approx v_{Germany} - v_{Berlin}$$
$$v_{Germany} - v_{Berlin} \approx v_{Portugal} - v_{Lisbon}$$

Assume that we consider the country and capital pairs in Figure 1 to be pairs of entities rather than word types. That is, we now represent country and capital entities by low-dimensional and dense vectors. The relational similarity between word pairs is presumably to capture a "is_capital_of" relationship between country and capital entities. Also, we represent this relationship by a translation vector $v_{is\_capital\_of}$ in the entity vector space. Thus, we expect:

$$v_{Tokyo} + v_{is\_capital\_of} - v_{Japan} \approx 0$$
$$v_{Berlin} + v_{is\_capital\_of} - v_{Germany} \approx 0$$
$$v_{Lisbon} + v_{is\_capital\_of} - v_{Portugal} \approx 0$$

This intuition inspired the TransE model—a well-known embedding model for KG completion or link prediction in KGs (Bordes et al., 2013).

Knowledge graphs are collections of real-world triples, where each triple or fact (h, r, t) in KGs represents some relation r between a head entity h and a tail entity t. KGs can thus be formalized as directed multi-relational graphs, where nodes correspond to entities and edges linking the nodes encode various kinds of relationships (García-Durán et al., 2016; Nickel et al., 2016a). Here entities are real-world things or objects such as persons, places, organizations, music tracks or movies. Each relation type defines a certain relationship between entities. For example, as illustrated in Figure 2, the relation type "child_of" relates person entities with each other, while the relation type "born_in" relates person entities

This work is licensed under a Creative Commons Attribution 4.0 International Licence. Licence details: `http://creativecommons.org/licenses/by/4.0/`.

Proceedings of the Graph-based Methods for Natural Language Processing (TextGraphs), pages 1–14
Barcelona, Spain (Online), December 13, 2020

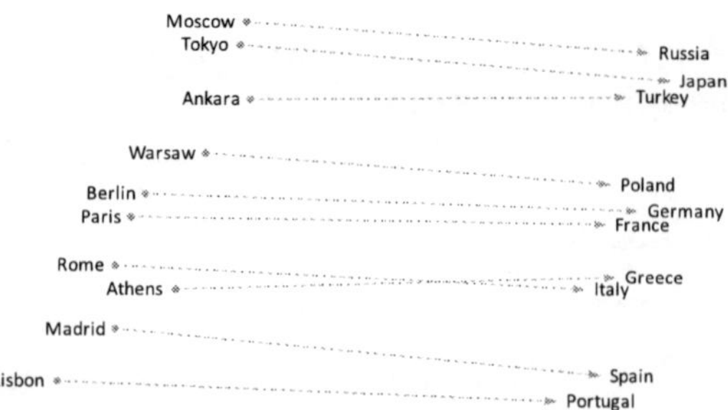

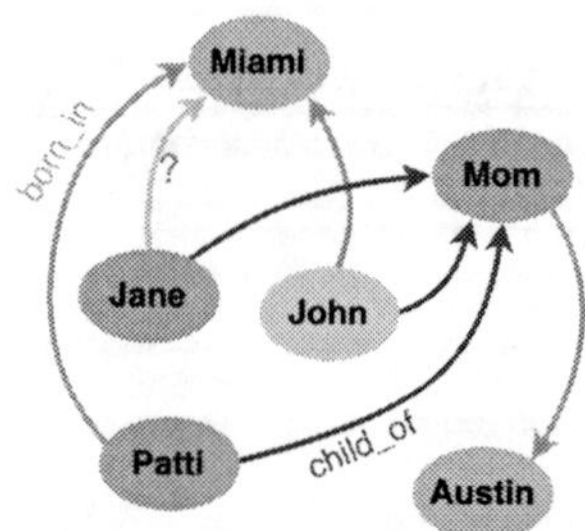

Figure 1: Two-dimensional projection of vectors of countries and their capitals. This figure is drawn based on Mikolov et al. (2013).

Figure 2: An illustration of (incomplete) knowledge base, with 4 person entities, 2 place entities, 2 relation types and total 6 triple facts. This figure is drawn based on Weston and Bordes (2014).

with place entities. Several KG examples include the domain-specific KG GeneOntology and popular generic KGs of WordNet (Fellbaum, 1998), YAGO (Suchanek et al., 2007), Freebase (Bollacker et al., 2008), NELL (Carlson et al., 2010) and DBpedia (Lehmann et al., 2015) as well as commercial KGs such as Google's Knowledge Graph, Microsoft's Satori and Facebook's Open Graph. Nowadays, KGs are used in a number of commercial applications including search engines such as Google, Microsoft's Bing and Facebook's Graph search. They also are useful resources for many natural language processing tasks such as question answering (Ferrucci, 2012; Fader et al., 2014), word sense disambiguation (Navigli and Velardi, 2005; Agirre et al., 2013), semantic parsing (Krishnamurthy and Mitchell, 2012; Berant et al., 2013) and co-reference resolution (Ponzetto and Strube, 2006; Dutta and Weikum, 2015).

A main issue is that even very large KGs, such as Freebase and DBpedia, which contain billions of fact triples about the world, are still far from complete. In particular, in English DBpedia 2014, 60% of person entities miss a place of birth and 58% of the scientists do not have a fact about what they are known for (Krompaß et al., 2015). In Freebase, 71% of 3 million person entities miss a place of birth, 75% do not have a nationality while 94% have no facts about their parents (West et al., 2014). So, in terms of a specific application, question answering systems based on incomplete KGs would not provide a correct answer given a correctly interpreted question. For example, given the incomplete KG in Figure 2, it would be impossible to answer the question "where was Jane born ?", although the question is completely matched with existing entity and relation type information (i.e. "Jane" and "born_in") in KG. Consequently, much work has been devoted towards knowledge graph completion to perform link prediction in KGs, which attempts to predict whether a relationship/triple not in the KG is likely to be true, i.e. to add new triples by leveraging existing triples in the KG (Lao and Cohen, 2010; Bordes et al., 2012; Gardner et al., 2014; García-Durán et al., 2016). For example, we would like to predict the missing tail entity in the incomplete triple $(\mathsf{Jane}, \mathsf{born\_in}, ?)$ or predict whether the triple $(\mathsf{Jane}, \mathsf{born\_in}, \mathsf{Miami})$ is correct or not.

Embedding models for KG completion have been proven to give state-of-the-art link prediction performances, in which entities are represented by latent feature vectors while relation types are represented by latent feature vectors and/or matrices and/or third-order tensors (Bordes et al., 2013; Socher et al., 2013). This paper: (1) surveys the embedding models for KG completion, then (2) summarizes up-to-date experimental results on the standard evaluation task of entity prediction—which is also referred to as the link prediction task (Bordes et al., 2013), and (3) points out potential future research directions.

2   A General Approach of Embedding Models for KG Completion

Let $\mathcal{E}$ denote the set of entities and $\mathcal{R}$ the set of relation types. Denote by $\mathcal{G}$ the knowledge graph consisting of a set of correct triples (h, r, t), such that $h, t \in \mathcal{E}$ and $r \in \mathcal{R}$. For each triple (h, r, t), the embedding models define a *score function* $f(h, r, t)$ of its plausibility. Their goal here is to:

Choose f such that the score $f(h, r, t)$ of a correct triple (h, r, t) is higher than the score $f(h', r', t')$ of an incorrect triple (h', r', t').

For example, TransE defines a score function of $f_{\text{TransE}}(h, r, t) = -\|\boldsymbol{v}_h + \boldsymbol{v}_r - \boldsymbol{v}_t\|$, where h, r and t are represented by low dimensional vectors $\boldsymbol{v}_h$, $\boldsymbol{v}_r$ and $\boldsymbol{v}_t$, respectively. As (Tokyo, is_capital_of, Japan) is a correct triple, while (Tokyo, is_capital_of, Portugal) and (Lisbon, is_capital_of, Japan) are incorrect ones, we would have: $-\|\boldsymbol{v}_{Tokyo} + \boldsymbol{v}_{is\_capital\_of} - \boldsymbol{v}_{Japan}\| > -\|\boldsymbol{v}_{Tokyo} + \boldsymbol{v}_{is\_capital\_of} - \boldsymbol{v}_{Portugal}\|$, and $-\|\boldsymbol{v}_{Tokyo} + \boldsymbol{v}_{is\_capital\_of} - \boldsymbol{v}_{Japan}\| > -\|\boldsymbol{v}_{Lisbon} + \boldsymbol{v}_{is\_capital\_of} - \boldsymbol{v}_{Japan}\|$. Table 1 in Section 3 summarizes different prominent score functions $f(h, r, t)$.

To learn model parameters (i.e. entity vectors, relation vectors or matrices), the embedding models minimize an objective loss $\mathcal{L}$. A conventional objective loss is the margin-based pairwise ranking loss (Bordes et al., 2013):

$$\mathcal{L}_{\text{Margin}} = \sum_{\substack{(h,r,t)\in\mathcal{G} \\ (h',r,t')\in\mathcal{G}'_{(h,r,t)}}} [\gamma - f(h, r, t) + f(h', r, t')]_+$$

where $[x]_+ = \max(0, x)$; γ is the margin hyper-parameter; and $\mathcal{G}'_{(h,r,t)}$ is the set of incorrect triples generated by corrupting the correct triple $(h, r, t) \in \mathcal{G}$.

Also, the negative log-likelihood (NLL) of softmax regression (Toutanova and Chen, 2015) and the NLL of logistic regression (Trouillon et al., 2016) are commonly used in recent KG completion research:[1]

$$\mathcal{L}_{\text{Softmax}} = -\sum_{(h,r,t)\in\mathcal{G}} \left(\frac{\exp\left(f\left(h, r, t\right)\right)}{\sum_{t' \in \mathcal{E}\backslash\{t\}} \exp\left(f\left(h, r, t'\right)\right)} \right.$$
$$\left. + \frac{\exp\left(f\left(h, r, t\right)\right)}{\sum_{h' \in \mathcal{E}\backslash\{h\}} \exp\left(f\left(h', r, t\right)\right)} \right)$$

$$\mathcal{L}_{\text{Logistic}} = \sum_{(h,r,t)\in\{\mathcal{G}\cup\mathcal{G}'\}} \log\left(1 + \exp\left(-\mathbf{I}_{(h,r,t)} \cdot f\left(h, r, t\right)\right)\right)$$
$$\text{with: } \mathbf{I}_{(h,r,t)} = \left\{ \begin{array}{l} 1 \text{ for } (h, r, t) \in \mathcal{G} \\ -1 \text{ for } (h, r, t) \in \mathcal{G}' \end{array} \right.$$

To corrupt the head or tail entities, a common strategy is to uniformly replace the entities when sampling incorrect triples (Bordes et al., 2013), however it results in many false negative labels (Wang et al., 2014). Domain sampling (Krompaß et al., 2015; Xie et al., 2017) generates corrupted triples by sampling entities from the same domain or from the set of relation-dependent entities. The "Bernoulli" trick (Wang et al., 2014) is widely used to set different probabilities for generating head or tail entities: For each relation type r, we calculate the averaged number $a_{r,1}$ of heads h for a pair (r, t) and the averaged number $a_{r,2}$ of tails t for a pair (h, r). We then define a Bernoulli distribution with success probability $\lambda_r = \frac{a_{r,1}}{a_{r,1} + a_{r,2}}$ for sampling: given a correct triple (h, r, t), we corrupt this triple by replacing head entity with probability λ_r while replacing the tail entity with probability $(1 - \lambda_r)$.

Recently, Cai and Wang (2018) and Sun et al. (2019) proposed adversarial learning-based strategies for sampling incorrect triples. However, they did not provide a comparison between the adversarial learning-based strategies and the "Bernoulli" trick.

3   Specific Models

3.1   Triple-based Embedding Models

Translation-based models: The Unstructured model (Bordes et al., 2012) assumes that the head and tail entity vectors are similar. As the Unstructured model does not take the relationship into account, it cannot distinguish different relation types. The Structured Embedding (SE) model (Bordes et al., 2011) assumes that the head and tail entities are similar only in a relation-dependent subspace, where each

---

[1]All the losses can also include an L2 regularization on the model parameters, which is not shown for simplification.

	Model	Score function $f(h, r, t)$
Translation	Unstructured	$-\|v_h - v_t\|_{\ell_{1/2}}$
	SE	$-\|W_{r,1}v_h - W_{r,2}v_t\|_{\ell_{1/2}}$ where $W_{r,1}, W_{r,2} \in \mathbb{R}^{k\times k}$
	TransE	$-\|v_h + v_r - v_t\|_{\ell_{1/2}}$ where $v_r \in \mathbb{R}^k$
	TransH	$-\|(I - r_p r_p^\top)v_h + v_r - (I - r_p r_p^\top)v_t\|_{\ell_{1/2}}$ where $r_p, v_r \in \mathbb{R}^k$, I denotes an identity matrix size $k \times k$
	TransR	$-\|W_r v_h + v_r - W_r v_t\|_{\ell_{1/2}}$ where $W_r \in \mathbb{R}^{n\times k}$, $v_r \in \mathbb{R}^n$
	STransE	$-\|W_{r,1}v_h + v_r - W_{r,2}v_t\|_{\ell_{1/2}}$ where $W_{r,1}, W_{r,2} \in \mathbb{R}^{k\times k}$, $v_r \in \mathbb{R}^k$
	TranSparse	$-\|W_{r,1}(\theta_{r,1})v_h + v_r - W_{r,2}(\theta_{r,2})v_t\|_{\ell_{1/2}}$ where $W_{r,1}, W_{r,2} \in \mathbb{R}^{n\times k}$; $\theta_{r,1}, \theta_{r,2} \in \mathbb{R}$; $v_r \in \mathbb{R}^n$
	TransD	$-\|(I + r_p h_p^\top)v_h + v_r - (I + r_p t_p^\top)v_t\|_{\ell_{1/2}}$ where $r_p, v_r, h_p, t_p \in \mathbb{R}^k$
	lppTransD	$-\|(I + r_{p,1}h_p^\top)v_h + v_r - (I + r_{p,2}t_p^\top)v_t\|_{\ell_{1/2}}$ where $r_{p,1}, r_{p,2}, v_r, h_p, t_p \in \mathbb{R}^k$
Bilinear & Tensor	Bilinear	$v_h^\top W_r v_t$ where $W_r \in \mathbb{R}^{k\times k}$
	DISTMULT	$v_h^\top W_r v_t$ where W_r is a diagonal matrix $\in \mathbb{R}^{k\times k}$
	SimplE	$\frac{1}{2}\left(v_{h,1}^\top W_r v_{t,2} + v_{t,1}^\top W_{r^{-1}} v_{h,2}\right)$ where $v_{h,1}, v_{h,2}, v_{t,1}, v_{t,2} \in \mathbb{R}^k$; W_r and $W_{r^{-1}}$ are diagonal matrices $\in \mathbb{R}^{k\times k}$
	SME(bilinear)	$v_h^\top(M_1 \times_3 v_r)^\top (M_2 \times_3 v_r)v_t$ where $v_r \in \mathbb{R}^k$; $M_1, M_2 \in \mathbb{R}^{n\times k\times k}$
	TuckER	$M \times_1 v_h \times_2 v_r \times_3 v_t$ where $v_r \in \mathbb{R}^n$, $M \in \mathbb{R}^{k\times n\times k}$; $\times_d$ denotes the tensor product along the d-th mode
	HolE	$\text{sigmoid}(v_t^\top (v_h \star v_r))$ where $\star$ denotes circular correlation
Neural network	NTN	$v_r^\top \tanh(v_h^\top M_r v_t + W_{r,1}v_h + W_{r,2}v_t + b_r)$ where $v_r, b_r \in \mathbb{R}^n$; $M_r \in \mathbb{R}^{k\times k\times n}$; $W_{r,1}, W_{r,2} \in \mathbb{R}^{n\times k}$
	ER-MLP	$\text{sigmoid}(w^\top \tanh(W\text{concat}(v_h, v_r, v_t)))$
	ConvE	$v_t^\top \text{ReLU}(W\text{vec}(\text{ReLU}(\text{concat}(\overline{v}_h, \overline{v}_r) * \Omega)))$
	ConvKB	$w^\top \text{concat}(\text{ReLU}([v_h, v_r, v_t] * \Omega))$
Complex vector	ComplEx	$\text{Re}\left(c_h^\top C_r \hat{c}_t\right)$ where $\text{Re}(c)$ denotes the real part of the complex value $c \in \mathbb{C}$ $c_h, c_t \in \mathbb{C}^k$; $C_r \in \mathbb{C}^{k\times k}$ is a diagonal matrix ; $\hat{c}_t$ is the conjugate of c_t
	RotatE	$-\|c_h \circ c_r - c_t\|_{\ell_{1/2}}$ where $c_h, c_r, c_t \in \mathbb{C}^k$; $\circ$ denotes the element-wise product
	QuatE	$q_h \otimes \frac{q_r}{|q_r|} \bullet q_t$ where $q_h, q_r, q_t \in \mathbb{H}^k$; $\otimes$ and $\bullet$ denote Hamilton and quaternion inner products, respectively
Path	TransE-COMP	$-\|v_h + v_{r_1} + v_{r_2} + ... + v_{r_m} - v_t\|_{\ell_{1/2}}$ where $v_{r_1}, v_{r_2}, ..., v_{r_m} \in \mathbb{R}^k$
	Bilinear-COMP	$v_h^\top W_{r_1} W_{r_2}...W_{r_m} v_t$ where $W_{r_1}, W_{r_2}, ..., W_{r_m} \in \mathbb{R}^{k\times k}$

Table 1: The score functions $f(h, r, t)$ of several prominent embedding models for KG completion. In these models, the entities h and t are represented by vectors v_h and $v_t \in \mathbb{R}^k$, respectively. $\ell_{1/2}$ denotes either the L$_1$-norm or the squared L$_2$-norm. In ConvE, $\overline{v}_h$ and $\overline{v}_r$ denote a 2D reshaping of v_h and v_r, respectively. In both ConvE and ConvKB models, $*$ and Ω denote a convolution operator and a set of filters, respectively.

relation is represented by two different matrices. TransE (Bordes et al., 2013) is inspired by models such as the Word2Vec Skip-gram model (Mikolov et al., 2013) where relationships between words often correspond to translations in latent feature space. In particular, TransE learns low-dimensional and dense vectors for every entity and relation type, so that each relation type corresponds to a translation vector operating on the vectors representing the entities, i.e. $v_h + v_r \approx v_t$ for each fact triple (h, r, t). TransE thus is suitable for 1-to-1 relationships, such as "is_capital_of", where a head entity is linked to at most one tail entity given a relation type. Because of using only one translation vector to represent each relation type, TransE is not well-suited for Many-to-1, 1-to-Many and Many-to-Many relationships,[2] such as for relation types "born_in", "place_of_birth" and "research_fields." For example in Figure 2, using one vector representing the relation type "born_in" cannot capture both the translating direction from "Patti" to "Miami" and its inverse direction from "Mom" to "Austin."

To overcome those issues of TransE, TransH (Wang et al., 2014) associates each relation with a relation-specific hyperplane and uses a projection vector to project entity vectors onto that hyperplane. TransD (Ji et al., 2015) and TransR/CTransR (Lin et al., 2015b) extend TransH by using two projection vectors and a matrix to project entity vectors into a relation-specific space, respectively. Similar to TransR, TransR-FT (Feng et al., 2016a) also uses a matrix to project head and tail entity vectors.

---

[2] A relation type r is classified Many-to-1 if multiple head entities can be connected by r to at most one tail entity. A relation type r is classified 1-to-Many if multiple tail entities can be linked by r from at most one head entity. A relation type r is classified Many-to-Many if multiple head entities can be connected by r to a tail entity and vice versa.

TEKE_H (Wang and Li, 2016) extends TransH to incorporate rich context information in an external text corpus. lppTransD (Yoon et al., 2016) extends TransD to additionally use two projection vectors for representing each relation. STransE (Nguyen et al., 2016b) and TranSparse (Ji et al., 2016) can be viewed as direct extensions of TransR, where head and tail entities are associated with their own projection matrices. Unlike STransE, TranSparse uses adaptive sparse matrices, whose sparse degrees are defined based on the number of entities linked by relations. TranSparse-DT (Chang et al., 2017) is an extension of TranSparse with a dynamic translation. ITransF (Xie et al., 2017) can be considered as a generalization of STransE, which allows the sharing of statistic regularities between relation projection matrices and alleviates data sparsity issue. Furthermore, TorusE (Ebisu and Ichise, 2018) embeds entities and relations on a torus to handle TransE's regularization problem which forces entity embeddings to be on a sphere in the embedding vector space.

Bilinear- & Tensor-based models: DISTMULT (Yang et al., 2015) is based on the Bilinear model (Nickel et al., 2011; Jenatton et al., 2012) where each relation is represented by a diagonal matrix rather than a full matrix. SimplE (Kazemi and Poole, 2018) extends DISTMULT to allow two embeddings of each entity to be learned dependently. Such quadratic forms are also used to model entities and relations in KG2E (He et al., 2015), TATEC (García-Durán et al., 2016), TransG (Xiao et al., 2016), RSTE (Tay et al., 2017), ANALOGY (Liu et al., 2017) and Dihedral (Xu and Li, 2019). SME-bilinear (Bordes et al., 2012) is proposed to first separately combine entity-relation pairs (h, r) and (r, t) and then semantically match these combinations, using tensor product. HolE (Nickel et al., 2016b) uses circular correlation– a compositional operator–which can be interpreted as a compression of the tensor product. In addition, TuckER (Balazevic et al., 2019) is a linear model based on the Tucker tensor decomposition of the binary tensor representation of KG triples.

Neural network-based models: The neural tensor network (NTN) model (Socher et al., 2013) also uses a bilinear tensor operator to represent each relation while ProjE (Shi and Weninger, 2017) can be viewed as simplified versions of NTN. The ER-MLP model (Dong et al., 2014) represents each triple by a vector obtained from concatenating head, relation and tail embeddings, then feeds this vector into a single-layer MLP with one-node output layer. ConvE (Dettmers et al., 2018) and ConvKB (Nguyen et al., 2018) are based on convolutional neural networks. ConvE uses a convolution layer directly over 2D reshaping of head-entity and relation embeddings, while ConvKB applies a convolution layer over the embedding triples (here each triple (h, r, t) is represented as a 3-column matrix where each column vector represents a triple element). HypER (Balažević et al., 2019) simplifies ConvE by using a hypernetwork to produce 1D convolutional filters for each relation, then extracts relation-specific features from head entity embeddings. Conv-TransE (Shang et al., 2019) extends ConvE to keep the translational characteristic between entities and relations. InteractE (Vashishth et al., 2020) uses a circular convolution operator and a checkered reshaping function instead of the standard convolution operator and 2D stack reshaping function in ConvE. The CapsE model (Nguyen et al., 2019) extends ConvKB by stacking a capsule network layer (Sabour et al., 2017) on top of the convolution layer.

Complex vector-based models: Instead of embedding entities and relations in the real-valued vector space, ComplEx (Trouillon et al., 2016) is an extension of DISTMULT in the complex vector space. ComplEx-N3 (Lacroix et al., 2018) extends ComplEx with weighted nuclear 3-norm. Also in the complex vector space, RotatE (Sun et al., 2019) defines each relation as a rotation from the head entity to the tail entity. QuatE (Zhang et al., 2019) represents entities by quaternion embeddings (i.e. hypercomplex-valued embeddings) and models relations as rotations in the quaternion space by employing the Hamilton and quaternion-inner products.

3.2 Relation Path-based Embedding Models

All embedding models mentioned above in Section 3.1 only take triples into account. Thus, these models ignore potentially useful information implicitly presented by the structure of the KG. For example, the relation path $h \xrightarrow{\text{born\_in\_city}} e \xrightarrow{\text{city\_in\_country}} t$ should indicate a relationship "nationality" between the h and t entities. Also, neighborhood information of entities could be useful for predicting the relationship between two entities as well. For example, in the KG NELL (Carlson et al., 2010), we have information such as if a person works for an organization and this person also leads that organization, then it is likely that this person is the CEO of that organization.

Recent research has also shown that relation paths between entities in KGs provide richer context information and improve the performance of embedding models for KG completion (Luo et al., 2015; Liang and Forbus, 2015; García-Durán et al., 2015; Guu et al., 2015; Toutanova et al., 2016; Durán and Niepert, 2018; Takahashi et al., 2018; Chen et al., 2018). In particular, Luo et al. (2015) constructed relation paths between entities and, viewing entities and relations in the path as pseudo-words, then applied Word2Vec (Mikolov et al., 2013) to produce pre-trained vectors for these pseudo-words. Luo et al. (2015) showed that using these pre-trained vectors for initialization helps to improve the performance of models TransE (Bordes et al., 2013), SME (Bordes et al., 2012) and SE (Bordes et al., 2011). Liang and Forbus (2015) used the plausibility score produced by SME to compute the weights of relation paths.

PTransE-RNN (Lin et al., 2015a) models relation paths by using a recurrent neural network (RNN). In addition, Das et al. (2017)'s model and ROPs (Yin et al., 2018) also apply RNN to model the path between an entity pair, however, in contrast to PTransE-RNN, they additionally take the intermediate entities present in the path into account. IRN (Shen et al., 2017) uses a shared memory and RNN-based controller to implicitly model multi-step structured relationships. RTransE (García-Durán et al., 2015), PTransE-ADD (Lin et al., 2015a) and TransE-COMP (Guu et al., 2015) extend TransE to represent a relation path by a vector which is the sum of the vectors of all relations in the path. In Bilinear-COMP (Guu et al., 2015) and PRUNED-PATHS (Toutanova et al., 2016), each relation is a matrix and so it represents the relation path by matrix multiplication. Durán and Niepert (2018) proposed the KB_{LRN} framework to combine relational paths with latent and numerical features.

The neighborhood mixture model TransE-NMM (Nguyen et al., 2016a) can be also viewed as a three-relation path model because it takes into account the neighborhood entity and relation information of both head and tail entities in each triple. ReInceptionE (Xie et al., 2020) employs the Inception network (Szegedy et al., 2016) to increase the interactions between head and relation embeddings for obtaining better representations of the head and relation pairs and then uses a relation-aware attention mechanism to enrich these pair representations with the local neighborhood and global entity information. Neighborhood information is also exploited in R-GCN (Schlichtkrull et al., 2018), SACN (Shang et al., 2019) and KBGAT (Nathani et al., 2019), which generalize graph convolutional networks (Kipf and Welling, 2017) and graph attention networks (Velikovi et al., 2018) for dealing with highly multi-relational data, e.g. KGs. For computing the final representation of an entity, they make use of layer-wise propagation to accumulate linearly-transformed embeddings of its neighboring entities through a normalized sum with different relational weights. For link prediction, R-GCN, SACN and KBGAT apply DISTMULT, Conv-TransE and ConvKB to compute triple scores, respectively.

3.3 Other KG Completion Models

The Path Ranking Algorithm (PRA) (Lao and Cohen, 2010) is a random walk inference technique which was proposed to predict a new relationship between two entities in KGs. Lao et al. (2011) used PRA to estimate the probability of an unseen triple as a combination of weighted random walks that follow different paths linking the head entity and tail entity in the KG. Gardner et al. (2014) made use of an external text corpus to increase the connectivity of the KG used as the input to PRA. Gardner and Mitchell (2015) improved PRA by proposing a subgraph feature extraction technique to make the generation of random walks in KGs more efficient and expressive, while Wang et al. (2016) extended PRA to couple the path ranking of multiple relations. PRA can also be used in conjunction with first-order logic in the discriminative Gaifman model (Niepert, 2016). In addition, Neelakantan et al. (2015) used a RNN to learn vector representations of PRA-style relation paths between entities in the KG. Other random-walk based learning algorithms for KG completion can be also found in Feng et al. (2016b), Liu et al. (2016), Wei et al. (2016), Mazumder and Liu (2017) and Das et al. (2018).

Yang et al. (2017) proposed a Neural Logic Programming (LP) framework to learning probabilistic first-order logical rules for KG reasoning, producing competitive link prediction performances. Feldman

Dataset	$\lvert \mathcal{E} \rvert$	$\lvert \mathcal{R} \rvert$	#Triples in train/valid/test		
FB15k (Bordes et al., 2013)	14,951	1,345	483,142	50,000	59,071
WN18 (Bordes et al., 2013)	40,943	18	141,442	5,000	5,000
FB15k-237 (Toutanova and Chen, 2015)	14,541	237	272,115	17,535	20,466
WN18RR Dettmers et al. (2018)	40,943	11	86,835	3,034	3,134

Table 2: Statistics of benchmark experimental datasets.

et al. (2019) presented an approach to generate sentences from triples via hand-craft templates, and then use the likelihoods produced by the pre-trained BERT (Devlin et al., 2019) for these generated sentences to score the plausibility of the corresponding triples. See other methods for learning from KGs and multi-relational data in Nickel et al. (2016a) and Wang et al. (2017).

4 Evaluation Task

The standard evaluation task of entity prediction, i.e. the link prediction task (Bordes et al., 2013), is proposed to evaluate embedding models for KG completion.[3]

Datasets: Information about benchmark datasets for KG completion evaluation is given in Table 2. FB15k and WN18 are derived from the large real-world KG Freebase (Bollacker et al., 2008) and the large lexical KG WordNet (Miller, 1995), respectively. Toutanova and Chen (2015) noted that FB15k and WN18 are not challenging datasets because they contain many reversible triples. Dettmers et al. (2018) showed a concrete example: A test triple (feline, hyponym, cat) can be mapped to a training triple (cat, hypernym, feline), thus knowing that "hyponym" and "hypernym" are reversible allows us to easily predict the majority of test triples. So, datasets FB15k-237 (Toutanova and Chen, 2015) and WN18RR (Dettmers et al., 2018) are created to serve as realistic KG completion datasets which represent a more challenging learning setting. FB15k-237 and WN18RR are subsets of FB15k and WN18, respectively.

4.1 Task Description

The entity prediction task, i.e. link prediction (Bordes et al., 2013), predicts the head or the tail entity given the relation type and the other entity, i.e. predicting h given $(?, r, t)$ or predicting t given $(h, r, ?)$ where ? denotes the missing element. The results are evaluated using a ranking induced by the function $f(h, r, t)$ on test triples.

Each correct test triple (h, r, t) is corrupted by replacing either its head or tail entity by each of the possible entities in turn, and then these candidates are ranked in descending order of their plausibility score. The "Filtered" setting protocol, described in Bordes et al. (2013), filters out before ranking any corrupted triples that appear in the KG. Ranking a corrupted triple appearing in the KG (i.e. a correct triple) higher than the original test triple is also correct, thus this "Filtered" setting provides a clear view on the ranking performance.

In addition to the mean rank and the Hits@10 (i.e. the proportion of test triples for which the target entity is ranked in the top 10 predictions), which were originally used in the entity prediction task (Bordes et al., 2013), recent work also reports the mean reciprocal rank (**MRR**).[4] Mean rank is always greater or equal to 1 and the lower mean rank indicates better entity prediction performance, while MRR and Hits@10 scores always range from 0.0 to 1.0, and higher score reflects better prediction result.

4.2 Main Results

Tables 3 and 4 list recent entity prediction results of KG completion models on FB15k and WN18 and on FB15k-237 and WN18RR, respectively. In Table 3, the first 28 rows report the performance of triple-based models that directly optimize a score function for the triples in a KG, i.e. they do not exploit information about alternative paths between head and tail entities. The next 9 rows report results

---

[3]Another evaluation task for KG completion is triple classification (Socher et al., 2013), however, it is not as widely used as the link prediction task. See the Supplementary file for a summary of triple classification results.

[4]See Baeza-Yates and Ribeiro-Neto (2011) for definitions of the mean rank, Hits@10 and MRR. Some recent work additionally reported Hits@1 (i.e. the proportion of test triples for which the target entity is ranked first). However, formulas of MRR and Hits@1 show a strong correlation between these two scores. So using Hits@1 might not reveal any additional insight.

Method	Filtered					
	FB15k			**WN18**		
	MR	@10	MRR	MR	@10	MRR
TransH (Wang et al., 2014)	87	64.4	-	303	86.7	-
TransR (Lin et al., 2015b)	77	68.7	-	225	92.0	-
CTransR (Lin et al., 2015b)	75	70.2	-	218	92.3	-
KG2E (He et al., 2015)	59	74.0	-	331	92.8	-
TransD (Ji et al., 2015)	91	77.3	-	212	92.2	-
lppTransD (Yoon et al., 2016)	78	78.7	-	270	94.3	-
TransG (Xiao et al., 2016)	98	79.8	-	470	93.3	-
TranSparse (Ji et al., 2016)	82	79.5	-	211	93.2	-
TranSparse-DT (Chang et al., 2017)	79	80.2	-	221	94.3	-
ITransF (Xie et al., 2017)	65	81.0	-	<u>205</u>	94.2	-
NTN (Socher et al., 2013) [♦]	-	41.4	0.25	-	66.1	0.53
TransE (Bordes et al., 2013) [■]	-	74.9	0.463	-	94.3	0.495
HolE (Nickel et al., 2016b)	-	73.9	0.524	-	94.9	0.938
ComplEx (Trouillon et al., 2016)	-	84.0	0.692	-	94.7	0.941
ANALOGY (Liu et al., 2017)	-	85.4	0.725	-	94.7	0.942
SimplE (Kazemi and Poole, 2018)	-	83.8	0.727	-	94.7	0.942
TorusE (Ebisu and Ichise, 2018)	-	83.2	0.733	-	95.4	0.947
STransE (Nguyen et al., 2016b)	69	79.7	0.543	206	93.4	0.657
ER-MLP (Dong et al., 2014) [♠]	81	80.1	0.570	299	94.2	0.895
DISTMULT (Yang et al., 2015) [♣]	42	89.3	<u>0.798</u>	655	94.6	0.797
ConvE (Dettmers et al., 2018)	64	87.3	0.745	504	95.5	0.942
HypER (Balažević et al., 2019)	44	88.5	0.790	431	95.8	<u>0.951</u>
RotatE (Sun et al., 2019)	40	88.4	0.797	309	<u>95.9</u>	0.949
QuatE (Zhang et al., 2019)	**17**	90.0	0.782	**162**	<u>95.9</u>	0.950
ComplEx-N3 (Lacroix et al., 2018)	-	<u>91</u>	**0.86**	-	**96**	0.95
TuckER (Balazevic et al., 2019)	-	89.2	0.795	-	95.8	**0.953**
IRN (Shen et al., 2017)	38	**92.7**	-	249	95.3	-
ProjE (Shi and Weninger, 2017)	<u>34</u>	88.4	-	-	-	-
RTransE (García-Durán et al., 2015)	50	76.2	-	-	-	-
PTransE-ADD (Lin et al., 2015a)	58	84.6	-	-	-	-
PTransE-RNN (Lin et al., 2015a)	92	82.2	-	-	-	-
GAKE (Feng et al., 2016b)	119	64.8	-	-	-	-
Gaifman (Niepert, 2016)	75	84.2	-	352	93.9	-
Hiri (Liu et al., 2016)	-	70.3	0.603	-	90.8	0.691
Neural LP (Yang et al., 2017)	-	83.7	0.76	-	94.5	**0.94**
R-GCN+ (Schlichtkrull et al., 2018)	-	84.2	0.696	-	**96.4**	0.819
KB$_{LRN}$ (Durán and Niepert, 2018)	**44**	**87.5**	**0.794**	-	-	-
TEKE_H (Wang and Li, 2016)	108	73.0	-	**114**	92.9	-
SSP (Xiao et al., 2017)	82	79.0	-	156	93.2	-

Table 3: Entity prediction results on WN18 and FB15k, which are taken from the corresponding papers. **MR** and **@10** denote metrics mean rank and Hits@10 (in %), respectively. [♦], [■], [♠] and [♣] denote results taking from Yang et al. (2015), Nickel et al. (2016b), Ravishankar et al. (2017) and Kadlec et al. (2017), respectively.

of models that exploit information about relation paths or neighborhood information. The last 2 rows present results for models which make use of textual mentions derived from a large external corpus. In Table 4, the last 5 rows report results of models that exploit the path or neighborhood information.

In general, Tables 3 and 4 show that the models using external corpus information or employing path information achieve better scores than the triple-based models that do not use such information. In terms of models not exploiting path or external information, the complex vector-based models (e.g. QuatE, CompleEx-N3 and RotatE) produce the strongest evaluation scores, followed by the neural network-based models (e.g. CapsE, InteractE and HypER).[5] Tables 3 and 4 also show that TransE and DIST-MULT, despite of theirs simplicity, can produce very competitive results (i.e. by performing a careful grid search of hyper-parameters).

---

[5]CapsE uses the pre-trained word embeddings for entity vector initialization on WN18RR. It is not surprising that CapsE produces the best MR on WN18RR as many entity names in WordNet are lexically meaningful. It is possible for all other embedding models to utilize the pre-trained word vectors as well. However, averaging the pre-trained word embeddings for initializing entity vectors is an open problem, and it is not always useful since entity names in many domain-specific KGs are not lexically meaningful (Wang et al., 2014; Guu et al., 2015).

Method	Filtered					
	FB15k-237			WN18RR		
	MR	@10	MRR	MR	@10	MRR
IRN (Shen et al., 2017)	211	46.4	-	-	-	-
KBGAN (Cai and Wang, 2018)	-	45.8	0.278	-	48.1	0.213
DISTMULT (Yang et al., 2015) [♦]	254	41.9	0.241	5110	49	0.43
ComplEx (Trouillon et al., 2016) [♦]	339	42.8	0.247	5261	51	0.44
ConvE (Dettmers et al., 2018)	246	49.1	0.316	5277	48	0.46
ER-MLP (Dong et al., 2014) [♠]	219	54.0	0.342	4798	41.9	0.366
HypER (Balažević et al., 2019)	250	52.0	0.341	5798	52.2	0.465
TransE (Bordes et al., 2013) [■]	347	46.5	0.294	<u>743</u>	56.0	0.245
ConvKB (Nguyen et al., 2018) [■]	254	53.2	<u>0.418</u>	763	56.7	0.253
CapsE (Nguyen et al., 2019)	303	**59.3**	**0.523**	**719**	56.0	0.415
InteractE (Vashishth et al., 2020)	<u>172</u>	53.5	0.354	5202	52.8	0.463
RotatE (Sun et al., 2019)	177	53.3	0.338	3340	<u>57.1</u>	0.476
QuatE (Zhang et al., 2019)	**87**	55.0	0.348	2314	**58.2**	**0.488**
ComplEx-N3 (Lacroix et al., 2018)	-	<u>56</u>	0.37	-	57	<u>0.48</u>
Conv-TransE (Shang et al., 2019)	-	51	0.33	-	52	0.46
TuckER (Balazevic et al., 2019)	-	54.4	0.358	-	52.6	0.470
Neural LP (Yang et al., 2017)	-	36.2	0.24	-	-	-
R-GCN+ (Schlichtkrull et al., 2018)	-	41.7	0.249	-	-	-
KB$_{LRN}$ (Durán and Niepert, 2018)	209	49.3	0.309	-	-	-
KBGAT (Nathani et al., 2019)	210	**62.6**	**0.518**	1940	58.1	0.440
ReInceptionE (Xie et al., 2020)	**173**	52.8	0.349	**1894**	**58.2**	**0.483**
SACN (Shang et al., 2019)	-	54	0.35	-	54	0.47

Table 4: Entity prediction results on WN18RR and FB15k-237, which are taken from the corresponding papers. [♦], [♠] and [■] denote results taking from Dettmers et al. (2018), Ravishankar et al. (2017) and Nguyen et al. (2019), respectively.

5   Discussion and Conclusion

The reasons why much work has been devoted towards developing triple-based models are: (1) additional information sources might not be available, e.g., for KGs for specialized domains, (2) models that do not exploit path information or external resources are simpler and thus typically much faster to train than the more complex models using path or external information, and (3) the more complex models that exploit path or external information are typically extensions of these simpler models, and are often initialized with parameters estimated by such simpler models, so improvements to the simpler models should yield corresponding improvements to the more complex models as well (Nguyen et al., 2016b).

It is worth to further explore those KG completion embedding models for a new application where we could formulate its corresponding data into triples. For example, in Web search engines, we observe user-oriented relationships between submitted queries and documents returned by the search engines. That is, we have triple representations (query, user, document) in which for each user-oriented relationship, we would have many queries and documents, resulting in a lot of Many-to-Many relationships. Inspired by this observation, Vu et al. (2017) applied STransE (Nguyen et al., 2016b) for search personalization to re-rank the search documents returned by a search engine for users' submitted queries. Other application examples can be also found for recommender systems (Zhang et al., 2016; He et al., 2017; Cao et al., 2019), social relation extraction (Tu et al., 2017) and visual relation detection (Zhang et al., 2017).

Future research directions might also include: (i) Combining logical rules which contain rich background information and KG triples in a unified KG completion framework, e.g. jointly embedding KGs and logical rules (Guo et al., 2016; Yang et al., 2017). (ii) Recent embedding models for KG completion hold a closed-world assumption where the KGs are fixed (i.e. new entities might not be added easily), therefore it would be worth exploring open-world KG completion models to connect unseen entities to the existing KGs (Shi and Weninger, 2018). (iii) Investigating efficient approaches which can be applied to large-scale KGs of millions of entities and relations (Zhang et al., 2020).

In this paper, we have presented a comprehensive survey of embedding models of entity and relationships for knowledge graph completion. This paper also provides update-to-date experimental results of the embedding models for the entity prediction (i.e. link prediction) task on benchmark datasets FB15k, WN18, FB15k-237 and WN18RR. We hope that this paper serves its purpose by providing a concrete foundation for future research and applications on the topic.

References

Eneko Agirre, Oier López de Lacalle, and Aitor Soroa. 2013. Random Walks for Knowledge-Based Word Sense Disambiguation. *Computational Linguistics*, 40(1):57–84.

Ricardo A. Baeza-Yates and Berthier A. Ribeiro-Neto. 2011. *Modern Information Retrieval - the concepts and technology behind search, Second edition*. Pearson Education Ltd., Harlow, England.

Ivana Balažević, Carl Allen, and Timothy M Hospedales. 2019. Hypernetwork knowledge graph embeddings. In *ICANN*, pages 553–565.

Ivana Balazevic, Carl Allen, and Timothy Hospedales. 2019. TuckER: Tensor factorization for knowledge graph completion. In *EMNLP-IJCNLP*, pages 5185–5194.

Jonathan Berant, Andrew Chou, Roy Frostig, and Percy Liang. 2013. Semantic Parsing on Freebase from Question-Answer Pairs. In *EMNLP*, pages 1533–1544.

Kurt Bollacker, Colin Evans, Praveen Paritosh, Tim Sturge, and Jamie Taylor. 2008. Freebase: A Collaboratively Created Graph Database for Structuring Human Knowledge. In *SIGMOD*, pages 1247–1250.

Antoine Bordes, Jason Weston, Ronan Collobert, and Yoshua Bengio. 2011. Learning Structured Embeddings of Knowledge Bases. In *AAAI*, pages 301–306.

Antoine Bordes, Xavier Glorot, Jason Weston, and Yoshua Bengio. 2012. A Semantic Matching Energy Function for Learning with Multi-relational Data. *Machine Learning*, 94(2):233–259.

Antoine Bordes, Nicolas Usunier, Alberto Garcia-Duran, Jason Weston, and Oksana Yakhnenko. 2013. Translating Embeddings for Modeling Multi-relational Data. In *NIPS*, pages 2787–2795.

Liwei Cai and William Yang Wang. 2018. KBGAN: Adversarial Learning for Knowledge Graph Embeddings. In *NAACL-HLT*, pages 1470–1480.

Yixin Cao, Xiang Wang, Xiangnan He, Zikun Hu, and Tat-Seng Chua. 2019. Unifying knowledge graph learning and recommendation: Towards a better understanding of user preferences. In *WWW*, page 151161.

Andrew Carlson, Justin Betteridge, Bryan Kisiel, Burr Settles, Estevam R. Hruschka, Jr., and Tom M. Mitchell. 2010. Toward an Architecture for Never-ending Language Learning. In *AAAI*, pages 1306–1313.

L. Chang, M. Zhu, T. Gu, C. Bin, J. Qian, and J. Zhang. 2017. Knowledge Graph Embedding by Dynamic Translation. *IEEE Access*, 5:20898–20907.

Wenhu Chen, Wenhan Xiong, Xifeng Yan, and William Yang Wang. 2018. Variational knowledge graph reasoning. In *NAACL-HLT*, pages 1823–1832.

Rajarshi Das, Arvind Neelakantan, David Belanger, and Andrew McCallum. 2017. Chains of Reasoning over Entities, Relations, and Text using Recurrent Neural Networks. In *EACL*, pages 132–141.

Rajarshi Das, Shehzaad Dhuliawala, Manzil Zaheer, Luke Vilnis, Ishan Durugkar, Akshay Krishnamurthy, Alex Smola, and Andrew McCallum. 2018. Go for a Walk and Arrive at the Answer: Reasoning Over Paths in Knowledge Bases using Reinforcement Learning. In *ICLR*.

Tim Dettmers, Pasquale Minervini, Pontus Stenetorp, and Sebastian Riedel. 2018. Convolutional 2D Knowledge Graph Embeddings. In *AAAI*, pages 1811–1818.

Jacob Devlin, Ming-Wei Chang, Kenton Lee, and Kristina Toutanova. 2019. BERT: Pre-training of deep bidirectional transformers for language understanding. In *NAACL-HLT*, pages 4171–4186.

Xin Dong, Evgeniy Gabrilovich, Geremy Heitz, Wilko Horn, Ni Lao, Kevin Murphy, Thomas Strohmann, Shaohua Sun, and Wei Zhang. 2014. Knowledge vault: A web-scale approach to probabilistic knowledge fusion. In *KDD*, pages 601–610.

Alberto García Durán and Mathias Niepert. 2018. KBLRN: End-to-end learning of knowledge base representations with latent, relational, and numerical features. In *UAI*.

Sourav Dutta and Gerhard Weikum. 2015. Cross-Document Co-Reference Resolution using Sample-Based Clustering with Knowledge Enrichment. *Transactions of ACL*, 3:15–28.

Takuma Ebisu and Ryutaro Ichise. 2018. TorusE: Knowledge Graph Embedding on a Lie Group. In *AAAI*, pages 1819–1826.

Anthony Fader, Luke Zettlemoyer, and Oren Etzioni. 2014. Open Question Answering over Curated and Extracted Knowledge Bases. In *KDD*, pages 1156–1165.

Joshua Feldman, Joe Davison, and Alexander M. Rush. 2019. Commonsense Knowledge Mining from Pretrained Models. In *EMNLP-IJCNLP*, pages 1173–1178.

Christiane D. Fellbaum. 1998. *WordNet: An Electronic Lexical Database*. MIT Press.

Jun Feng, Minlie Huang, Mingdong Wang, Mantong Zhou, Yu Hao, and Xiaoyan Zhu. 2016a. Knowledge graph embedding by flexible translation. In *KR*, pages 557–560.

Jun Feng, Minlie Huang, Yang Yang, and xiaoyan zhu. 2016b. GAKE: Graph Aware Knowledge Embedding. In *COLING*, pages 641–651.

David Angelo Ferrucci. 2012. Introduction to "This is Watson". *IBM Journal of Research and Development*, 56(3):235–249.

Alberto García-Durán, Antoine Bordes, and Nicolas Usunier. 2015. Composing Relationships with Translations. In *EMNLP*, pages 286–290.

Alberto García-Durán, Antoine Bordes, Nicolas Usunier, and Yves Grandvalet. 2016. Combining Two and Three-Way Embedding Models for Link Prediction in Knowledge Bases. *Journal of Artificial Intelligence Research*, 55:715–742.

Matt Gardner and Tom Mitchell. 2015. Efficient and Expressive Knowledge Base Completion Using Subgraph Feature Extraction. In *EMNLP*, pages 1488–1498.

Matt Gardner, Partha P. Talukdar, Jayant Krishnamurthy, and Tom M. Mitchell. 2014. Incorporating Vector Space Similarity in Random Walk Inference over Knowledge Bases. In *EMNLP*, pages 397–406.

Shu Guo, Quan Wang, Lihong Wang, Bin Wang, and Li Guo. 2016. Jointly embedding knowledge graphs and logical rules. In *EMNLP*, pages 192–202.

Kelvin Guu, John Miller, and Percy Liang. 2015. Traversing Knowledge Graphs in Vector Space. In *EMNLP*, pages 318–327.

Shizhu He, Kang Liu, Guoliang Ji, and Jun Zhao. 2015. Learning to Represent Knowledge Graphs with Gaussian Embedding. In *CIKM*, pages 623–632.

Ruining He, Wang-Cheng Kang, and Julian McAuley. 2017. Translation-based recommendation. In *RecSys*, page 161169.

Rodolphe Jenatton, Nicolas L. Roux, Antoine Bordes, and Guillaume R Obozinski. 2012. A latent factor model for highly multi-relational data. In *NIPS*, pages 3167–3175.

Guoliang Ji, Shizhu He, Liheng Xu, Kang Liu, and Jun Zhao. 2015. Knowledge Graph Embedding via Dynamic Mapping Matrix. In *ACL-IJCNLP*, pages 687–696.

Guoliang Ji, Kang Liu, Shizhu He, and Jun Zhao. 2016. Knowledge Graph Completion with Adaptive Sparse Transfer Matrix. In *AAAI*, pages 985–991.

Seyed Mehran Kazemi and David Poole. 2018. Simple embedding for link prediction in knowledge graphs. In *NIPS*, pages 4284–4295.

Thomas N. Kipf and Max Welling. 2017. Semi-Supervised Classification with Graph Convolutional Networks. In *ICLR*.

Jayant Krishnamurthy and Tom Mitchell. 2012. Weakly Supervised Training of Semantic Parsers. In *EMNLP-CoNLL*, pages 754–765.

Denis Krompaß, Stephan Baier, and Volker Tresp. 2015. Type-Constrained Representation Learning in Knowledge Graphs. In *ISWC*, pages 640–655.

Timothée Lacroix, Nicolas Usunier, and Guillaume Obozinski. 2018. Canonical Tensor Decomposition for Knowledge Base Completion. In *ICML*, pages 2869–2878.

Ni Lao and William W. Cohen. 2010. Relational retrieval using a combination of path-constrained random walks. *Machine Learning*, 81(1):53–67.

Ni Lao, Tom Mitchell, and William W. Cohen. 2011. Random Walk Inference and Learning in a Large Scale Knowledge Base. In *EMNLP*, pages 529–539.

Jens Lehmann, Robert Isele, Max Jakob, Anja Jentzsch, Dimitris Kontokostas, Pablo N. Mendes, Sebastian Hellmann, Mohamed Morsey, Patrick van Kleef, Sören Auer, and Christian Bizer. 2015. DBpedia - A Large-scale, Multilingual Knowledge Base Extracted from Wikipedia. *Semantic Web*, 6(2):167–195.

Chen Liang and Kenneth D. Forbus. 2015. Learning Plausible Inferences from Semantic Web Knowledge by Combining Analogical Generalization with Structured Logistic Regression. In *AAAI*, pages 551–557.

Yankai Lin, Zhiyuan Liu, Huanbo Luan, Maosong Sun, Siwei Rao, and Song Liu. 2015a. Modeling Relation Paths for Representation Learning of Knowledge Bases. In *EMNLP*, pages 705–714.

Yankai Lin, Zhiyuan Liu, Maosong Sun, Yang Liu, and Xuan Zhu. 2015b. Learning Entity and Relation Embeddings for Knowledge Graph Completion. In *AAAI*, pages 2181–2187.

Qiao Liu, Liuyi Jiang, Minghao Han, Yao Liu, and Zhiguang Qin. 2016. Hierarchical Random Walk Inference in Knowledge Graphs. In *SIGIR*, pages 445–454.

Hanxiao Liu, Yuexin Wu, and Yiming Yang. 2017. Analogical Inference for Multi-relational Embeddings. In *ICML*, pages 2168–2178.

Yuanfei Luo, Quan Wang, Bin Wang, and Li Guo. 2015. Context-Dependent Knowledge Graph Embedding. In *EMNLP*, pages 1656–1661.

Sahisnu Mazumder and Bing Liu. 2017. Context-aware Path Ranking for Knowledge Base Completion. In *IJCAI*, pages 1195–1201.

Tomas Mikolov, Ilya Sutskever, Kai Chen, Greg S Corrado, and Jeff Dean. 2013. Distributed Representations of Words and Phrases and their Compositionality. In *NIPS*, pages 3111–3119.

George A. Miller. 1995. WordNet: A Lexical Database for English. *Communications of the ACM*, 38(11):39–41.

Deepak Nathani, Jatin Chauhan, Charu Sharma, and Manohar Kaul. 2019. Learning attention-based embeddings for relation prediction in knowledge graphs. In *ACL*, pages 4710–4723.

Roberto Navigli and Paola Velardi. 2005. Structural Semantic Interconnections: A Knowledge-Based Approach to Word Sense Disambiguation. *IEEE Transactions on Pattern Analysis and Machine Intelligence*, 27(7):1075–1086.

Arvind Neelakantan, Benjamin Roth, and Andrew McCallum. 2015. Compositional Vector Space Models for Knowledge Base Completion. In *ACL-IJCNLP*, pages 156–166.

Dat Quoc Nguyen, Kairit Sirts, Lizhen Qu, and Mark Johnson. 2016a. Neighborhood Mixture Model for Knowledge Base Completion. In *CoNLL*, pages 40–50.

Dat Quoc Nguyen, Kairit Sirts, Lizhen Qu, and Mark Johnson. 2016b. STransE: a novel embedding model of entities and relationships in knowledge bases. In *NAACL-HLT*, pages 460–466.

Dai Quoc Nguyen, Tu Dinh Nguyen, Dat Quoc Nguyen, and Dinh Phung. 2018. A Novel Embedding Model for Knowledge Base Completion Based on Convolutional Neural Network. In *NAACL-HLT*, pages 327–333.

Dai Quoc Nguyen, Thanh Vu, Tu Dinh Nguyen, Dat Quoc Nguyen, and Dinh Phung. 2019. A Capsule Network-based Embedding Model for Knowledge Graph Completion and Search Personalization. In *NAACL-HLT*, pages pages 2180–2189.

Maximilian Nickel, Volker Tresp, and Hans-Peter Kriegel. 2011. A Three-Way Model for Collective Learning on Multi-Relational Data. In *ICML*, pages 809–816.

Maximilian Nickel, Kevin Murphy, Volker Tresp, and Evgeniy Gabrilovich. 2016a. A Review of Relational Machine Learning for Knowledge Graphs. *the IEEE*, 104(1):11–33.

Maximilian Nickel, Lorenzo Rosasco, and Tomaso Poggio. 2016b. Holographic embeddings of knowledge graphs. In *AAAI*, pages 1955–1961.

Mathias Niepert. 2016. Discriminative Gaifman Models. In *NIPS*, pages 3405–3413.

Jeffrey Pennington, Richard Socher, and Christopher Manning. 2014. Glove: Global Vectors for Word Representation. In *EMNLP*, pages 1532–1543.

Simone Paolo Ponzetto and Michael Strube. 2006. Exploiting Semantic Role Labeling, WordNet and Wikipedia for Coreference Resolution. In *NAACL*, pages 192–199.

Sara Sabour, Nicholas Frosst, and Geoffrey E Hinton. 2017. Dynamic Routing Between Capsules. In *NIPS*, pages 3856–3866.

Michael Sejr Schlichtkrull, Thomas N. Kipf, Peter Bloem, Rianne van den Berg, Ivan Titov, and Max Welling. 2018. Modeling Relational Data with Graph Convolutional Networks. In *ESWC*, pages 593–607.

Chao Shang, Yun Tang, Jing Huang, Jinbo Bi, Xiaodong He, and Bowen Zhou. 2019. End-to-end Structure-Aware Convolutional Networks for Knowledge Base Completion. In *AAAI*, pages 3060–3067.

Yelong Shen, Po-Sen Huang, Ming-Wei Chang, and Jianfeng Gao. 2017. Modeling Large-Scale Structured Relationships with Shared Memory for Knowledge Base Completion. In *Rep4NLP*, pages 57–68.

Baoxu Shi and Tim Weninger. 2017. ProjE: Embedding Projection for Knowledge Graph Completion. In *AAAI*, pages 1236–1242.

Baoxu Shi and Tim Weninger. 2018. Open-world knowledge graph completion. In *AAAI*, pages 1957–1964.

Richard Socher, Danqi Chen, Christopher D Manning, and Andrew Ng. 2013. Reasoning With Neural Tensor Networks for Knowledge Base Completion. In *NIPS*, pages 926–934.

Fabian M. Suchanek, Gjergji Kasneci, and Gerhard Weikum. 2007. YAGO: A Core of Semantic Knowledge. In *WWW*, pages 697–706.

Zhiqing Sun, Zhi-Hong Deng, Jian-Yun Nie, and Jian Tang. 2019. RotatE: Knowledge Graph Embedding by Relational Rotation in Complex Space. In *ICLR*.

C. Szegedy, V. Vanhoucke, S. Ioffe, J. Shlens, and Z. Wojna. 2016. Rethinking the Inception Architecture for Computer Vision. In *CVPR*, pages 2818–2826.

Ryo Takahashi, Ran Tian, and Kentaro Inui. 2018. Interpretable and Compositional Relation Learning by Joint Training with an Autoencoder. In *ACL*, pages 2148–2159.

Yi Tay, Anh Tuan Luu, Siu Cheung Hui, and Falk Brauer. 2017. Random Semantic Tensor Ensemble for Scalable Knowledge Graph Link Prediction. In *WSDM*, pages 751–760.

Kristina Toutanova and Danqi Chen. 2015. Observed Versus Latent Features for Knowledge Base and Text Inference. In *CVSC*, pages 57–66.

Kristina Toutanova, Victoria Lin, Wen-tau Yih, Hoifung Poon, and Chris Quirk. 2016. Compositional Learning of Embeddings for Relation Paths in Knowledge Base and Text. In *ACL*, pages 1434–1444.

Théo Trouillon, Johannes Welbl, Sebastian Riedel, Éric Gaussier, and Guillaume Bouchard. 2016. Complex Embeddings for Simple Link Prediction. In *ICML*, pages 2071–2080.

Cunchao Tu, Zhengyan Zhang, Zhiyuan Liu, and Maosong Sun. 2017. TransNet: Translation-Based Network Representation Learning for Social Relation Extraction. In *IJCAI*, pages 2864–2870.

Shikhar Vashishth, Soumya Sanyal, Vikram Nitin, Nilesh Agrawal, and Partha Talukdar. 2020. InteractE: Improving Convolution-based Knowledge Graph Embeddings by Increasing Feature Interactions. In *AAAI*.

Petar Velikovi, Guillem Cucurull, Arantxa Casanova, Adriana Romero, Pietro Li, and Yoshua Bengio. 2018. Graph attention networks. In *ICLR*.

Thanh Vu, Dat Quoc Nguyen, Mark Johnson, Dawei Song, and Alistair Willis. 2017. Search Personalization with Embeddings. In *ECIR*, pages 598–604.

Zhigang Wang and Juan-Zi Li. 2016. Text-Enhanced Representation Learning for Knowledge Graph. In *IJCAI*, pages 1293–1299.

Zhen Wang, Jianwen Zhang, Jianlin Feng, and Zheng Chen. 2014. Knowledge Graph Embedding by Translating on Hyperplanes. In *AAAI*, pages 1112–1119.

Quan Wang, Jing Liu, Yuanfei Luo, Bin Wang, and Chin-Yew Lin. 2016. Knowledge Base Completion via Coupled Path Ranking. In *ACL*, pages 1308–1318.

Q. Wang, Z. Mao, B. Wang, and L. Guo. 2017. Knowledge graph embedding: A survey of approaches and applications. *IEEE Transactions on Knowledge and Data Engineering*, 29(12):2724–2743.

Zhuoyu Wei, Jun Zhao, and Kang Liu. 2016. Mining Inference Formulas by Goal-Directed Random Walks. In *EMNLP*, pages 1379–1388.

Robert West, Evgeniy Gabrilovich, Kevin Murphy, Shaohua Sun, Rahul Gupta, and Dekang Lin. 2014. Knowledge Base Completion via Search-based Question Answering. In *WWW*, pages 515–526.

Jason Weston and Antoine Bordes. 2014. Embedding Methods for NLP. In *EMNLP 2014 tutorial*.

Han Xiao, Minlie Huang, and Xiaoyan Zhu. 2016. TransG : A Generative Model for Knowledge Graph Embedding. In *ACL*, pages 2316–2325.

Han Xiao, Minlie Huang, and Xiaoyan Zhu. 2017. SSP: semantic space projection for knowledge graph embedding with text descriptions. In *AAAI*, pages 3104–3110.

Qizhe Xie, Xuezhe Ma, Zihang Dai, and Eduard Hovy. 2017. An Interpretable Knowledge Transfer Model for Knowledge Base Completion. In *ACL*, pages 950–962.

Zhiwen Xie, Guangyou Zhou, Jin Liu, and Jimmy Xiangji Huang. 2020. ReInceptionE: Relation-aware inception network with joint local-global structural information for knowledge graph embedding. In *ACL*, pages 5929–5939.

Canran Xu and Ruijiang Li. 2019. Relation Embedding with Dihedral Group in Knowledge Graph. In *ACL*, pages 263–272.

Bishan Yang, Wen-tau Yih, Xiaodong He, Jianfeng Gao, and Li Deng. 2015. Embedding Entities and Relations for Learning and Inference in Knowledge Bases. In *ICLR*.

Fan Yang, Zhilin Yang, and William W Cohen. 2017. Differentiable Learning of Logical Rules for Knowledge Base Reasoning. In *NIPS*, pages 2316–2325.

Wenpeng Yin, Yadollah Yaghoobzadeh, and Hinrich Schütze. 2018. Recurrent One-Hop Predictions for Reasoning over Knowledge Graphs. In *COLING*, pages 2369–2378.

Hee-Geun Yoon, Hyun-Je Song, Seong-Bae Park, and Se-Young Park. 2016. A Translation-Based Knowledge Graph Embedding Preserving Logical Property of Relations. In *NAACL-HLT*, pages 907–916.

Fuzheng Zhang, Nicholas Jing Yuan, Defu Lian, Xing Xie, and Wei-Ying Ma. 2016. Collaborative knowledge base embedding for recommender systems. In *KDD*, page 353362.

Hanwang Zhang, Zawlin Kyaw, Shih-Fu Chang, and Tat-Seng Chua. 2017. Visual translation embedding network for visual relation detection. In *CVPR*, pages 5532–5540.

Shuai Zhang, Yi Tay, Lina Yao, and Qi Liu. 2019. Quaternion knowledge graph embeddings. In *Advances in Neural Information Processing Systems 32*, pages 2735–2745.

Yuyu Zhang, Xinshi Chen, Yuan Yang, Arun Ramamurthy, Bo Li, Yuan Qi, and Le Song. 2020. Efficient probabilistic logic reasoning with graph neural networks. In *ICLR*.

Graph-based Aspect Representation Learning
for Entity Resolution

Zhenqi Zhao[1*], Yuchen Guo[2*], Dingxian Wang[1†]
Yufan Huang[1], Xiangnan He[3], Bin Gu[4]

[1]**eBay Inc.** {zhenqzhao, diwang, yufhuang}@ebay.com
[2]**Nanjing University** mf1814036@smail.nju.edu.cn
[3]**University of Science and Technology of China** xiangnanhe@gmail.com
[4]**Mohamed bin Zayed University of Artificial Intelligence** jsgubin@gmail.com

Abstract

Entity Resolution (ER) identifies records that refer to the same real-world entity. Deep learning approaches improved the generalization ability of entity matching models, but hardly overcame the impact of noisy or incomplete data sources. In real scenes, an entity usually consists of multiple semantic facets, called aspects. In this paper, we focus on entity augmentation, namely retrieving the values of missing aspects. The relationship between aspects is naturally suitable to be represented by a knowledge graph, where entity augmentation can be modeled as a link prediction problem. Our paper proposes a novel graph-based approach to solve entity augmentation. Specifically, we apply a dedicated random walk algorithm, which uses node types to limit the traversal length, and encodes graph structure into low-dimensional embeddings. Thus, the missing aspects could be retrieved by a link prediction model. Furthermore, the augmented aspects with fixed orders are served as the input of a deep Siamese BiLSTM network for entity matching. We compared our method with state-of-the-art methods through extensive experiments on downstream ER tasks. According to the experiment results, our model outperforms other methods on evaluation metrics (accuracy, precision, recall, and f1-score) to a large extent, which demonstrates the effectiveness of our method.

1 Introduction

Entity resolution has a tremendous impact on applications and research, such as deduplication, record linkage and canonicalization. It is a common challenge in various domains including digital libraries, E-commerce, natural language understanding, etc. Applying deep learning methods to solve ER problems has become a current research hotspot. These kinds of approaches have good generalization capability to improve the accuracy of prediction values on unseen data. One of the remaining challenges in tackling ER tasks is the poor quality of data, such as missing values and ambiguity. This makes pairwise distance measures approaches less effective with noisy content and context. In real-world applications, different types of aspects often interact with each other to form heterogeneous relations (Shi et al., 2018) in almost all networks. Another challenge of ER lies in how to express the relationships between the heterogeneous nature of aspects by proper data structure.

Advanced Graph Representation Learning (GRL), also called graph embedding, aiming to learn low-dimensional representations of nodes in networks, has attracted considerable attention in many real applications of networks (Perozzi et al., 2014). The universal pattern of these learning approaches is employing various types of random walk to generate node sequences and applying language models to map nodes into the same semantic vector space. In Knowledge Graph (KG), several related nodes often jointly represent a structural identity. An example of graph embedding in an aspect-based KG is shown in Figure 1.

---

[*]The first two authors contributed equally to this paper.
[†]Dingxian Wang is the corresponding author.

This work is licensed under a Creative Commons Attribution 4.0 International License. License details: http://creativecommons.org/licenses/by/4.0/.

Proceedings of the Graph-based Methods for Natural Language Processing (TextGraphs), pages 15–23
Barcelona, Spain (Online), December 13, 2020

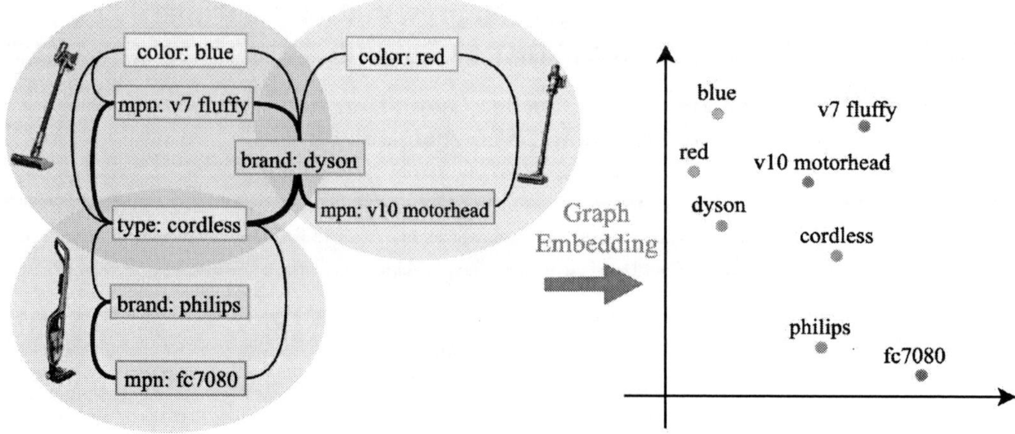

Figure 1: Schema of graph embedding in an aspect-based KG. The edges between aspects represent their co-occurrence in entities. Node colors in the graph represent different aspects types, and the thickness of the edge represents its weight. This method learns a latent space representation of aspects, which can be applied by downstream machine learning tasks.

An entity is composed of a set of aspects, and the relationship of aspects is easy to be represented in the form of graphs. In this paper, GRL is introduced to resolve entity augmentation in ER problems. We apply a heuristic feedback mechanism to the GRL field, which has long been proven successful in handling combinatorial optimization problems. This mechanism can significantly reduce the aggregation phenomenon caused by the long tail distribution of aspects, and generate more diverse and reasonable traversal sequences. We develop an algorithm (ASPECT2VEC) that learns the latent representation of aspects in a KG, by modeling a stream of random walks. ASPECT2VEC applies neural language models to process a special language composed of a set of heuristically-generated walks. The latent space representation of aspects would capture neighborhood similarity.

We apply ASPECT2VEC to resolve entity augmentation. In the first place, link prediction in KG is implemented and used to estimate the likelihood of linkages between aspects. This step can retrieve missing aspects of entities. Then, deep Siamese networks are constructed to generate high-quality hash codes based on semantic-preserving vectors of aspect sequences. Finally, the hashing method is employed to evaluate the performance of pairwise matching in ER.

Our main contributions are as follows:

* ASPECT2VEC. We propose a flexible aspect representation learning framework. The framework adopts a novel heuristic feedback method to generate reasonable subgraphs in an aspect-based KG, while preventing long tails phenomenon due to high-frequency aspects. Moreover, we encode aspects into a continuous vector space while preserving the semantic associations. These enrich the connotation of representation learning.

* Novel Problem Modeling. We model entity augmentation in ER as a link prediction task in KG. Normally KG is constructed from the observed interactions between aspects, which may be incomplete or inaccurate. Thus the challenge of data augmentation lies in measuring the likelihood of links between aspects.

* Evaluation. Here, we evaluate the quality of our aspect representations on downstream pairwise matching problems. The method shows significant improvements over several state-of-the-art methodologies on real public E-commerce data sets. This starts new directions for exploring data quality problems in the E-commerce field.

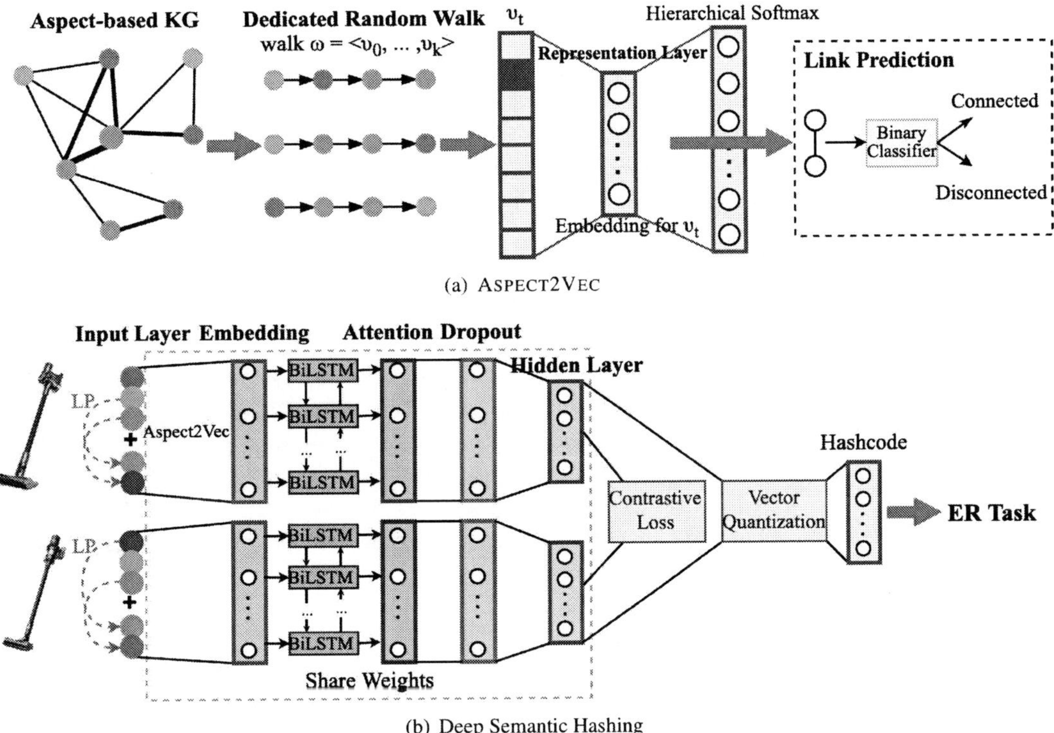

Figure 2: ASPECT2VEC (2a) employs a dedicated random walk algorithm to generate reasonable aspect sequences. Then SkipGram and Hierarchical Softmax are applied to convert the aspects into low-dimensional vector space for downstream tasks. In (2b), Link Prediction (LP) helps retrieve missing aspects for entity augmentation. Deep semantic hashing uses attention-based BiLSTM networks and vector quantization to generate discriminative hash codes, therefore similar pairs could be easily distinguished from dissimilar ones.

2 Proposed Approach

2.1 Problem Formulation

Given a set of entities U and a set of aspects A, each $u_i \in U$ corresponds to a series of $\{a_1, a_2, \cdots, a_m\} \subset A$. In this paper, entity resolution is scaled to a pairwise matching problem. The target of ER is employing aspects to generate discriminative hash codes so that similar pairs could be easily distinguished from dissimilar ones.

Let $G = (V, E, W)$ denote a weighted undirected graph, where V, E and W represent nodes set, edges set and weights set respectively. Each node $v \in V$ refers to an aspect, and edges refer to the co-occurrence of aspects in entities. Each weight $w \in W$ represents the co-occurrence times of aspects. A pairwise labeled dataset T is created with triples$\{(u_i, u_j, y)\}$, where $u_i, u_j \in U$ are the combinations of entities and y is a boolean label representing whether the pair of entities are matching or not.

2.2 Aspect Representation Learning

Aspect representation learning encodes aspects into a continuous vector space while preserving the semantic associations in the graph. To dig deep into the problem, we propose ASPECT2VEC, which leverages dedicated random walk to learn latent representations of nodes in the aspect-based KG. Figure 2 (a) shows a schematic diagram of ASPECT2VEC. Considering that aspects often have fixed types, the dedicated random walk helps generate reasonable sequences of aspects and avoid exhaustive search. This method lays the foundation for downstream entity augmentation.

2.2.1 Dedicated Walk

Swarm intelligence like ant colony optimization (ACO) (Dorigo and Stützle, 2019) algorithm has excellent performance in solving combination optimization problems. Artificial ants in ACO communicate with each other via pheromone, leading to a heuristic positive feedback mechanism. Inspired by this idea, we propose a novel traversal approach, which applies a heuristic feedback mechanism and tabu search to generate reasonable subgraphs. A walk $\omega = \langle v_0, \ldots, v_n \rangle$ is defined as a sequence of nodes where $(v_i, v_{i+1}) \in E$. Specifically, the k-th walk moves from node v_i to node v_j with probability $p_{i,j}^k$, as defined in equation 1:

$$p_{i,j}^k = \frac{\tau_{i,j}^\alpha \cdot \eta_{i,j}^\beta}{\sum_{r \in \Gamma(i)} \tau_{i,r}^\alpha \cdot \eta_{i,r}^\beta} \tag{1}$$

where $\tau_{i,j}$ represents degree of *freshness* of the hop from node v_i to node v_j. $\alpha \geq 0$ is a parameter to control the influence of $\tau_{i,j}$. *Freshness* is initiated with a constant τ_0, and indicates the visited frequency of edge (v_i, v_j) during traversal. $\eta_{i,j}$ describes the attractiveness of the hop from v_i to v_j, which is typically set to $w_{i,j}$. $\beta \geq 1$ is a parameter to control the influence of $\eta_{i,j}$. $\Gamma(i)$ is the 1-hop neighbors of v_i.

Degrees of *freshness* are updated when a walk is completed, decreasing the value corresponding to its moves. An example of a global *freshness* updating rule is

$$\tau_{i,j} \leftarrow \begin{cases} (1 - \rho)\tau_{i,j} & \text{if } (v_i, v_j) \text{ belongs to the } k\text{-th walk} \\ \tau_{i,j} & \text{otherwise} \end{cases} \tag{2}$$

where ρ is the *freshness* decay coefficient. The value of ρ depends on $\sum_k d_{i,j}^k$, which is the total length of k-th walk. $d_{i,j} = 1/w_{i,j}$ is the shortest distance between v_i and v_j.

$$\rho = \frac{1}{1 + \sum_k d_{i,j}^k} \tag{3}$$

2.2.2 Roulette Wheel Selection

To guarantee the stochastic properties of the walk, a roulette wheel selection method is adopted to choose the next hop in a walk, as shown in Algorithm 1. This method keeps the algorithm from falling into greedy search.

Algorithm 1: Roulette Wheel Selection

    Input: v_x: current node; $\Gamma(x)$: one-hop neighbors of v_x; N_k: forbidden nodes in k-th walk;
    Output: φ: the next hop node;

1 $\varphi = -1$;
2 $\mu = random(0.0, 1.0)$;
3 **for** *each* $v_z \in \Gamma(x)$ **do**
4     $\mu \leftarrow \mu - p_{x,z}$;
5   **if** $(\mu < 0)$ **&&** $(v_z \notin N_k)$ **then**
6         $\varphi = v_z$;
7   **break**;
8 **if** $(\varphi == -1)$ **then**
9     $\varphi = random(v \in \Gamma(x))$;
10 $update(N_k)$;
11 **return** φ;

Aspects that connect to similar others and have the same types in a graph are considered structural equivalence. Here, each entity only owns one specific value for a certain aspect type. Thus we restrict the walk length to the number of aspect types. If an aspect is visited during a walk, then the nodes that are with the same type as it will be added to the forbidden node set N_k.

Algorithm 2 shows procedures of how a dedicated walk generates total subgraphs. At the start of the algorithm, all parameters are initialized, including distance matrix and *freshness* matrix. In this method, degrees of *freshness* are the key to achieve heuristics. And the randomness of the algorithm is achieved through roulette wheel selection.

Algorithm 2: Dedicated Random Walk

Input: V: node set; χ: node type constrains;
Output: λ: all walks;
1 Initialize all parameters;
2 **for** *each* $v \in V$ **do**
3     $\omega = dedicatedRandomWalk(v, \chi)$;
4     $updateGlobalFreshness()$;
5     $\lambda.add(\omega)$;
6 **return** λ

2.2.3 ASPECT2VEC

SkipGram works as a language model to maximize the co-occurrence probability among the words appearing within a window. Compared to continuous bag-of-words (CBOW), SkipGram weighs nearby context words more heavily than distant context words. In ASPECT2VEC, SkipGram is applied to convert the aspects into low-dimensional vector space.

Algorithm 2 generates almost all reasonable aspect sequences. After that, each aspect node will be encoded to a corresponding representation vector. Moreover, to maximize the appearance probability of its neighbors in the walk, Hierarchical Softmax is used to approximate the probability distribution.

2.2.4 Entity Augmentation

Entity augmentation is modeled as a link prediction problem, namely predicting whether two nodes in a graph should have a link. The challenge lies in identifying spurious interactions and predicting missing links. The original connection information between aspects can be obtained from the KG and utilized to train a supervised model for LP.

We complete the entity augmentation task with a two-step solution-recall and classification. The original aspects are mapped into vector space, and the nearest neighbors that belong to the missing aspect types are recalled as candidates(the default size of the recall set is 10). Then the neighbors that are most likely to have connections with the query aspects are selected as supplement aspects. We build the LP model with a Siamese MLP structure. The input of the model is two aspect vectors, and the objective function is the contrastive loss. Accurate aspect representations facilitate entity augmentation, which greatly helps resolve downstream ER problems.

2.3 Deep Semantic Hashing

Deep semantic hashing uses deep neural networks to generate discriminative hash codes so that similar pairs could be easily distinguished from dissimilar ones (Suthee et al., 2018). Our semantic hashing method is implemented by a deep Siamese network and vector quantization.

2.3.1 Siamese Network

In the pairwise-preserving hashing method, the Siamese network is applied to explore the inner representation of symmetrical objects. We construct a deep bidirectional long short-term memory (BiLSTM) network with hierarchical attention (Z. et al., 2016) as the base structure. This model takes symmetrical input, as shown in Figure 2 (b). During the training process, the symmetrical parts share the neural weights of the network. The loss function applied here is contrastive loss (Nicosia and Moschitti, 2017) based on Euclidean distance, which can be defined as:

$$\min \ell = \frac{1}{2N} \sum_{n=1}^{N} y_n \varepsilon_n^2 + (1 - y_n) \max(margin - \varepsilon_n, 0)^2$$

$$\varepsilon_n = ||a_n - b_n||_2$$

$$(4)$$

where y_n denotes whether the pair is matching or not, ε_n is the Euclidean distance between two output vectors a_n and b_n, and $margin$ is the default threshold. The loss function makes a mapping from high to low dimensional space which maps similar input vectors to nearby points on the output manifold and dissimilar vectors to distant points. In the deepest layer of the Siamese network, we apply a fully connected neural layer with Softsign activation function, which polarizes the activation value and easily converts it to binary code.

2.3.2 Vector Quantization

Hash codes are widely used in information retrieval for O(1) time complexity and data compression. Vector quantization works by dividing a large set of vectors into groups, and each group is represented by its centroid point. Utilizing the output of the last layer of the network, we can get the vectors corresponding to the aspect sequences. We apply k-means clustering to **every dimension** of the output vectors, fitting the distribution of binary codes. It means that for each dimension there will be two clusters. For a multidimensional vector, dimension independent quantization divides values into discrete groups.

3 Experimental Evaluation

Our experiments on ASPECT2VEC consist of two parts, namely link prediction and entity resolution. Each experiment compares ASPECT2VEC with several state-of-the-art graph embedding methods, including DEEPWALK (Perozzi et al., 2014), LINE (Tang et al., 2015), NODE2VEC (Grover and Leskovec, 2016) and STRUC2VEC (Ribeiro et al., 2017) on two E-commerce datasets. The comparison includes link prediction as well as pairwise matching by hash codes.

3.1 Dataset

We select two public E-commerce datasets with different sizes and sparsity for experiments. The Flipkart dataset[i] contains 20000 products, the density of aspect data is 0.08% (32569 nodes, 426202 edges). The eBay dataset[ii] contains more than 8000 vacuum cleaner items, the density of aspect data is 0.15% (22841 nodes, 401973 edges). More than one hundred thousand entity pairs are constructed from each data set, where the label is generated from UPC/EAN[iii] in eBay and item title in Flipkart. The ratio of the training set to test set is controlled at four to one by random sampling.

3.2 Experiment Setting

Each kind of product entities have their main aspect types, so the length and order of the generated sequences can be determined by restricting the aspect types, which is also utilized in tabu search. For ASPECT2VEC, α and β are both set to 1, enabling balanced heuristic weight between $\tau_{i,j}$ and $\eta_{i,j}$. τ_0 is set to 1 to initialize the *freshness* matrix. For a fair comparison, parameters of neural networks used by different algorithms are the same. The deep models for link prediction and entity resolution are Siamese network with dense layers and deep Siamese BiLSTM, respectively. And the bits of hash code is set to 64 in pairwise matching, which is corresponding to the dimensions of the output vector.

3.3 Evaluation Results

Table 1 shows the evaluation result on link prediction between aspects, and ASPECT2VEC obviously outperforms all other methods on accuracy, precision, recall, and f1-score metrics. In ASPECT2VEC, the dedicated random walk takes the co-occurrence between aspects as the heuristic factor to choose the next

---

[i] https://www.kaggle.com/PromptCloudHQ/flipkart-products
[ii] https://www.kaggle.com/zhenqizhao/ebay-vacuum-cleaner-products
[iii] UPC stands for Universal Product Code and EAN stands for European Article Number, both for product identification.

Table 1: Comparison of aspect representation methods on link prediction

Datasets	Methods	accuracy	precision	recall	f1-score
Flipkart	DEEPWALK	0.7964	0.9424	0.6315	0.7562
	LINE	0.7831	0.9245	0.6166	0.7398
	NODE2VEC	0.6748	0.9373	0.3745	0.5352
	STRUC2VEC	0.7225	0.9141	0.4911	0.6390
	ASPECT2VEC	**0.8183**	**0.9525**	**0.6701**	**0.7867**
eBay	DEEPWALK	0.6797	0.9756	0.3596	0.5255
	LINE	0.8190	0.9709	0.6524	0.7804
	NODE2VEC	0.7012	0.9764	0.4039	0.5714
	STRUC2VEC	0.6746	0.9632	0.3536	0.5173
	ASPECT2VEC	**0.8534**	**0.9825**	**0.7155**	**0.8280**

Table 2: Comparison of aspect representation methods on pairwise matching

Datasets	Methods	accuracy	precision	recall	f1-score
Flipkart	DEEPWALK	0.9151	0.9623	0.4889	0.6484
	LINE	0.9472	**0.9786**	0.6855	0.8062
	NODE2VEC	0.9204	0.9694	0.5192	0.6762
	STRUC2VEC	0.9107	0.9688	0.4570	0.6210
	ASPECT2VEC	**0.9608**	0.9512	**0.7959**	**0.8667**
eBay	DEEPWALK	0.8987	0.9909	0.6232	0.7652
	LINE	0.9140	0.9909	0.6815	0.8076
	NODE2VEC	0.9124	0.9887	0.6771	0.8038
	STRUC2VEC	0.8943	**0.9915**	0.6063	0.7524
	ASPECT2VEC	**0.9187**	0.9900	**0.7001**	**0.8201**

hop, and captures deep potential connections rather than random hopping. Higher accuracy indicates that the method can not only connect missing links, but also identify spurious or incorrect links. Accurate link prediction facilitates entity augmentation. Table 2 shows the result of different methods on resolving pairwise matching. Attention-based BiLSTM can accurately capture the contribution of different aspect types to the final result, and the pairwise learning method fully understands symmetrical and asymmetric information between different pairs. Compared to other methods, ASPECT2VEC sacrifices a little precision but greatly improves the recall rate. The improved accuracy proves the ability to identify different kinds of entities, and the hashing method enables very fast matching. The experimental result shows the effectiveness of our method to entity augmentation, and the increase in overall performance on entity resolution.

4 Related Work

Entity resolution has attracted the interest of a large number of researchers in recent years. With the development of deep learning (DL), a growing number of DL methods are applied to solve ER problems (Mudgal et al., 2018). End-to-end deep matching models (Nie et al., 2019; Fu et al., 2020; Zhao and He, 2019) adopt similarity measures or semantic features of attributes for ER, especially dealing with heterogeneous entities. DL often requires a lot of labeled data as a training set, which is expensive to obtain. Therefore, transfer learning methods, based on a pre-trained model, are employed to solve ER tasks with little or no training data (Zhao and He, 2019). Besides, there have been many unsupervised methods to solve the data labeling problem, particularly focusing on machine labeling and error label correction (B. et al., 2019; R. et al., 2020; Chen et al., 2020). Some of the methods mentioned above pay attention to overcoming the dirty or heterogeneous data. However, how to deal with incomplete data and augment data quality in ER still needs further research. The method we proposed applies graph representation learning to resolve this problem.

Graph representation learning is dedicated to mapping nodes in networks into the same vector space, while maintaining the semantic association between nodes(Perozzi et al., 2014; Grover and Leskovec, 2016; Ribeiro et al., 2017; Shi et al., 2018; Tang et al., 2015; Wang et al., 2016; Ristoski and Paulheim, 2016). This kind of technique has received significant attention in the last few years with the development of natural language processing. The quality of the generated vectors is often measured by link prediction and node classification (Zhang and Chen, 2018; Ying et al., 2018; Trouillon et al., 2016). Previous researchers focused on the breadth and depth of graph traversal, but few of them take the node type into consideration during the progress of the random walk. In addition, how to avoid the long tail phenomenon as well as generating reasonable sequences in the traversal process is also a problem worth exploring.

5 Conclusion

In this paper, we proposed a novel aspect representation learning framework ASPECT2VEC, which resolves the entity augmentation problem in ER by modeling it as a link prediction problem in KG. ASPECT2VEC collaboratively explores dedicated random walks and captures semantic information between nodes in a network. Moreover, through extensive experiments on link prediction and deep semantic hashing, we demonstrated the superiority of the proposed framework to several state-of-the-art methods. Furthermore, dedicated random walk is flexible and also has great potential capability of parallelism to be explored in future research.

Acknowledgements

The research is supported by th Key Projects of Philosophy and Social Sciences Research of Chinese Ministry of Education under Grant 19JZD021. Assistance provided by eBay, Ads Shanghai Director Hua Yang, Director Wei Fang, Manager Hansi Wu was greatly appreciated.

References

Hou B., Chen Q., Shen J., Liu X., Zhong P., Wang Y., Chen Z., and Li Z. 2019. Gradual machine learning for entity resolution. In *WWW 2019*, pages 3526–3530.

Zhaoqiang Chen, Qun Chen, Boyi Hou, Zhanhuai Li, and Guoliang Li. 2020. Towards interpretable and learnable risk analysis for entity resolution. In *Proceedings of the 2020 ACM SIGMOD International Conference on Management of Data*, pages 1165–1180.

Marco Dorigo and Thomas Stützle. 2019. Ant colony optimization: overview and recent advances. In *Handbook of metaheuristics*, pages 311–351. Springer.

Cheng Fu, Xianpei Han, Jiaming He, and Le Sun. 2020. Hierarchical matching network for heterogeneous entity resolution. pages 3637–3643, 07.

Aditya Grover and Jure Leskovec. 2016. node2vec: Scalable feature learning for networks. In *Proceedings of the 22nd ACM SIGKDD international conference on Knowledge discovery and data mining*, pages 855–864.

Sidharth Mudgal, Han Li, Theodoros Rekatsinas, AnHai Doan, Youngchoon Park, Ganesh Krishnan, Rohit Deep, Esteban Arcaute, and Vijay Raghavendra. 2018. Deep learning for entity matching: A design space exploration. In *Proceedings of the 2018 International Conference on Management of Data*, pages 19–34.

Massimo Nicosia and Alessandro Moschitti. 2017. Accurate sentence matching with hybrid siamese networks. In *Proceedings of the 2017 ACM on Conference on Information and Knowledge Management*, pages 2235–2238.

Hao Nie, Xianpei Han, Ben He, Le Sun, Bo Chen, Wei Zhang, Suhui Wu, and Hao Kong. 2019. Deep sequence-to-sequence entity matching for heterogeneous entity resolution. In *Proceedings of the 28th ACM International Conference on Information and Knowledge Management(CIKM)*, pages 629–638.

Bryan Perozzi, Rami Al-Rfou, and Steven Skiena. 2014. Deepwalk: Online learning of social representations. In *Proceedings of the 20th ACM SIGKDD international conference on Knowledge discovery and data mining*, pages 701–710.

Wu R., Chaba S., Sawlani S., Chu X., and Thirumuruganathan S. 2020. Zeroer: Entity resolution using zero labeled examples. In *Proceedings of the 2020 ACM SIGMOD International Conference on Management of Data*, pages 1149–1164.

Leonardo FR Ribeiro, Pedro HP Saverese, and Daniel R Figueiredo. 2017. struc2vec: Learning node representations from structural identity. In *Proceedings of the 23rd ACM SIGKDD international conference on knowledge discovery and data mining*, pages 385–394.

Petar Ristoski and Heiko Paulheim. 2016. Rdf2vec: Rdf graph embeddings for data mining. In *International Semantic Web Conference*, pages 498–514. Springer.

Yu Shi, Huan Gui, Qi Zhu, Lance Kaplan, and Jiawei Han. 2018. Aspem: Embedding learning by aspects in heterogeneous information networks. In *Proceedings of the 2018 SIAM International Conference on Data Mining*, pages 144–152. SIAM.

Chaidaroon Suthee, Ebesu Travis, and Fang Yi. 2018. Deep semantic text hashing with weak supervision. In *The 41st International ACM SIGIR Conference on Research & Development in Information Retrieval*, pages 1109–1112.

Jian Tang, Meng Qu, Mingzhe Wang, Ming Zhang, Jun Yan, and Qiaozhu Mei. 2015. Line: Large-scale information network embedding. In *Proceedings of the 24th international conference on world wide web*, pages 1067–1077.

Théo Trouillon, Johannes Welbl, Sebastian Riedel, Éric Gaussier, and Guillaume Bouchard. 2016. Complex embeddings for simple link prediction. International Conference on Machine Learning (ICML).

Daixin Wang, Peng Cui, and Wenwu Zhu. 2016. Structural deep network embedding. In *Proceedings of the 22nd ACM SIGKDD international conference on Knowledge discovery and data mining*, pages 1225–1234.

Zhitao Ying, Jiaxuan You, Christopher Morris, Xiang Ren, Will Hamilton, and Jure Leskovec. 2018. Hierarchical graph representation learning with differentiable pooling. In *Advances in neural information processing systems*, pages 4800–4810.

Yang Z., Yang D., Dyer C., He X., Smola A., and Hovy E. 2016. Hierarchical attention networks for document classification. In *Proceedings of the 2016 conference of the North American chapter of the association for computational linguistics: human language technologies*, pages 1480–1489.

Muhan Zhang and Yixin Chen. 2018. Link prediction based on graph neural networks. In *Advances in Neural Information Processing Systems*, pages 5165–5175.

Chen Zhao and Yeye He. 2019. Auto-em: End-to-end fuzzy entity-matching using pre-trained deep models and transfer learning. In *The World Wide Web Conference*, pages 2413–2424.

Merge and Recognize: A Geometry and 2D Context Aware Graph Model for Named Entity Recognition from Visual Documents

Chuwei Luo[1], Yongpan Wang[1], Qi Zheng[1], Liangcheng Li[2], Feiyu Gao[1], Shiyu Zhang[1]

Alibaba Group[1]

College of Computer Science, Zhejiang University, No.38, Zheda Road[2]

`chuwei.lcw@alibaba-inc.com`, `{yongpan,yongqi.zq}@taobao.com`,
`liangcheng_li@zju.edu.cn`,
`{feiyu.gfy,rickzhang.zsy}@alibaba-inc.com`

Abstract

Named entity recognition (NER) from visual documents, such as invoices, receipts or business cards, is a critical task for visual document understanding. Most classical approaches use a sequence-based model (typically BiLSTM-CRF framework) without considering document structure. Recent work on graph-based model using graph convolutional networks to encode visual and textual features have achieved promising performance on the task. However, few attempts take geometry information of text segments (text in bounding box) in visual documents into account. Meanwhile, existing methods do not consider that related text segments which need to be merged to form a complete entity in many real-world situations. In this paper, we present GraphNEMR, a graph-based model that uses graph convolutional networks to jointly merge text segments and recognize named entities. By incorporating geometry information from visual documents into our model, richer 2D context information is generated to improve document representations. To merge text segments, we introduce a novel mechanism that captures both geometry information as well as semantic information based on pre-trained language model. Experimental results show that the proposed GraphNEMR model outperforms both sequence-based and graph-based SOTA methods significantly.

1 Introduction

With the rapid progresses in natural language processing and computer vision, visual documents become a mainstream media for expressing abundant information. Extracting the named entities from these visual documents is a critical step for further understanding. In the perspective of traditional natural language processing, the layout and the format information of documents is discarded. Only plain text that simply consists of sequential words do the researchers focus on and are necessary to be extracted entities. However, visual documents consist of many discrete text segments with a large variety of layouts and formats as Figure 1 shows. The combination of different text segments with different positions may represent different semantic information. Without the layout structure and the 2D semantic context information in it, the named entity recognition in visual documents could be much harder.

Although the named entity recognition in visual documents is a newly proposed under-researched task. Recently, in the attempt to make use of the structure information of visual documents, many works (Palm et al., 2017; Yang et al., 2017; Katti et al., 2018; Liu et al., 2018; Qian et al., 2019; Denk and Reisswig, 2019; Zhao et al., 2019) have designed NLP/CV/NLPCV based methods for visual-documents-related tasks. These approaches mostly focus on the coordinate of text segments to make features or learn embeddings. However, most of these methods do not consider the two problems:

1. Existing models often ignore the geometric information between text segments which is crucial for constructing 2D context for visual documents to extract named entities. It is hard to analyze the semantic meaning only through the plain text inside the bounding box and its coordinates.

This work is licensed under a Creative Commons Attribution 4.0 International License. License details: `http://creativecommons.org/licenses/by/4.0/`.

Proceedings of the Graph-based Methods for Natural Language Processing (TextGraphs), pages 24–34

Barcelona, Spain (Online), December 13, 2020

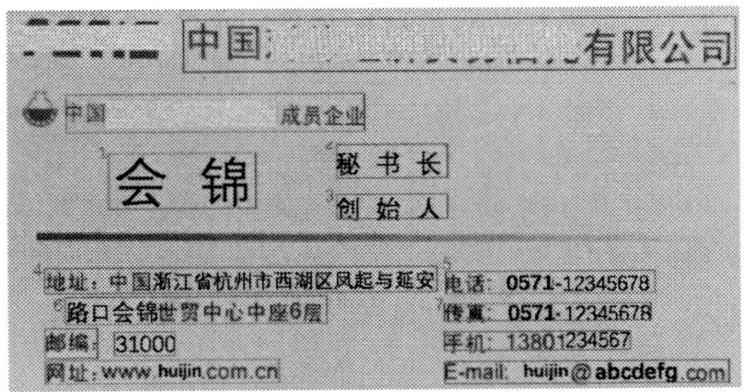

Figure 1: Example of a visual documents: visual business card. The red rectangular boxes are different text segments.

2. Because of the layout design, a complete named entity may be separated into several segments and cannot represent its full meaning. Meanwhile, some of text segments may lose the semantic information of their prefix ones and get incorrect tagging results. It is necessary and important to merge text segments into a complete named entity.

Specifically, for the first problem, as illustrated in Figure 1, it is hard to tell whether "会锦"("HuiJin") in text segment 1 is a named entity only according to its own plain text. While according to some of the nearest text segments, "秘书长"("Secretary General") in text segment 2 and "创始人"("The Founder") in text segment 3, human can help infer that text segment 1 is a person entity.

For the second, as Figure 1 shows, neither text segment 4 nor text segment 6 is a complete named entity. However, the two segments (segment 4 and segment 6) together represent a complete location entity that is *6/F, Middle Block, Huijin World Trade Center, at the intersection of Fengqi Road and Yan'an Road, Xihu District, Hangzhou, Zhejiang, China*. Apparently, the ability to merge text segments into a complete entity is important for NER from visual document.

To solve the above two problems, in this paper, we propose GraphNEMR, a graph neural end-to-end joint model for named entity recognition and merging tokens into named entities from visual documents. GraphNEMR incorporates the geometric information with the semantics to automatically extract non-sequential context-aware hidden features for each text segments in the visual documents. Specifically, We regard a visual document as a graph structure and all text segments in it are the graph nodes. The geometric information is represented by the adjacency matrix of the graph. In each text segment, a BiLSTM structure is used to sequentially encode tokens to represent semantic features. Then the graph convolutional network (GCN) (Kipf and Welling, 2017) encoder integrates information between neighbor nodes to learn the final representation of each text segment. Then the representations are used as the inputs of the merge module we proposed to decide the relation between text segments. After GCN encoder and the merge module, a LSTM+CRF decoder is used to get the named entity tagging. Our main contributions of this paper are as follows:

- To address the visual text merge problem, we propose a general method that captures the geometry information and semantics information. To the best of our knowledge, our approach is the first work to merge tokens in different text segments into complete named entity in visual documents.

- We propose the 8-geometry neighbors relation for each text bounding boxes in visual documents to represent geometry information in merge layer. Meanwhile, we design a geometry-distance-related adjacency matrix for graph representation with GCN.

- We propose a loss called $Loss_{nsp/sop}$ for semantically supervising merging text segments. Furthermore, we can obtain the right prefix semantic information for each text segments via merging results.

Extensive experiments show that our model outperforms both the strong sequence-based baseline model (BiLSTM-CRF) and the SOTA graph-based model (GraphIE) in visual document named entity recognition task.

2 Related Work

Our model builds on recent research of information extraction in visual documents and nested named entity recognition.

Recently, there is a lot interest in the task of information extraction in visual documents. Most of these works combined approaches from NLP, CV and document analysis. Lample et al. (2016) propose model BiLSTM-CRF that is a strong and a wildly used baseline for NER. Many researchers apply BiLSTM-CRF directly in visual information extraction without structure information consideration. Palm et al. (2017) use the sequential recurrent neural network (RNN) to extract key-value information from invoices. Their work shows the ability of neural network approach for extracting information in visual documents. However, their RNN model also treats documents as sequential text. Yang et al. (2017) consider document information extraction as a pixel-wise segmentation task and applied a end-to-end multimodal network to in visual documents. Their experiments showed that the textual features help layout segmentation. Katti et al. (2018) try to preserves visual documents' 2D layout by incorporating coordinate of characters for information extraction from invoices. Zhao et al. (2019) also found that in documents key information extraction, spatial information plays intrinsic roles. Denk and Reisswig (2019) extended the work of (Katti et al., 2018) to incorporate contextualized embedding by BERT language model and Xu et al. (2019) propose a pre-trained LayoutLM with the text and coordinates of text segments as inputs. They showed the effectiveness of using a pre-trained language model to invoice information extraction. Based on graph convolution network (GCN), Qian et al. (2019) and Liu et al. (2018) introduced the graph-based model that integrate textual and position attribute (i.e., coordinate, font size) to do visual information extraction task. They show that graph-based model outperforms the sequence-based baseline BiLSTM-CRF and confirms the benefits of using layout structure in visual information extraction.

The task of nested NER (Finkel and Manning, 2009) focuses on recognizing entities that can be nested within each other. This can be considered as related problems to ours on how to merge text segments in visual document. Recently, a number of approaches have been proposed for nested NER (Ju et al., 2018; Wang and Lu, 2018; Fisher and Vlachos, 2019). Specifically, Fisher and Vlachos (2019) decomposes nested NER into two stages, that first merge tokens into entities and then do recognition. But compared with our merging tokens problems, their approaches applied on serialized 1-D text instead of visual documents.

As we can see, 2D layout documents features is crucial for most existing work on visual documents information extraction. These models however simply equipped position features (i.e., absolute/relative coordinate) but ignore the geometry of neighbourhood and geometry distance information. Inevitably, simply combining position features with neural models may help little with 2D semantic context, as the layout of the different document varies a lot. And in many cases, text segments should be merged to represent a complete named entity. Thus we are thus motivated to look into the relative geometry of neighbourhood, exploring how to integrate geometry distance to build better 2D semantic context of each text segments and researching on how to merge text segments into complete named entity in visual documents.

3 Proposed Model

3.1 Overview

Text segments (characters in text segments and the bounding box position coordinates of the text segments) of a visual document are acquired by an OCR engine. Mathematically, let a visual document be $D = (t_0, t_1, ..., t_n)$, where t_i stands for a text segments and n is the number of text segments in the visual document D. An overview of our proposed model is illustrated in Figure 2. Firstly, we model a visual document D as a weighted fully connected graph by a graph convolution network encoder into geometry&2D context aware hidden representations, where each text segments t_i is the node of the graph. Secondly, given these hidden representations, a *merge layer* is applied to infer text segments merge decision. Lastly, we combine the graph hidden representations with merge information to reconstruct the

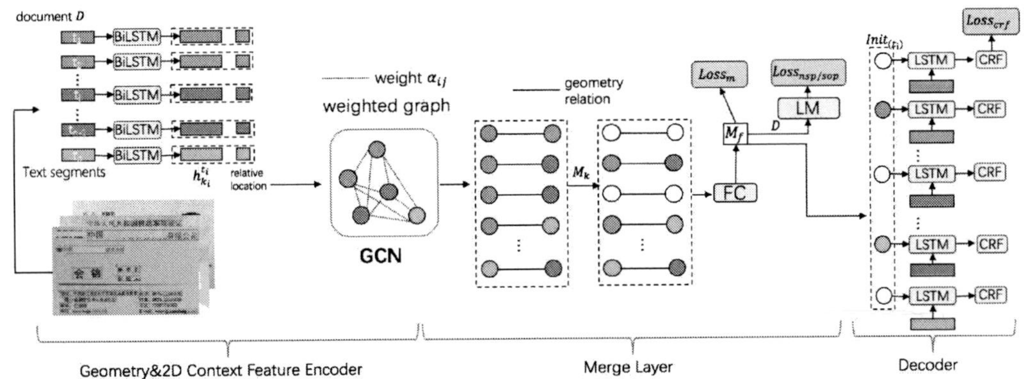

Figure 2: GraphNEMR Architecture

sequential front state of text segments and apply LSTM+CRF for named entity recognition.

3.2 Geometry&2D Context Feature Encoder

Given a text segment t_i, let the text in t_i be $S_{t_i} = (w_1^i, w_2^i, ..., w_{k_i}^i)$ where k_i stands for the length of S_{t_i} and w_j^i is the j-th character in sequence S_{t_i}. We first use Bi-LSTM to calculate sequential text embeddings:

$$h_{1:k_i}^{(t_i)} = BiLSTM(S_{t_i}) \tag{1}$$

where $h_{1:k_i}^{(t_i)}$ denotes the hidden states. We then use the last hidden states $h_{k_i}^{(t_i)}$ to represent the text sequence. To encode basic 2D information, relative coordinates and relative text segment size are concatenated to text embeddings. So the hidden representation node t_i is defined as follows,

$$e_{(t_i)} = [h_{k_i}^{(t_i)}, \frac{x^{(t_i)} - x_{min}}{s}, \frac{y^{(t_i)} - y_{min}}{s}, \frac{w^{(t_i)}}{s}, \frac{h^{(t_i)}}{s}] \tag{2}$$

where $x^{(t_i)}$ and $y^{(t_i)}$ are x-coordinate and y-coordinate of text segments respectively, x_{min} and y_{min} are the circumscribed square's minimum xy-coordinates of all text segments' bounding boxes, s is the side length of the circumscribed square.

Then, a graph convolution is applied to capture 2D context and geometry features from input embeddings that contain text and position information. Intuitively, from the perspective of 2D context, the closer the distance between text segments, the stronger the relevant information they represents. Different from exist gcn-based methods that use mean/max aggregation, to better build a 2D context with geometry information considered, we utilize the distance between text segments as a *weighted aggregation information*. For node t_i, our model retrieves new node features as follows,

$$g_{t_i}^{l+1} = ReLU(\sum_{t_j \in D} \alpha_{ij}(W^{l+1}g_{t_j}^l + b^{l+1})) \tag{3}$$

where $g_{t_j}^l \in R^f$ denotes the hidden feature of node t_j at layer l, W^{l+1} and b^{l+1} are learnable weights. Our model aggregates information from the neighbors of each node by the weight α_{ij} that is denoted as

$$\alpha_{ij} = \frac{(s - d_{ij})}{s} \tag{4}$$

where the $d_{ij} = |t_i, t_j|$ is the geometry distance between t_i and t_j. Intuitively, the closer the distance between t_i and t_j, the greater the value of α_{ij}. Thus, by using this weighted aggregation, closer relevant information between text segments can be encoded.

Since our GCN layer propagates information between nodes by every connected nodes with distance-based weight to construct 2D context. And the node embedding consist of semantics and geometry information. After we do graph convolution by L layers, each node t_i can capture both 2D context and geometry information. So, given document D, after getting each node hidden representations by our encoder, we get tensor D_g of shape $[n, f]$,

$$D_g = [g_{t_0}^L, g_{t_1}^L, ..., g_{t_n}^L] \tag{5}$$

3.3 Merge Layer

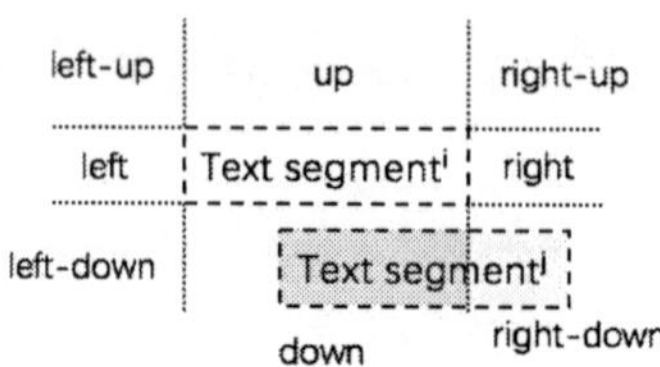

Figure 3: 8-geometry neighbors relation from Text segment^i (t_i) to Text segment^i (t_j)

The merge layer is responsible for merging text segments into a complete entity. Intuitively, one text segment can only be merged with its nearest text segments of 8-geometry neighborhoods. We obtain relative position between two text segments by 8-geometry neighbors. Given a text segment t_i with its bounding box area p^{t_i}, its 8-geometry neighbors areas are defined as a set $P^{t_i} = \{p_{left-up}^{t_i}, p_{up}^{t_i}, p_{right-up}^{t_i}, p_{right}^{t_i}, p_{right-down}^{t_i}, p_{down}^{t_i}, p_{left-down}^{t_i}, p_{left}^{t_i}\}$ where represent the left-up, up, right-up, right, right-down, down, left-down and left area of t_i respectively in visual document D. Given another text segment t_j with its bounding box area p^{t_j}, then the geometry position relation $p_{t_i:t_j}$ can be denoted by a 9-dim-one-hot vector where the first eight dimensions stand for 8-geometry neighbors and the last dimension represent the self-area of given text segments. Notice that p^{t_j} may intersect with more than one area in P^{t_i}, we choose the area which has the largest intersection with p^{t_j}. For example in Figure 3, the size of the intersecting area between text segments t_j and $p_{down}^{t_i}$ is larger than the others, the relation from t_i to t_j is *down*. Following encoder, by tiling and expanding dim on D_g with $p_{t_i:t_j}$ being added, we have

$$\mathbf{D_M} = \begin{bmatrix} [m_{00}] & [m_{01}] & \cdots & [m_{0n}] \\ [m_{10}] & [m_{11}] & \cdots & [m_{1n}] \\ \vdots & \vdots & \ddots & \vdots \\ [m_{n0}] & [m_{n1}] & \cdots & [m_{nn}] \end{bmatrix} = [[m_{ij}]] \tag{6}$$

$$m_{ij} = [g_{t_i}^L, p_{t_i:t_j}, g_{t_j}^L] \tag{7}$$

where $\mathbf{D_M} \in R^{n \times n \times (2f+9)}$ denotes all nodes pair features, $m_{ij} \in R^{2f+9}$ is the concatenation of $g_{t_i}^L$, $p_{t_i:t_j}$ and $g_{t_j}^L$. Then, a fully-connected network with sigmoid activation function is applied to learn a merge matrix M^f as

$$M^f = FC(D_M) \tag{8}$$

where $M_f \in R^{n \times n}$ represents whether two text segments should be merged and which text segment is the front segment. Here, the merge decisions are trained using cross entropy (CE) loss:

$$Loss_m = CE(M^f \cdot M^k, M_{label}^f) \tag{9}$$

where M_{label}^f is the label of M^f with binary value of 0 or 1. M^k is also a binary matrix where $M^k[i, j] == 1$ means that t_j is one of the top k nearest text segments from one of t_i's 8-geometry neighbors. By doing $\cdot$ (dot product operation) between M^f and M^k, only the top k nearest text segments in each 8-geometry neighbors can be merged. During inference, for example, if $M^f[i, j] == 1$, it means that text segment t_i should be merged with t_j and t_i is in front of t_j. $M^f[i, j] == 0$ means t_i and t_j should not be merged.

To leverage sequential language semantics, inspired by the next sentence prediction (NSP) training in BERT (Devlin et al., 2019) and sentence-order prediction (SOP) training in ALBERT (Lan et al., 2019), we propose a loss called $Loss_{nsp/sop}$ for semantically supervising merging text segments as follows,

$$Loss_{nsp/sop} = -LM_{nsp/sop}(D \times M^f) \tag{10}$$

where $LM_{nsp/sop}$ is the pre-trained language model that use NSP or SOP training. $\times$ represents matrix multiplication. The language model's parameters are fixed during training. By doing matrix multiplication between D and M^f, we can get the pair that our model hope to be merged in equation (8). The BERT model then get the pairwise input and by maximizing $Loss_{nsp/sop}$, the parameters of our model will be upgraded to make the merge decision in language model's perspective.

3.4 NER Decoder

The last NER Decoder is for named entity tagging. The structure is a standard LSTM+CRF. But different from previous works that use LSTM+CRF for tagging, we utilize the front text segment information that we get from *Merge Layer* as an initial state $Init_{(t_i)}$ for LSTM+CRF, for every node in D,

$$h_{lstm}^{t_i} = LSTM(u_{1:k_i}^{(t_i)}, Init_{(t_i)}) \tag{11}$$

$$u_{1:k_i}^{(t_i)} = [h_1^{t_i}|g_{t_i}^L, h_2^{t_i}|g_{t_i}^L, ..., h_{k_i}^{t_i}|g_{t_i}^L] \tag{12}$$

where $h_{lstm}^{t_i}$ is the hidden state of LSTM. $|$ is the concatenate operation. $Init_{(t_i)}$ is the initial state for the LSTM that is denoted as follows,

$$Init_{(t_i)} = \begin{cases} g_{t_j}^L & if(M^f[i,j] == 1) \\ 0 & otherwise, \end{cases} \tag{13}$$

where we can easily get the front text segment by doing matrix multiplication between D_g and M^f to get $Init_{(t_i)}$.

Then, a conditional random fields (CRF) is applied to perform entity tagging,

$$Loss_{crf} = CRF(h_{lstm}^{t_i}) \tag{14}$$

Finally, the objective function to be optimized is as follows,

$$Loss = Loss_m + Loss_{nsp/sop} + Loss_{crf} \tag{15}$$

In this way, the geometry information and 2D context is encoded into to our model's hidden layer, and with the *Merge Layer* and the last decoder, our model perform merge and recognize in visual documents.

4 Experiments

We first introduce the datasets for evaluating our proposed model. Then we describe baselines we compared with, the evaluation metrics and briefly explain our implementation details. Next, we show the results for two datasets. Finally, we demonstrate the improved effect of our model via ablation study.

4.1 Dataset

The aim of ICDAR 2019 SROIE task3[1] is to extract different kinds of text of several keys which are *company, address, date and total* from given receipts. The SROIE dataset consists of 1,000 scanned receipt images. Since the annotation of this task is incomplete and not well applied to our problem, we relabeled all the named entities in this dataset and get the text and corresponding bounding boxes

---

[1] https://rrc.cvc.uab.es/?ch=13&com=evaluation&task=3

according to the ground truth OCR annotations of SROIE. We build the dataset as SROIE-VNER. Our goal is to extract all the named entities (location, organization, date) in SROIE's receipt images. For our relabeled SROIE-VNER dataset, we split the dataset in 70% for training, 30% for testing.

The BCD dataset consists of 13,498 real-world business card images that is much larger than SROIE-VNER dataset. The collection is provided by user-uploading. We get the text and corresponding bounding boxes with Alibaba's OCR API[2]. Each character in text is manually labelled with B/I/E named entity tagging. Our goal is to extract all named entities (person, organization, location) in business card images. Business card styles of different companies are usually different and they are in large layout variability. So the layout of the images in the BCD dataset is more diverse than the SROIE-VNER dataset. 80% images in BCD dataset are used as training data. The left 20% images in BCD dataset are used for testing.

4.2 Baselines and Evaluation Metrics

We implement BiLSTM-CRF as a sequential tagger baseline as many researchers do in invoice/receipt images information extraction. According to (Palm et al., 2017) and (Liu et al., 2018), text segments in a document are concatenated from left to right and from top to bottom. And then they apply BiLSTM-CRF model to the concatenated document. We also compared our model to a graph-based tagging model GraphIE (Qian et al., 2019) which is probably the SOTA graph-based model in visual information extraction.

1 | O,B-ORG,I-ORG   3 | I-ORG,I-ORG

2 | I-ORG,I-ORG   4 | E-ORG,O,O

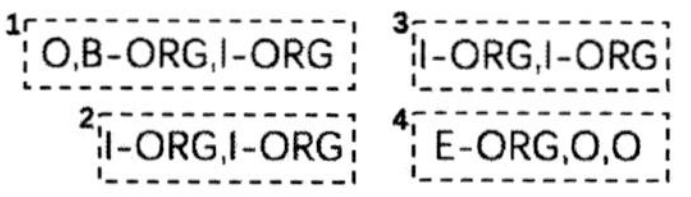

Figure 4: Example text segments in a visual document

The evaluation metrics are the standard named entity recognition precision, recall and F1 score. However, even if the tags of each text segments are completely correct, it cannot achieve extracting the complete entity correctly due to the order of the text segments. The traditional NER CoNLL evaluation method can not cover this problem. For example in Figure 4, assuming that entity tags in text segments 1-4 are correct. It is difficult for humans to determine whether the order (1,2,3,4) or the order (1,3,2,4) is right. And without the right order, we can not extract the right complete named entity. To address this problem, we evaluate the precision, recall and F1 score on complete entities recognition.

4.3 Implementation Details

We calculate the distance between text segments and determine whether the two regions intersect by the Shapely Python package[3]. For LSTM in our model, the dimension of hidden state is 256. The 300-dimensional pre-trained fasttext English word embeddings are used in SROIE-VNER experiments and 300-dimensional pre-trained fasttext Chinese character embeddings are used in BCD experiments. We use an one-layer GCN that is the same with GraphIE and the hidden size is 256. For language model for supervision, we utilize the sentence-order prediction (SOP) of ALBERT.

4.4 Results

Table 1 shows the precision, recall, and F1 score of the tagging results in SROIE-VNER dataset and BCD dataset for BiLSTM-CRF, GraphIE, and GraphNEMR. In SROIE-VNER dataset, both graph-based model GraphIE and our GraphNEMR have over 5.7% improvement compared to the sequential-based BiLSTM-CRF model. But from named entity character tagging results, GraphNEMR* dose not have significant improvement over GraphIE. In BCD dataset, which has a large diversity of layouts, GraphNEMR further surpasses GraphIE by 5.34% and yields 10.60% improvement over BiLSTM-CRF.

---

[2] https://duguang.aliyun.com/
[3] https://shapely.readthedocs.io/en/stable/manual.html

dataset	Entity	BiLSTM-CRF			GraphIE			GraphNEMR*		
		P	R	F1	P	R	F1	P	R	F1
SROIE-VNER	LOC	86.75	86.18	86.46	91.42	94.43	**92.90**	89.88	94.43	92.10
	ORG	75.71	75.71	75.71	80.95	86.29	**83.54**	84.38	82.23	83.29
	DATE	94.15	84.73	89.19	87.18	89.47	88.31	90.96	90.00	**90.48**
	ALL	85.37	82.08	83.69	87.70	91.18	89.40	88.81	90.28	**89.54**
BCD	PER	85.35	88.72	87.00	83.66	94.14	88.59	94.32	93.71	**94.02**
	LOC	80.67	85.47	83.00	84.42	95.59	89.66	93.84	94.12	**93.98**
	ORG	69.75	70.93	70.34	74.10	79.58	76.74	83.17	82.46	**82.81**
	ALL	76.92	79.60	78.24	79.58	87.82	83.50	89.05	88.63	**88.84**

Table 1: Visual documents named entity character tagging results. For a fair comparison, here we use GraphNEMR* that removes the pre-trained language model $Loss_{nsp/sop}$ supervision in equantion (10).

dataset	Entity	BiLSTM-CRF			GraphIE			GraphNEMR*		
		P	R	F1	P	R	F1	P	R	F1
SROIE-VNER	LOC	86.75	86.18	86.46	55.33	42.03	47.77	90.53	94.43	**92.44**
	ORG	75.71	75.71	75.71	80.95	86.29	**83.54**	84.38	82.23	83.29
	DATE	94.15	84.73	89.19	88.54	89.47	89.01	90.96	90.00	**90.48**
	ALL	85.37	82.08	83.69	72.08	64.71	68.19	89.14	90.28	**89.71**
BCD	PER	85.35	88.72	87.00	83.11	92.07	87.36	94.28	93.68	**93.98**
	LOC	80.67	85.47	83.00	74.53	84.05	79.00	93.64	93.86	**93.75**
	ORG	69.70	70.89	70.29	72.70	77.02	74.80	82.23	80.73	**81.48**
	ALL	76.90	79.58	78.22	75.95	82.86	79.25	88.58	87.75	**88.16**

Table 2: Visual documents NER results, evaluating on complete entities recognition.

Table 2 presents the comparisons of our model with the sequence-based model and the graph-based model on complete named entities recognition. Intuitively, this is a more suitable evaluation method for visual documents related tasks. Since GraphIE model doesn't have the ability to merge text segments, on this evaluating method, the LOC result of GraphIE has dropped significantly in SROIE-VNER dataset. Sequence-based model BiLSTM-CRF merges the text from left-to-right and from up-to-down and our model GraphNEMR* learns to merge. GraphNEMR* significantly outperforms the sequence-based model BiLSTM-CRF by 6.02% and the graph-based model GraphIE by 21.52% separately. In BCD dataset, GraphNEMR also obtains significant improvements over BiLSTM-CRF by 9.94% and GraphIE by 8.91%.

4.5 Analysis

From the dataset perspective, the layout of SROIE-VNER dataset is relatively simple. But many text segments need to be merged. The BCD dataset is quite different from SROIE-VNER. Since the style of each business card image is quite different, the BCD dataset has large layout varieties and also many text segments that need to be merged.

Since the sequence-based BiLSTM-CRF concatenate text segments in a document based on a common order which many layouts follow in real-world situations. So in SROIE-VNER dataset that is in a relatively simple layout, no matter what evaluation methods, the sequence-based BiLSTM-CRF can achieve relatively stable and comparable results. But the order that is from left-to-right and from top-to-bottom may not be guaranteed. The sequence order of entities like *location* and *organization* that often appear as multiple lines or multiple text segments are broken by such concatenations. So in BCD dataset that is in large varieties layouts, the performance of the sequence-based model suffers from significant performance degradation. Entities that usually have a short text length and in most cases are in left-to-right order in single text segment, i.e. *person*, are not influenced by concatenations and can keep a relatively stable performance in different layout varieties.

GraphNEMR	P	R	F1
k=1	86.57	85.49	86.03
k=2	88.33	89.21	88.77
k=3	87.70	90.10	**88.88**
k=+∞	86.62	88.61	87.60

Table 3: Results of different k nearest text segments from 8-geometry neighbors. $+\infty$ means using all text segments from the document.

Model	F1
GraphNEMR-FULL	88.88
- relative location	88.49($\downarrow$ 0.39)
- merge with geometry	87.48($\downarrow$ **1.4**)
- $Loss_{nsp/sop}$ supervise	88.16($\downarrow$ 0.72)

Table 4: Ablation study ("-" means removing the sub-component from GraphNEMR.

In BCD dataset, visual documents have diverse layouts and many text segments need to be merged. Because graph-based models take the visual layout into account, both GraphIE and GraphNEMR* achieve better results on visual documents with diverse layout changes than sequence-based model BiLSTM-CRF. So under these circumstances, the gap between our proposed GraphNEMR* and GraphIE mainly comes from the geometry features. While the visual documents in SROIE-VNER have simple layouts and a lot of text segments need to be merged, both GraphNEMR* and GraphIE have a better performance than BiLSTM-CRF in character tagging results. Since GraphIE doesn't have the ability of mergence and BiLSTM-CRF uses a naive merging strategy, GraphNEMR* performs much better than other models.

We also evaluate the impact of different numbers of k nearest text segments from 8-geometry neighbors. In theory, a text segment wouldn't be merged with a long-distance text segment. And a text segment will not only be merged with its nearest neighbors. Table 3 presents the results of using different k nearest text segments from 8-geometry neighbors. As we can see, using all text segments as candidates do not help the merging task and only setting the nearest neighbors as merging candidates will hurt the model performance.

4.6   Ablation Study

To better understand the contributions of each sub-component of GraphNEMR, we perform ablation studies in BCD dataset. Table 4 presents the results. In each study, we exclude the relative location, geometry information in merge layer and the use of the pre-trained ALBERT language model as $Loss_{nsp/sop}$ to supervise sentence order respectively. As we can see that the geometry information plays a more important role than others. The semantic $Loss_{nsp/sop}$ is also very helpful for recognize complete named entities. Intuitively, with the 8-geometry neighbors information considered, a richer 2D context and layout information is provided to better merge and recognize named entities.

5   Conclusions

In this paper, we propose GraphNEMR, a graph-based model that uses graph convolutional networks to jointly merge text segments and recognize named entities from visual documents. We model the visual document as a graph and incorporate geometry information into graph convolution network to build richer 2D context. To address the problem that text segments need to be merged into a complete entity, we combine geometry features with semantic features for learning to merge and recognize named entities. We evaluate our model on relabeled SROIE-VNER dataset and a real-world BCD dataset. Results show that our model outperforms sequence-based model (BiLSTM-CRF) and graph-based model (GraphIE) for named entity recognition from visual documents.

References

Piotr Bojanowski, Edouard Grave, Armand Joulin, and Tomas Mikolov. 2017. Enriching word vectors with subword information. *Transactions of the Association for Computational Linguistics*, 5:135–146.

Timo I Denk and Christian Reisswig. 2019. Bertgrid: Contextualized embedding for 2d document representation and understanding.

Jacob Devlin, Ming-Wei Chang, Kenton Lee, and Kristina Toutanova. 2019. Bert: Pre-training of deep bidirectional transformers for language understanding. In *NAACL*.

Jenny Rose Finkel and Christopher D Manning. 2009. Nested named entity recognition. In *Proceedings of the 2009 Conference on Empirical Methods in Natural Language Processing: Volume 1-Volume 1*, pages 141–150. Association for Computational Linguistics.

Joseph Fisher and Andreas Vlachos. 2019. Merge and label: A novel neural network architecture for nested ner. In *ACL*.

Tsu-Jui Fu, Peng-Hsuan Li, and Wei-Yun Ma. 2019. Graphrel: Modeling text as relational graphs for joint entity and relation extraction. In *Proceedings of the 57th Annual Meeting of the Association for Computational Linguistics*, pages 1409–1418.

Rinon Gal, Nimrod Morag, and Roy Shilkrot. 2018. Visual-linguistic methods for receipt field recognition. In *Asian Conference on Computer Vision*, pages 542–557. Springer.

Meizhi Ju, Makoto Miwa, and Sophia Ananiadou. 2018. A neural layered model for nested named entity recognition. In *Proceedings of the 2018 Conference of the North American Chapter of the Association for Computational Linguistics: Human Language Technologies, Volume 1 (Long Papers)*, pages 1446–1459.

Anoop Raveendra Katti, Christian Reisswig, Cordula Guder, Sebastian Brarda, Steffen Bickel, Johannes Höhne, and Jean Baptiste Faddoul. 2018. Chargrid: Towards understanding 2d documents. In *EMNLP*.

Thomas N. Kipf and Max Welling. 2017. Semi-supervised classification with graph convolutional networks. In *International Conference on Learning Representations (ICLR)*.

Sai Chandra Kosaraju, Mohammed Masum, Nelson Zange Tsaku, Pritesh Patel, Tanju Bayramoglu, Girish Modgil, and Mingon Kang. 2019. Dot-net: Document layout classification using texture-based cnn. In *2019 International Conference on Document Analysis and Recognition (ICDAR)*, pages 1029–1034. IEEE.

Guillaume Lample, Miguel Ballesteros, Sandeep Subramanian, Kazuya Kawakami, and Chris Dyer. 2016. Neural architectures for named entity recognition. In *NAACL*.

Zhenzhong Lan, Mingda Chen, Sebastian Goodman, Kevin Gimpel, Piyush Sharma, and Radu Soricut. 2019. Albert: A lite bert for self-supervised learning of language representations. *arXiv preprint arXiv:1909.11942*.

Anh Duc Le, Dung Van Pham, and Tuan Anh Nguyen. 2019. Deep learning approach for receipt recognition. In *International Conference on Future Data and Security Engineering*, pages 705–712. Springer.

Xiaojing Liu, Feiyu Gao, Qiong Zhang, and Huasha Zhao. 2018. Graph convolution for multimodal information extraction from visually rich documents. In *NAACL*.

Devashish Lohani, A Belaïd, and Yolande Belaïd. 2018. An invoice reading system using a graph convolutional network. In *Asian Conference on Computer Vision*, pages 144–158. Springer.

Ying Luo, Fengshun Xiao, and Hai Zhao. 2020. Hierarchical contextualized representation for named entity recognition. In *AAAI*.

Rasmus Berg Palm, Ole Winther, and Florian Laws. 2017. Cloudscan-a configuration-free invoice analysis system using recurrent neural networks. In *2017 14th IAPR International Conference on Document Analysis and Recognition (ICDAR)*, volume 1, pages 406–413. IEEE.

Rasmus Berg Palm, Florian Laws, and Ole Winther. 2018. Attend, copy, parse-end-to-end information extraction from documents. In *arXiv preprint arXiv:1812.07248*.

Yujie Qian, Enrico Santus, Zhijing Jin, Jiang Guo, and Regina Barzilay. 2019. Graphie: A graph-based framework for information extraction. In *NAACL*.

Rizlene Raoui-Outach, Cecile Million-Rousseau, Alexandre Benoit, and Patrick Lambert. 2017. Deep learning for automatic sale receipt understanding. In *2017 Seventh International Conference on Image Processing Theory, Tools and Applications (IPTA)*, pages 1–6. IEEE.

Bailin Wang and Wei Lu. 2018. Neural segmental hypergraphs for overlapping mention recognition. In *EMNLP*.

Bailin Wang and Wei Lu. 2019. Combining spans into entities: A neural two-stage approach for recognizing discontiguous entities.

Yiheng Xu, Minghao Li, Lei Cui, Shaohan Huang, Furu Wei, and Ming Zhou. 2019. Layoutlm: Pre-training of text and layout for document image understanding. *arXiv preprint arXiv:1912.13318*.

Xiao Yang, Ersin Yumer, Paul Asente, Mike Kraley, Daniel Kifer, and C Lee Giles. 2017. Learning to extract semantic structure from documents using multimodal fully convolutional neural networks. In *Proceedings of the IEEE Conference on Computer Vision and Pattern Recognition*, pages 5315–5324.

Xiaohui Zhao, Zhuo Wu, and Xiaoguang Wang. 2019. Cutie: Learning to understand documents with convolutional universal text information extractor. *arXiv preprint arXiv:1903.12363*.

Joint Learning of the Graph and the Data Representation
for Graph-Based Semi-Supervised Learning

Mariana Vargas-Vieyra[1], Aurélien Bellet[2], and Pascal Denis[3]

[1,2,3]Magnet Team, Inria Lille - Nord Europe
[1]Université de Lille, CNRS, UMR 9189 - CRIStAL
59650 Villeneuve d'Ascq, France
`first-last@inria.fr`

Abstract

Graph-based semi-supervised learning is appealing when labels are scarce but large amounts of
unlabeled data are available. These methods typically use a heuristic strategy to construct the
graph based on some fixed data representation, independently of the available labels. In this paper, we propose to jointly learn a data representation and a graph from both labeled and unlabeled
data such that (i) the learned representation indirectly encodes the label information injected into
the graph, and (ii) the graph provides a smooth topology with respect to the transformed data.
Plugging the resulting graph and representation into existing graph-based semi-supervised learning algorithms like label spreading and graph convolutional networks, we show that our approach
outperforms standard graph construction methods on both synthetic data and real datasets.

1   Introduction

An important bottleneck for the development of accurate Natural Language Processing (NLP) tools for
many applications and languages is the lack of annotated data. A natural remedy to this issue lies in
semi-supervised learning (SSL) methods, which are able to leverage smaller labeled datasets in combination with large amounts of unannotated text data (which are often more easily available). In particular,
graph-based SSL algorithms (Subramanya and Talukdar, 2014), among which variants of label propagation (Zhu and Ghahramani, 2002; Zhu et al., 2003; Zhou et al., 2004) and more recently graph
convolutional networks (Kipf and Welling, 2017; Chen et al., 2018; Wu et al., 2019), have attracted
a lot of attention due to their interesting theoretical properties and good empirical performance. They
have successfully been applied to several NLP problems, such as sentiment analysis (Goldberg and Zhu,
2006), word sense disambiguation (Alexandrescu and Kirchhoff, 2007), text categorization (Subramanya and Bilmes, 2008), POS tagging (Subramanya et al., 2010), semantic parsing (Das and Smith,
2011), machine translation (Saluja et al., 2014), or lexicon induction (Faruqui et al., 2016). As their
name suggests, graph-based SSL methods represent all data points (that is, labeled and unlabeled) as
nodes in a graph with weighted edges encoding the similarity between pairs of points. This graph is then
used as a propagation operator to transfer labels from labeled to unlabeled points. Despite differences in
the way this propagation is achieved, graph-based SSL approaches all rely on two assumptions: (i) the
graph representing the data provides a faithful approximation of the manifold on which the data actually
live, and (ii) the underlying labels are smooth with respect to this manifold.

In many NLP problems, there is often no *a priori*-known graph, which raises the question of how to
best construct this graph over the dataset given some data representation. Most existing work rely on
classic graph construction heuristics such as k-nn graphs, ϵ-graphs or radial kernel graphs (Subramanya
and Talukdar, 2014), which may poorly adapt to the intrinsic structure of the data manifold and hence
violate assumption (i). More recently, in the machine learning and signal processing communities, some
algorithms were proposed to learn more flexible graphs by enforcing the topology to be smooth with
respect to the input data (Daitch et al., 2009; Kalofolias, 2016; Dong et al., 2016). All these approaches

This work is licensed under a Creative Commons Attribution 4.0 International License.   License details: `http://
creativecommons.org/licenses/by/4.0/`.

Proceedings of the Graph-based Methods for Natural Language Processing (TextGraphs), pages 35–45
Barcelona, Spain (Online), December 13, 2020

heavily depend on the choice of data representation and disregard the label information, making them unable to adapt to the prediction task and therefore potentially violating assumption (ii). While supervised representation learning techniques such as metric learning (Bellet et al., 2015) could be used to adapt the representation to the task of interest, for instance by bringing closer points with the same label, the lack of labeled data in the semi-supervised learning scenario makes them prone to overfitting.

In this paper, we propose an original semi-supervised algorithm for graph construction that adapts to both the data and the predictive task. Specifically, our approach leverages the labeled and unlabeled data to jointly learn a graph and a data representation. On the one hand, the graph is learned to provide a smooth topology with respect to the learned representation. On the other hand, the representation should bring closer (labeled and unlabeled) points that are neighbors in the graph as well as similarly labeled points, while pulling away points of different labels. A key feature of our approach is that the learned representation indirectly encodes and injects label information into the graph beyond the labeled points alone. We formulate our problem as a joint optimization problem over the representation and the graph weights, with a hyperparameter to easily control the sparsity of the resulting graph and thereby obtain a good approximation of the underlying manifold. We discuss some appropriate parameterizations for learning the representation, which revolve around adapting pre-trained embeddings so as to avoid overfitting. We then propose to solve our joint problem by alternating optimization on the representation and the graph. We validate our approach through several graph-based SSL experiments using label spreading (Zhou et al., 2004) and graph convolutional networks (GCN) (Kipf and Welling, 2017), both on synthetic and real text classification datasets. Incidentally, note that our approach is generic and could in principle be used in combination with any existing graph-based SSL framework. The results show that our approach outperforms previous methods which rely on heuristic graphs, generally by a considerable margin. Interestingly, we also observe that our approach effectively bridges the accuracy gap between a simple method like label spreading and a richer neural-based approach like GCN.

The rest of this paper is organized as follows. We introduce some notations and discuss the related work in Section 2. We then describe our approach and algorithm in Section 3. Our experimental results are presented in Section 4, and we conclude with future work directions in Section 5.

2 Notations and Related Work

Our work lies in the intersection of two topics: graph-based semi-supervised learning and graph learning. In this section, we start by introducing some useful notations. We then briefly review some related work in both areas.

2.1 Notations

We consider a dataset consisting of l labeled points $L = \{(x_i, y_i)\}_{i=1}^{l}$ and u unlabeled points $U = \{x_i\}_{i=l+1}^{l+u}$, where data points x_i lie in some space $\mathcal{X}$ (typically $\mathcal{X} \subset \mathbb{R}^d$) and labels $y_i \in \{1, \ldots, C\}$ are discrete. We denote the combined data by $X \in \mathbb{R}^{n \times d}$, where $n = l+u$. We place ourselves in the typical semi-supervised scenario where $l \ll u$, and the goal is to predict $y_{l+1}, \ldots, y_{l+u}$. Let $G = (V, W)$ be a graph composed of a set of nodes $V = \{v_1, \ldots, v_n\}$ and a symmetric nonnegative weighted adjacency matrix $W \in \mathbb{R}^{n \times n}$. We denote the set $\mathcal{W}$ of admissible weighted adjacency matrices by

$$\mathcal{W} = \{W : W \geq 0, \operatorname{diag}(W) = 0, W^\top = W\}. \tag{1}$$

Every observation x_i (labeled or unlabeled) can be seen as a signal occurring at node v_i, and W assigns a weight to each pair of nodes. We say that two nodes v_i and v_j are connected when $W_{ij} > 0$.

2.2 Graph-based SSL

Graph-based SSL takes as input a graph $G = (V, W)$ over the labeled and unlabeled data, the known labels and optionally some feature representation $X \in \mathbb{R}^{n \times d}$ of the data, and aims to predict the labels of the unlabeled points.

Many approaches exist for graph-based SSL, see (Subramanya and Talukdar, 2014) for a review of standard approaches. Classic algorithms take as input only the graph and use it to propagate the known labels to the unlabeled points (Zhu and Ghahramani, 2002; Zhou et al., 2004; Bengio et al., 2006). A popular approach is label spreading (Zhou et al., 2004), which can be formulated as a convex optimization problem implementing a trade-off between two terms. The first term is a graph Laplacian regularization term which encourages similar predictions for strongly connected points in the graph, while the second one tries to keep the predictions accurate for points with known labels. There also exist algorithms formalized as graph partitioning problems inspired from spectral clustering (Joachims, 2003).

Graph-based SSL methods can also leverage a feature representation of the data in addition to the graph. A generic strategy is to add the graph Laplacian regularization term to existing supervised learning algorithms such as SVM or neural networks (Belkin et al., 2006; Weston et al., 2012). Following a different direction, (Yang et al., 2016) builds upon graph embeddings approaches to propose a method to predict labels based on the input representation as well as some embeddings learned from the input graph and known labels. Finally, there has been some recent interest in graph convolutional networks (GCN) (Kipf and Welling, 2017; Chen et al., 2018; Wu et al., 2019). Much like CNNs for images, they rely on an (approximation of) a notion of graph convolution, allowing them to learn a nonlinear transformation of the input representation while encoding the graph structure when propagating inputs from a layer to the next.

In all these approaches, the graph is fixed and given as input to the algorithm (for several methods, this is also true for the data representation). Their performance is thus very sensitive to the relevance of the graph for the task at hand: in particular, the underlying labeling should be smooth with respect to the graph. Our method is a principled approach to learn such a task-specific graph, and also infers a relevant data representation.

2.3 Graph Construction and Learning

As pointed out by (Subramanya and Talukdar, 2014), graph-based SSL methods typically rely on graphs constructed from the input data representation with a simple heuristic strategy. Popular choices include k-nearest neighbor graphs (connecting pairs of points that are among the k-closest to each other), ϵ-graph (connecting points that are within distance ϵ), and radial kernel graphs (building a fully connected graph with exponentially decreasing weights $W_{ij} = e^{-\gamma \|x_i - x_j\|^2}$). Recently, more sophisticated methods that learn the graph weights as the solution of an optimization problem have been introduced (Daitch et al., 2009; Kalofolias, 2016; Dong et al., 2016). Essentially, the weights are learned to be smooth over the data representation (i.e., assigning large weights to nearby points) with some regularization to enforce or control some properties such as connectedness and sparsity. In any case, the graphs obtained with the above approaches are task-independent in the sense that they ignore the labels.

To the best of our knowledge, there have been very few attempts to learn task-specific graphs for SSL. (Alexandrescu and Kirchhoff, 2007) propose to train a supervised classifier on labeled points and using the soft label predictions as the representation to build the graph. While this gives a way to incorporate label information, the supervised predictions are very dependent on the initial representation and the classifier itself can heavily overfit due to scarce labels.

3 Proposed Model

Our approach learns a graph and a data representation for use in downstream graph-based SSL algorithms. In this section, we start by introducing our formulation as a joint optimization problem over the representation and the graph. We then discuss some relevant choices for the parameterization of the learned representation, and finally present our alternating optimization scheme.

3.1 Problem Formulation

For the sake of generality, in this section we formulate our problem with respect to a generic representation function $\phi_\Theta : \mathcal{X} \to \mathbb{R}^k$, parameterized by Θ, which represents any data point $x \in \mathcal{X}$ as a k-dimensional vector $\phi_\Theta(x) \in \mathbb{R}^k$. We discuss some relevant choices of representation functions in Section 3.2.

We propose to learn a weighted adjacency matrix W^* and a representation function ϕ_{Θ^*} by minimizing a joint objective function f that involves both the labeled and unlabeled data points:

$$W^*, \Theta^* = \underset{W \in \mathcal{W}, \Theta}{\arg\min} \, f(W, \Theta).$$

Once the above optimization problem has been solved, the learned graph W^* (which is based on the learned representation function ϕ_{Θ^*}) and possibly the representation ϕ_{Θ^*} can then be given as input to any graph-based SSL algorithm to obtain predictions for the unlabeled data.

Our objective function $f(W, \Theta)$ decomposes into three terms:

$$f(W, \Theta) = f_1(\Theta) + \alpha[f_2(W) + f_3(W, \Theta)] \tag{2}$$

where $f_1(\Theta)$ and $f_2(W)$ are respectively the representation and graph specific terms, while $f_3(W, \Theta)$ is the joint term. Hyperparameter $\alpha \geq 0$ controls the trade-off between the (supervised) representation learning term f_1 and the unsupervised part (f_2 and f_3).

We now define these three terms. For notational convenience, let us denote by $Z \in \mathbb{R}^{n \times n}$ the matrix whose entries are the normalized squared Euclidean distances between data points in the transformed space, i.e. $(Z_\Theta)_{ij} = \frac{\|\phi_\Theta(x_i) - \phi_\Theta(x_j)\|^2}{\sum_{i<j} \|\phi_\Theta(x_i) - \phi_\Theta(x_j)\|^2}$. The normalization conveniently removes the dependency on the scale of the data and Θ. The representation term $f_1(\Theta)$ is defined on the labeled data points only and takes the following form:

$$f_1(\Theta) = \sum_{\substack{x_i, x_j, x_k \in L \\ y_i = y_j, y_i \neq y_k}} \left[(Z_\Theta)_{ij} - (Z_\Theta)_{ik} + 1\right]_+, \tag{3}$$

where $[\cdot]_+ = \max(0, \cdot)$. This is a large-margin triplet loss similar to those used in metric learning (Bellet et al., 2015): it attempts to learn a representation function ϕ_Θ that brings each point x_i closer to points x_j with the same label than to differently labeled points x_k, with a safety margin of 1. In practice, we can subsample instead of summing over all possible triplets.

The graph term $f_2(W)$ is inspired from the (unsupervised) graph learning approach proposed by (Kalofolias, 2016):

$$f_2(W) = \beta\|W\|_F^2 - \mathbf{1}^\top \log(\mathbf{1}^\top W), \tag{4}$$

The log-barrier term on the degrees prevents any node from being isolated in the graph, while the Frobenius norm is a shrinkage term over the graph weights. Combined with our joint term (6) defined below, hyperparameter $\beta \geq 0$ directly controls the sparsity of the learned graph: the smaller β, the more concentrated the weights of each point on its nearest neighbors in the learned representation (hence the sparser the graph). On the other hand, as $\beta \to +\infty$, the graph becomes complete with uniform weights. Sparsity allows to enforce the locality property (only close points are connected in the graph) which is necessary to obtain a good approximation of the data manifold. It also reduces the computational cost in downstream graph-based SSL algorithms, whose complexity typically depends on the number of edges in the graph.

Other options are possible for $f_2(W)$ depending on the prior we want to have on the structure of the graph. For instance, one may use

$$f_2(W) = (1/\gamma) \sum_{i,j} W_{ij}[\log(W_{ij}) - 1], \tag{5}$$

where $\gamma > 0$ is a hyperparameter. This will force the graph to be fully connected.

Finally, we introduce the joint term bringing together the graph and the representation:

$$f_3(W, \Theta) = \text{tr}(W Z_\Theta) = \sum_{i,j} W_{ij}(Z_\Theta)_{ij}. \tag{6}$$

This can be seen as a weighted L_1 norm term on W (which is why it induces sparsity), and equivalently written as a quadratic form of the Laplacian matrix of the graph encoded by the symmetric matrix W.

It is also used in approaches based on graph Laplacian regularization (see Section 2), but in our case both the graph and the representation are learned in joint manner. This term makes the graph and the representation as smooth as possible with respect to each other on *both labeled and unlabeled points*.

Overall, our joint objective function (2) is designed to produce a sparse topology that tends to be smooth with respect to the data manifold and the underlying labeling function through an appropriate representation. We now discuss the choice of representation function ϕ_Θ.

3.2 Choices of Representation Functions

Many options are possible for the representation function ϕ_Θ depending on the nature of the data and task at hand. However, it is important to keep in mind that the amount of labeled information is scarce, hence learning complex text representations from scratch is likely to lead to severe overfitting. We argue that it is preferable to adapt pre-trained representations, which generally requires to optimize much fewer parameters. We give some concrete examples below.

Linear transformation. Pre-trained word embeddings (Mikolov et al., 2013; Pennington et al., 2014) are commonly used to represent texts in a vectorial space, e.g. by averaging the embeddings of the words occurring in a document. In order to adapt the representation to the task, we can learn a simple linear mapping $\phi_\Theta(x) = \Theta x$ which transforms the initial d-dimensional representation into a k-dimensional one, with $\Theta \in \mathbb{R}^{k \times d}$ and $k \leq d$. Such a strategy has been previously explored in the supervised setting to "re-embed" words in a task-specific manner (Denis and Ralaivola, 2017). This is the representation function that we use in our experiments (see Section 4).

Weighted combination. Recent work in learning deep contextualized word representations such as ELMo (Peters et al., 2018) and BERT (Devlin et al., 2019) allows to learn a task-specific combination of the token representations obtained at the K layers of the model, which typically capture different aspects of tokens (from syntax to semantics). In this case, we have K initial d-dimensional representations $x \in \mathbb{R}^{K \times d}$ for each text x and we learn a weighted combination $\phi_\Theta(x) = \Theta x \in \mathbb{R}^d$ where $\Theta \in \mathbb{R}^K$ is simply a K-dimensional parameter vector.

3.3 Optimization

We propose to optimize the cost function $f(W, \Theta)$ by alternating minimization over W and Θ, which is guaranteed to converge to a local optimum. This is a natural approach: one step learns a smooth graph given the current representation Θ, while the other learns a smooth representation with respect to the current graph (this can be seen as a regularizer for Θ based on unlabeled data) and also tries to keep labeled points of the same class closer than points of different class.

As the joint problem is nonconvex, initialization plays an important role. We propose to initialize the graph weights to zero and to start by optimizing Θ so that the initial representation focuses only on the (scarce) labeled data. The graph learned on this representation will thus strongly connect together the labeled points as well as unlabeled points that are very close to the labeled points and are thus likely to share the same label. At the next iteration, these unlabeled points will then contribute in learning a better representation and in turn a graph which strongly connects new unlabeled points. This process can be seen as a principled version of self-training heuristics popular in traditional (non-graph-based) semi-supervised learning (Triguero et al., 2015).

The subproblem of optimizing W given Θ is convex regardless of whether we define $f_2(W)$ as (4) or (5). Using (5) is computationally convenient as the subproblem has a closed-form solution: the weights are exponentially decreasing with the distance in the current representation ϕ_Θ, as given by the radial kernel $W_{ij} = \exp(-\gamma(Z_\Theta)_{ij})$ (Kalofolias, 2016). Note that unlike the classic radial kernel baseline construction method mentioned in Section 2.3, our graph is computed based on the learned representation ϕ_Θ by minimizing the joint objective function with respect to W. One drawback of using (5) is that the resulting graphs are always fully connected. Using (4) instead, we can obtain sparse graphs but the solution must be computed with an iterative algorithm. We found that the primal-dual algorithm introduced by (Kalofolias, 2016) converges slowly in practice — we instead optimize W by simple gradient descent over the "effective" $n(n-1)/2$ weights, adding a small positive constant inside the log term in (4) to make the objective function smooth.

As ϕ_Θ is typically differentiable in Θ (as in the examples outlined in Section 3.2), we also solve the subproblem in Θ by (stochastic) gradient descent. Note that this subproblem is generally nonconvex due to the distance difference in $f_1(\Theta)$.

Remark. *Updating W requires to optimize over $O(n^2)$ variables, which was manageable for the datasets used in our experiments. To scale to larger datasets, one can restrict the optimization to the weights corresponding to pairs of points that are close enough in the learned representation space[1] (other weights are kept to 0). This has a negligible impact on the solution in sparse regimes (small β).*

4   Experiments

In this section, we study the practical behavior of our method by comparing the accuracy of downstream graph-based SSL algorithms when the graph (along with the underlying representation) is learned with our approach (**ours**) rather than constructed with the following baseline strategies:

- **radial**: Complete graph with weights $W_{ij} = \exp(-\gamma \|x_i - x_j\|^2)$.

- **knn**: $W_{ij} = 1$ for x_i in the k-neighborhood of x_j (or vice versa), and $W_{ij} = 0$ otherwise.

- **kalo**: Unsupervised graph learning with the method of (Kalofolias, 2016). This corresponds to our approach when using the graph term (4) and keeping the original representation fixed.

In all cases the graph is constructed over the union of labeled (train set) and unlabeled data (validation and test sets). For experiments with our method, the learned representation is a linear transformation of the initial features as explained in Section 3.2.

We perform experiments with two graph-based SSL approaches: Label Spreading (LS) (Zhou et al., 2004) and the Graph Convolutional Network (GCN) method of (Kipf and Welling, 2017). We used the scikit-learn (Pedregosa et al., 2011) implementation of LS. For GCN, we used the TensorFlow implementation provided by the authors[2] and follow the recommended architecture:

$$\hat{Y} = \mathrm{softmax}(\tilde{L}\max(0, \tilde{L}XH_0)H_1), \tag{7}$$

where $\tilde{L} = \tilde{D}^{1/2}\tilde{W}\tilde{D}^{1/2}$ is the normalized Laplacian corresponding to the graph $\tilde{W} = W + \lambda I$ (the input graph augmented with self-loops), $\tilde{D}$ is the diagonal degree matrix ($\tilde{D}_{ii} = \sum_j \tilde{D}_{ij}$), and $H_0 \in \mathbb{R}^{d \times h}$, $H_1 \in \mathbb{R}^{h \times C}$ are the parameters to be learned. We set the number of hidden units h to 16 and λ to 1 as done in (Kipf and Welling, 2017).

To illustrate the behavior of our approach, we first present some experiments on synthetic data. We then show some results on real text classification datasets.

4.1   Synthetic Data

We generated a 3-dimensional dataset consisting of 100 points evenly distributed in two classes (Figure 1). We have two clusters per class placed far from each other while keeping clusters from different classes closer. We randomly picked 60% of the points and removed their labels.

We compare the classification error of GCN and Label Spreading when the input graph is given by our approach instead of using baseline graph construction methods. For GCN, we also give as input the representation learned with our approach. For our approach, we use the graph term (4) and for each labeled point x_i, we random sample 2 points x_j of the same class and 3 points x_k of different class and construct all combinations (x_i, x_j, x_k), leading to 6 triplets for each x_i in the triplet loss (3). The results given in Table 1 show that our approach clearly and consistently outperforms all methods in both GCN and Label Spreading.[3] The improvements are especially large for Label Spreading, as LS makes

---

[1] These can be identified in near-linear time using approximate nearest-neighbor techniques (Muja and Lowe, 2014).
[2] `https://github.com/tkipf/gcn`
[3] For this illustrating experiment, we picked the values of hyperparameters giving the best results for each method.

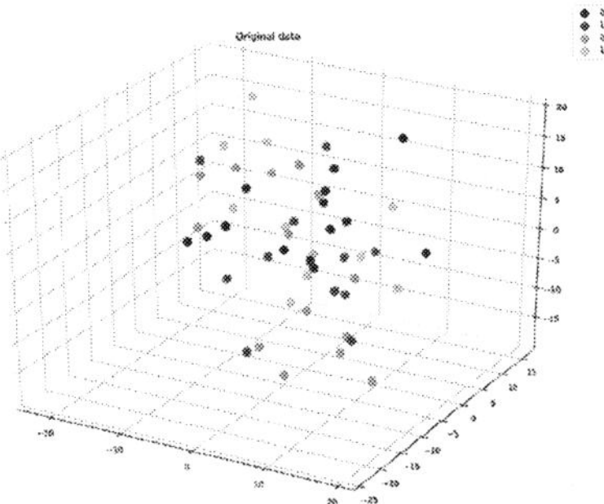

Figure 1: Original 3-dimensional synthetic data. Semi-transparent points are unlabeled.

	Label Spreading	GCN
radial	50.7	93.3
knn	81.3	93.3
kalo	77.3	88.0
ours	**96.0**	**96.0**

Table 1: Classification accuracy on the synthetic dataset.

predictions based on the graph only. In contrast, GCN learns its own (nonlinear) transformation of the representation given as input in an end-to-end manner. Still, our method is able to provide some gains for GCN as well, by providing it with a better graph. Note for instance the significant improvement compared to **kalo**, which learns the graph on the original representation.

To visualize this difference, Figure 2a shows the graph learned by **kalo**. Although the graph is learned to minimize the smoothness criterion with respect to the data, it fails to accurately capture the label distribution due to the limitations of the initial representation. Our alternating optimization approach overcomes this issue by learning a task-specific graph through an appropriate representation. In Figure 2b-2c-2d, we can see how label information is gradually injected at each step: after the first iteration, the graph is already significantly more smooth with respect to the underlying labeling and the graph is also sparser, but some edges between differently labeled points as well as an overly connected point remain. The following iterations further improve the graph quality. This explains the better performance obtained in downstream semi-supervised algorithms.

4.2 Real Data

We now evaluate our method on three text classification tasks derived from the 20NewsGroups dataset,[4] a collection of documents categorized into 20 topics, each one of which is partitioned into sub-topics. We chose the topics of *computers* with classes IBM and Mac ($n = 1945$ documents), *religion* with classes atheism and Christian ($n = 1796$), and *sports* with classes baseball and hockey ($n = 1993$).

For all datasets, we represent data points using the average token embedding based on word2vec (Mikolov et al., 2013). These embeddings are of dimension $d = 300$ and were trained on a 100B word corpus of Google news data (vocabulary size is 3M).[5]

We experiment with different proportions of unlabeled points in the training set (90%, 75%, 60% and 40%), while the rest of the data is evenly split into a validation and a test set. As commonly done in semi-supervised learning, we train on the union of the (labeled) training set and the (unlabeled) validation and test sets, select the values of hyperparameters based on the accuracy on the validation set, and report the corresponding accuracy on the test set.

To evaluate our approach we optimize the objective (2) as described in Section 3.3 with the graph term defined as in (4). To compute the representation term of our objective defined in (3), we construct triplets

---

[4] http://qwone.com/~jason/20Newsgroups/

[5] https://code.google.com/archive/p/word2vec/

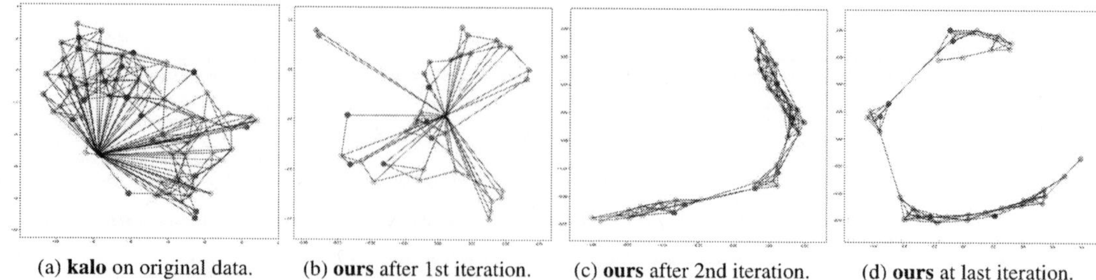

(a) **kalo** on original data.	(b) **ours** after 1st iteration.	(c) **ours** after 2nd iteration.	(d) **ours** at last iteration.

Figure 2: Force-directed drawing (spring layout) of graphs learned with **kalo**, and with our method at several iterations of our alternating optimization algorithm. Semi-transparent points are unlabeled.

dataset	%	radial	knn	kalo	ours
comp	90	62.76	61.89	63.63	**67.10**†
comp	75	67.35	67.35	69.87	**74.67**
comp	60	70.92	67.76	72.84	**75.58**
comp	40	76.58	70.99	75.86	**77.48**
rel	90	80.47	79.53	80.59	**83.88**†
rel	75	84.74	85.05	84.66	**85.18**
rel	60	85.74	83.36	87.22	**88.26**
rel	40	84.60	85.77	**86.74**	85.96
sports	90	84.11	81.78	86.55	**95.66**†
sports	75	89.81	90.87	89.93	**96.02**†
sports	60	92.77	91.43	92.64	**97.19**
sports	40	95.43	93.32	95.08	**97.36**

(a) Label spreading

dataset	%	radial	knn	kalo	ours
comp	90	69.60	65.91	**70.36**†	67.97
comp	75	74.55	67.95	73.71	**75.15**
comp	60	**77.78**	68.86	74.21	76.82
comp	40	**81.08**	67.21	80.72	76.76
rel	90	83.06	82.35	81.53	**83.41**
rel	75	83.49	83.62	83.88	**85.57**†
rel	60	83.36	83.21	**86.92**	86.03
rel	40	**88.30**	82.65	87.33	86.16
sports	90	94.70	92.48	93.33	**95.13**†
sports	75	**96.84**	94.85	95.78	96.25
sports	60	**98.80**†	95.85	97.19	96.92
sports	40	**98.77**	97.01	97.72	97.89

(b) GCN

Table 2: Classification accuracies of Label Spreading and GCN for different graph construction methods and proportions of unlabeled data. McNemar test to compare **ours** vs. the best baseline is statistically significant for those results marked with a dagger symbol †.

as follows: for each pair (x_i, y_i) in the labeled set we obtain the closest points with labels other than y_i ("imposters"), and the closest points with label y_i ("targets"). We picked 8 imposters and 3 targets. We tune the hyperparameters α from $\{0.001, 0.01, 1\}$, β from $\{0.00001, 0.001, 0.1, 1\}$, the dimension k of the learned representation from $\{16, 32, 64\}$, and perform early stopping with respect to the number of alternating steps between learning the graph and learning the representation (up to 10 alternating steps). We also tuned the hyperparameters of each baseline method (γ for **radial**, k for **knn** and β for **kalo**) and the trade-off hyperparameter of Label Spreading. Finally, we computed the McNemar test of significance (McNemar Quinn, 1947) to compare the performance of our method against the best baseline. Results marked with a dagger symbol † yield a statistically significant test for a significance level of 0.05.

Label Spreading. Table 2a reports test classification accuracies obtained on the test set for each configuration of dataset and proportion of unlabeled data. Our approach clearly outperforms all baselines, most of the time by a large margin. Also, McNemar test indicates that we tend to be significantly better than the best baseline in the more challenging settings where labeled data is the most scarce. The results also show that learning the representation along with the graph makes a clear difference compared to learning the graph only (as seen by the superior performance of **ours** over **kalo**).

As LS only uses the graph to make predictions, these results provide strong evidence of the superior quality of the graphs learned with our method.

Graph Convolutional Networks. We now turn to the more complex GCN prediction model. We reuse the same setup as for LS and feed GCN with both the learned representation and the learned graph. Table 2b summarizes the results. The gains obtained with our approach are smaller than those ob-

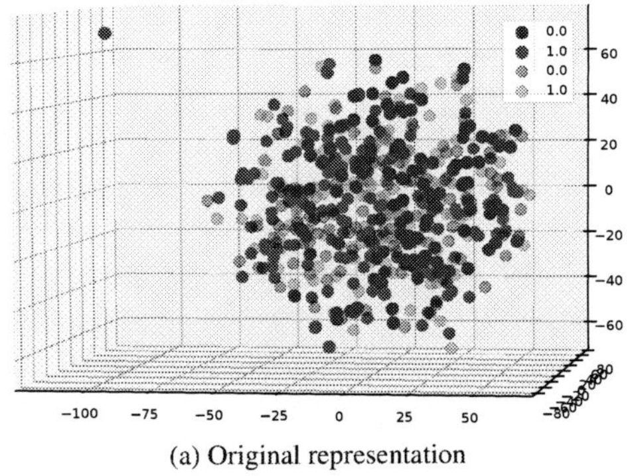
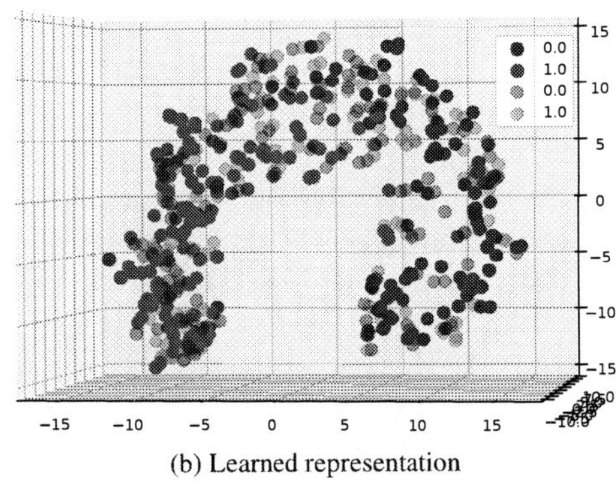

(a) Original representation

(b) Learned representation

Figure 3: 3D PCA visualization of the original representation (left) and the representation learned with our approach (right) on the *rel* dataset (%75 unlabeled). Transparent dots represent unlabeled documents.

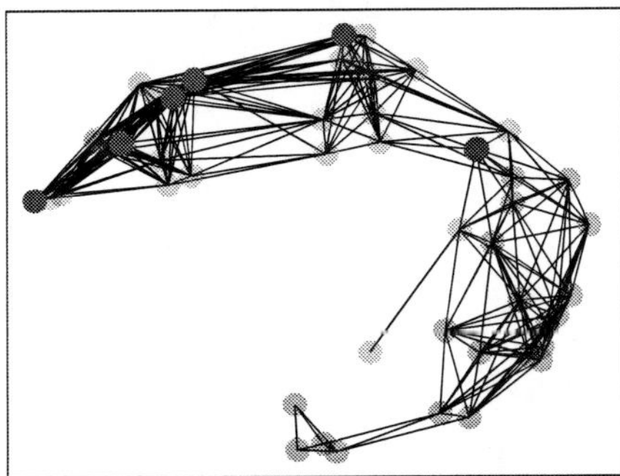

Figure 4: Force-directed drawing (spring layout) of a random 50-node subgraph of the graph learned with our approach on the *rel* dataset (%75 labeled).

tained in LS, which is to be expected since GCN has the ability to learn nonlinear transformations of the data. Nevertheless, we do observe some performance gains, as our approach generally improves upon or closely matches the performance of the best baseline. An interesting finding is that our method tends to close the gap of performance between LS and the richer neural-based GCN model. This suggests that simple propagation approaches may be sufficient in practice for many datasets, if provided with the right graph.

Visualization. We provide visualizations of the representation and the graph learned with our approach on the *rel* dataset. Figure 3 shows 3D PCA visualizations of the original representation and the representation learned with our approach. We see that the two classes are quite mixed up in the original representation while the learned representation is much smoother with respect to the underlying labeling (even in this crude low-dimensional summary). Figure 4 gives a snapshot of the graph learned with our approach by showing a subgraph of 50 randomly sampled nodes (subsampling helps to avoid clutter). The graph is very smooth with respect to the underlying labeling, and suggests that the learned high-dimensional representation has a nice manifold structure, with some regions of higher densities.

5 Discussion and Future Work

We presented a novel method bringing together graph learning, representation learning and SSL by jointly inferring the graph and the representation from semi-supervised data. The output of our approach can then be plugged into any graph-based SSL algorithm in place of using common graph constructions. Our experimental results suggest that the gains are especially significant for graph-based SSL algorithms that are unable to adapt the data representation (like label spreading and its variants), although we observe some gains also for GCN. To further improve the performance with richer models like GCNs, a promising direction is to extend our approach to learn the graph, the representation and the classifier in an end-to-end manner. We note that there has been very recent attempts in this general direction (Franceschi et al., 2019), though specific to GCN and with completely different modeling and assumptions.

The ideas underlying our approach could also be useful to tackle transfer learning settings and in particular domain adaptation (Ben-David et al., 2010). The latter can be seen as a SSL problem where the distribution of the target (unlabeled) data follows a different distribution that the source (training) data. Our objective function could be modified to encourage the learned representation and graph to serve as a "bridge" between the source and target distributions.

Acknowledgements

The authors would like to thank the Agence Nationale de la Recherche for funding this project with the grant number ANR-16-CE33-0011, and the reviewers for their feedback and suggestions. We also thank Grid5000 team for providing the necessary resources and technical support for this project, and CPER Nord-Pas de Calais/FEDER DATA Advanced data science and technologies 2015-2020.

References

Andrei Alexandrescu and Katrin Kirchhoff. 2007. Data-Driven Graph Construction for Semi-Supervised Graph-Based Learning in NLP. In *HLT-NAACL*.

Mikhail Belkin, Partha Niyogi, and Vikas Sindhwani. 2006. Manifold Regularization: A Geometric Framework for Learning from Labeled and Unlabeled Examples. *Journal of Machine Learning Research*, 7:2399–2434.

Aurélien Bellet, Amaury Habrard, and Marc Sebban. 2015. *Metric Learning*. Morgan & Claypool Publishers.

Shai Ben-David, John Blitzer, Koby Crammer, Alex Kulesza, Fernando Pereira, and Jennifer Wortman Vaughan. 2010. Transductive Learning via Spectral Graph Partitioning. *Machine Learning*, 79(1–2):151–175.

Yoshua Bengio, Olivier Delalleau, and Nicolas Le Roux. 2006. Label Propagation and Quadratic Criterion. In Olivier Chapelle, Bernhard Schölkopf, and Alexander Zien, editors, *Semi-Supervised Learning*, pages 193–216. MIT Press.

Jie Chen, Tengfei Ma, and Cao Xiao. 2018. FastGCN: Fast Learning with Graph Convolutional Networks via Importance Sampling. In *ICLR*.

Samuel I. Daitch, Jonathan A. Kelner, and Daniel A. Spielman. 2009. Fitting a graph to vector data. In *ICML*.

Dipanjan Das and Noah A Smith. 2011. Semi-supervised frame-semantic parsing for unknown predicates. In *ACL*.

Pascal Denis and Liva Ralaivola. 2017. Online Learning of Task-specific Word Representations with a JointBi-convex Passive-Aggressive Algorithm. In *EACL*.

Jacob Devlin, Ming-Wei Chang, Kenton Lee, and Kristina Toutanova. 2019. BERT: Pre-training of Deep Bidirectional Transformers for Language Understanding. In *NAACL-HLT*.

Xiaowen Dong, Dorina Thanou, Pascal Frossard, and Pierre Vandergheynst. 2016. Learning Laplacian Matrix in Smooth Graph Signal Representations. *IEEE Transactions on Signal Processing*, 64(23):6160–6173.

Manaal Faruqui, Ryan McDonald, and Radu Soricut. 2016. Morpho-syntactic lexicon generation using graph-based semi-supervised learning. *Transactions of the Association for Computational Linguistics*, 4:1–16.

Luca Franceschi, Mathias Niepert, Massimiliano Pontil, and Xiao He. 2019. Learning Discrete Structures for Graph Neural Networks. In *ICML*.

Andrew Goldberg and Xiaojin Zhu. 2006. Seeing stars when there aren't many stars: Graph-based semi-supervised learning for sentiment categorization. In *HLT-NAACL 2006 Workshop on Textgraph*.

Thorsten Joachims. 2003. Transductive Learning via Spectral Graph Partitioning. *Machine Learning*, 20(1):290–297.

Vassilis Kalofolias. 2016. How to learn a graph from smooth signals. In *AISTATS*.

Thomas N Kipf and Max Welling. 2017. Semi-supervised Classification with Graph-convolutional Neural Networks. In *ICLR*.

McNemar Quinn. 1947. Note on the sampling error of the difference between correlated proportions or percentages. *Psychometrika*, 12(2):153–157.

Tomas Mikolov, Kai Chen, Greg Corrado, and Jeffrey Dean. 2013. Efficient Estimation of Word Representations in Vector Space. *arXiv:1301.3781*.

Marius Muja and David G. Lowe. 2014. Scalable Nearest Neighbor Algorithms for High Dimensional Data. *IEEE Transactions on Pattern Analysis and Machine Intelligence*, 36(11):2227–2240.

F. Pedregosa, G. Varoquaux, A. Gramfort, V. Michel, B. Thirion, O. Grisel, M. Blondel, P. Prettenhofer, R. Weiss, V. Dubourg, J. Vanderplas, A. Passos, D. Cournapeau, M. Brucher, M. Perrot, and E. Duchesnay. 2011. Scikit-learn: Machine Learning in Python. *Journal of Machine Learning Research*, 12:2825–2830.

Jeffrey Pennington, Richard Socher, and Christopher Manning. 2014. Glove: Global vectors for word representation. In *EMNLP*.

Matthew E. Peters, Mark Neumann, Mohit Iyyer, Matt Gardner, Christopher Clark, Kenton Lee, and Luke Zettlemoyer. 2018. Deep contextualized word representations. In *NAACL*.

Avneesh Saluja, Hany Hassan, Kristina Toutanova, and Chris Quirk. 2014. Graph-based semi-supervised learning of translation models from monolingual data. In *ACL*.

Amarnag Subramanya and Jeff Bilmes. 2008. Soft-supervised Learning for Text Classification. In *EMNLP*.

Amarnag Subramanya and Partha Pratim Talukdar. 2014. *Graph-Based Semi-Supervised Learning*. Morgan & Claypool Publishers.

Amarnag Subramanya, Slav Petrov, and Fernando Pereira. 2010. Efficient Graph-based Semi-supervised Learning of Structured Tagging Models. In *EMNLP*.

Isaac Triguero, Salvador García, and Francisco Herrera. 2015. Self-labeled techniques for semi-supervised learning: taxonomy, software and empirical study. *Knowledge and Information Systems*, 42(2):245–284.

Jason Weston, Frédéric Ratle, Hossein Mobahi, and Ronan Collobert. 2012. Deep Learning via Semi-supervised Embedding. In *Neural Networks: Tricks of the Trade - Second Edition*, pages 639–655.

Felix Wu, Tianyi Zhang, Amauri Holanda de Souza Jr., Christopher Fifty, Tao Yu, and Kilian Q. Weinberger. 2019. Simplifying Graph Convolutional Networks. *arXiv:1902.07153*.

Zhilin Yang, William W Cohen, and Ruslan Salakhutdinov. 2016. Revisiting semi-supervised learning with graph embeddings. In *ICML*.

Dengyong Zhou, Olivier Bousquet, Thomas Navin Lal, Jason Weston, and Bernhard Schölkopf. 2004. Learning with Local and Global Consistency. In *NIPS*.

Xiaojin Zhu and Zoubin Ghahramani. 2002. Learning from Labeled and Unlabeled Data with Label Propagation. Technical Report CMU-CALD-02-107, Carnegie Mellon University.

Xiaojin Zhu, Z Ghahramani, and John Lafferty. 2003. Semi-supervised learning using Gaussian fields and harmonic functions. In *ICML*.

Contextual BERT:
Conditioning the Language Model Using a Global State

Timo I. Denk
Zalando SE
Berlin, Germany
`timo.denk@zalando.de`

Ana Peleteiro Ramallo
Zalando SE
Berlin, Germany
`ana.peleteiro.ramallo@zalando.de`

Abstract

BERT is a popular language model whose main pre-training task is to fill in the blank, i.e., predicting a word that was masked out of a sentence, based on the remaining words. In some applications, however, having an additional context can help the model make the right prediction, e.g., by taking the domain or the time of writing into account. This motivates us to advance the BERT architecture by adding a global state for conditioning on a fixed-sized context. We present our two novel approaches and apply them to an industry use-case, where we complete fashion outfits with missing articles, conditioned on a specific customer. An experimental comparison to other methods from the literature shows that our methods improve personalization significantly.

1 Introduction

Since its publication, the BERT model by Devlin et al. (2019) has enjoyed great popularity in the natural language processing (NLP) community. To apply the model to a specific problem, it is commonly pre-trained on large amounts of unlabeled data, and subsequently fine-tuned on a target task. During both stages, the model's only input is a variably-sized sequence of words.

There are use-cases, however, where having an additional context can help the model. Consider a query intent classifier whose sole input is a user's text query. Under the assumption that users from different age groups and professions express the same intent in different ways, the classifier would benefit from having access to that user context in addition to the query. Alternatively, one might consider training multiple models on separate, age group- and profession-specific samples. However, this approach does not scale well, requires more training data, and does not share knowledge between the models.

To the best of our knowledge, there is a shortcoming in effective methods for conditioning BERT on a fixed-sized context. Motivated by this, and inspired by the graph-networks perspective on self-attention models (Battaglia et al., 2018), we advance BERT's architecture by adding a global state that enables conditioning. With our proposed methods [GS] and [GSU], we combine two previously independent streams of work. The first is centered around the idea of explicitly adding a global state to BERT, albeit without using it for conditioning. The second is focused on injecting additional knowledge into the BERT model. By using a global state for conditioning, we enable the application of BERT in a range of use-cases that require the model to make context-based predictions.

We use the outfit completion problem to test the performance of our new methods: The model predicts fashion items to complete an outfit and has to account for both style coherence and personalization. For the latter, we condition on a fixed-sized customer representation containing information such as customer age, style preferences, hair color, and body type. We compare our methods against two others from the literature and observe that ours are able to provide more personalized predictions.

2 Related Work

BERT's Global State In the original BERT paper, Devlin et al. (2019) use a `[CLS]` token which is prepended to the input sequence (e.g., a sentence of natural language). The assumption is that the model

This work is licensed under a Creative Commons Attribution 4.0 International License.
License details: `http://creativecommons.org/licenses/by/4.0/`.

Proceedings of the Graph-based Methods for Natural Language Processing (TextGraphs), pages 46–50
Barcelona, Spain (Online), December 13, 2020

aggregates sentence-wide, global knowledge at the position of the [CLS] token. This intuition was confirmed through attention score analysis (Clark et al., 2019), however, the BERT architecture does not have an inductive bias that aids it. Recent work therefore treats the [CLS] token differently. Zaheer et al. (2020) constrain their BERT variant Big Bird to local attention only, with the exception that every position may always attend to [CLS] regardless of its spatial proximity.

Ke et al. (2020) also observe that the [CLS] attention exhibits peculiar patterns. This motivates them to introduce a separate set of weights for attending to and from [CLS]. The authors thereby explicitly encode into the architecture that the sequence's first position has a special role and different modality than the other positions. The result is an increased performance on downstream GLUE tasks.

It is important to note that all related work on BERT's global state does not use the global state for conditioning. Instead, the architectural changes are solely being introduced to improve the performance on non-contextual NLP benchmarks.

Conditioning on a Context   To the best of our knowledge, Wu et al. (2018) are the first to provide sentence-wide information to the model to ease the masked language model (MLM) pre-training task. The authors inject the target label (e.g., positive or negative review) of sentiment data by adding it to the [CLS] token embedding. In a similar application, Li et al. (2020) process the context separately and subsequently combine it with the model output to make a sentiment prediction.

Xia et al. (2020) condition on richer information, namely an *intent*, which can be thought of as a task descriptor given to the model. The intent is represented in text form, is variably sized, and prepended to the sequence. This is very similar to a wide range of GPT (Radford et al., 2019) applications.

Chen et al. (2019) condition on a customer's variably-sized click history using a Transformer (Vaswani et al., 2017). The most similar to our work are Wu et al. (2020) who personalize by concatenating every position in the input sequence with a user embedding – method [C] from Section 3. Their approach, however, lacks an architectural bias that makes the model treat the user embedding as global information.

BERT as a Graph Neural Network (GNN)   Battaglia et al. (2018) introduce a framework that unites several lines of research on GNNs. In the Appendix, the authors show that – within their framework – the Transformer architecture is a type of GNN; Joshi (2020) supports this finding. In both cases the observation is that a sentence can be seen as a graph, where words correspond to nodes and the computation of an attention score is the assignment of a weight to an edge between two words.

In the GNN framework, a global state is accessible from every *transfer function* and can be individually updated from layer to layer.[1] Neither Transformer nor BERT, however, have a global state in that sense. Inspired by this observation, we introduce a global state and use it for conditioning. We explain our two novel methods in the following section, alongside with two that are derived from the literature.

3   Conditioning BERT With a Global State

Let w denote a sequence of n words $w_i \in \mathbb{V}$ from a fixed-sized vocabulary $\mathbb{V}$. Further, let w_{-i} be the sequence without the ith word. Recall that a vanilla BERT model (Devlin et al., 2019) can predict the probability $\Pr(M = w_i \mid w_{-i})$ that a word w_i is masked-out in a sequence ($M = w_i$ being the masking event), conditioned on the other words in the sequence. Next, we introduce four methods to additionally condition BERT on a context vector $c \in \mathbb{R}^{d_{\text{context}}}$, which allows it to predict $\Pr(M = w_i \mid w_{-i}, c)$.

Concat [C]   Similar to Wu et al. (2020), we concatenate the context vector with every position in the input sequence. Let $x_i \in \mathbb{R}^{d_{\text{model}}}$ denote the embedding of word w_i at position i. The resulting input matrix is $I_{[C]} := W \begin{bmatrix} x_1 & \cdots & x_n \\ c & \cdots & c \end{bmatrix}$. $W \in \mathbb{R}^{d_{\text{model}} \times (d_{\text{model}} + d_{\text{context}})}$ is a trainable weight matrix that reduces the input dimensionality.

New Position [NP]   This method adds a new position to the input sequence at which the context is stored. It is comparable to how Wu et al. (2018) add label information. Instead of feeding the word sequence $\begin{bmatrix} x_1 & \cdots & x_n \end{bmatrix}$ into the model, we prepend the transformed context $W c$ to the sequence, where

---

[1]For details on the GNN definition of a global state we refer the reader to Section 3.2 in Battaglia et al. (2018).

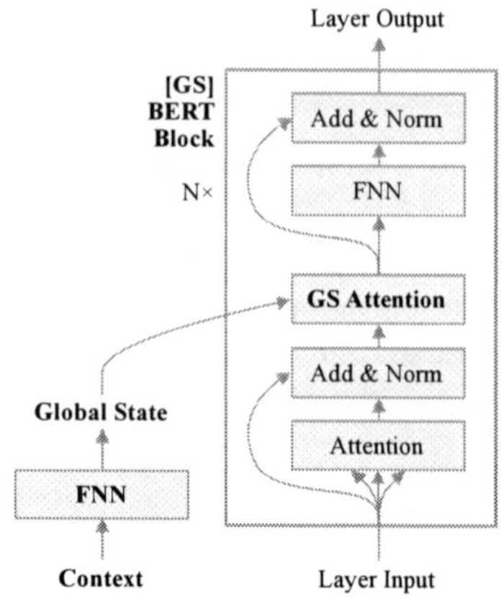

Figure 1: A BERT block with global state. Boxes have learned parameters; our additions are bold.

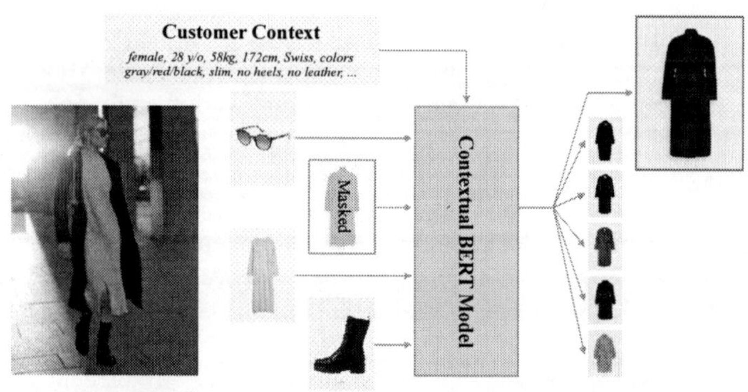

Figure 2: The fill-in-the-blank task on fashion outfits. Given a set of articles (left-hand side) and customer context, the model makes several predictions (right-hand side) for a masked out item (here: the coat). The predictions are personalized, because the model is utilizing the customer context.

$W \in \mathbb{R}^{d_{\text{model}} \times d_{\text{context}}}$ is a trainable weight matrix. The resulting input is $I_{\text{[NP]}} := \begin{bmatrix} Wc & x_1 & \dots & x_n \end{bmatrix}$. The model's attention masks are adjusted, such that every position can attend to the new first position.

Global State [GS] Our method is inspired by the GNN perspective on BERT. Its implementation is similar to the way the Transformer (Vaswani et al., 2017) decoder attends to the encoder. [GS] treats the context as a read-only global state from which the internal representations can be updated. In order to adjust the architecture of BERT accordingly, we insert a *global state attention layer* between the intra-sequence attention and the (originally) subsequent feed-forward neural network (FNN). Figure 1 shows how the inserted elements fit into the vanilla BERT block.

More formally, let $X^{(l)} \in \mathbb{R}^{n \times d_{\text{model}}}$ be the output of the lth BERT block (of which there are N); let $X^{(0)} := \begin{bmatrix} x_1 & \dots & x_n \end{bmatrix}$ be the model input; and let $\tilde{c} := \text{FNN}(c)$ be the global state derived from the context vector using a non-linear transformation $\text{FNN}(x) := W_2 \max(0, W_1 x + b_1) + b_2$. With our modification, $X^{(l)}$ is defined by first performing the normal intra-sequence attention as in BERT $A := \text{Attention}(W^Q X^{(l-1)}, W^K X^{(l-1)}, W^V X^{(l-1)})$; multi-head attention can be used here as well. Then, also unchanged, $\hat{A} := \text{LayerNorm}(\text{Dropout}(A) + X^{(l-1)})$. The internal representation is then updated once more by reading[2] from the global state $\tilde{c}$ with

$$B := \text{Attention}\left(V^Q \hat{A}, V^K [\tilde{c}], V^V [\tilde{c}]\right) = V^V [\tilde{c}], \tag{1}$$

and computing $\hat{B} := \text{LayerNorm}\left(\text{Dropout}(B) + \hat{A}\right)$. Lastly, the BERT layer output is computed as $X^{(l)} := \text{LayerNorm}\left(\text{FNN}\left(\hat{B}\right) + \hat{B}\right)$. The definitions of $\text{Attention}(\cdot)$, $\text{LayerNorm}(\cdot)$, and $\text{Dropout}(\cdot)$ are identical to Vaswani et al. (2017). The weight matrices W and V are not shared between layers. The layer indices $^{(l)}$ of A, B, and the weight matrices are omitted to aid readability.

Global State With Update [GSU] Note that in the [GS] method the global state $\tilde{c}$, which is being added to the internal representation in Equation 1, is the same for all blocks. With [GSU], a global state transfer function $\tilde{c}^{(l+1)} := \text{FNN}\left(\tilde{c}^{(l)}\right)$ updates the global state, with its initial value being derived from the context: $\tilde{c}^{(1)} := \text{FNN}(c)$. The weights of FNN are not shared between layers. Equation 1 is updated to read from the global state belonging to the lth layer:

$$B^{(l)}_{\text{[GSU]}} := V^V [\tilde{c}^{(l)}]. \tag{2}$$

---

[2]Note that the global state *sequence* $[\tilde{c}]$ does not admit for attention in the sense of selecting a weighted average of multiple vectors, because it consists only of a single vector. Instead, Equation 1 is reduced to the possibility for the lth layer to transform the context and update its internal state based on it.

Method	Cross-entropy loss	Recall@1	Recall@5	Recall@250	Parameters
[None]	5.2636 ± 0.0038	$8.53\% \pm 0.06$	$21.44\% \pm 0.04$	$87.14\% \pm 0.09$	546 432
[C]	4.9428 ± 0.0047	$10.26\% \pm 0.16$	$25.75\% \pm 0.09$	$90.76\% \pm 0.10$	673 664
[NP]	4.9260 ± 0.0078	$10.53\% \pm 0.06$	$26.27\% \pm 0.25$	$90.80\% \pm 0.11$	640 768
[GS]	4.8542 ± 0.0084	$11.19\% \pm 0.06$	$27.56\% \pm 0.28$	$91.35\% \pm 0.13$	723 328
[GSU]	4.7459 ± 0.0043	$12.21\% \pm 0.17$	$29.40\% \pm 0.06$	$92.19\% \pm 0.08$	921 856

Table 1: Comparison of the different conditioning methods on validation data. [None] provides no customer context to the model. Values are means across three training runs reported with standard error.

4 Empirical Evaluation and Discussion

We evaluate the performance of our proposed methods on a real-world industry problem: personalized fashion outfit completion (see Figure 2) for Europe's largest fashion platform. Our proprietary dataset consists of 380k outfits, created by professional stylists for individual customers. When styling a customer, i.e., putting together an outfit, the stylist has access to all customer features that we later use to condition the model. Therefore, customer data and outfit are statistically dependent.

The customer features are individually embedded using trainable, randomly initialized embedding spaces. The per-feature embedding vectors are subsequently concatenated, yielding a context vector of $d_{\text{context}} = 736$. Features include the customer's age, gender, country, preferred brands/colors/styles, no-go types, clothing sizes, price preferences, and the occasion for which the outfit is needed. The second model input, namely the outfit itself, is constructed from learned embeddings for every individual fashion article, with $d_{\text{model}} = 128$. We stack $N = 4$ BERT blocks with multi-head attention (eight heads). For a masked-out item, the model predicts a probability distribution over $|\mathbb{V}| = 30\,000$ articles.

While not being an NLP dataset, our data resembles many of the important traits of a textual corpus: the vocabulary size is comparable to the one of word-piece vocabularies commonly used with BERT models. Fashion outfits are similar to sentences in that some articles appear often together (match style-wise) and others do not. Different is the typical sequence length which ranges from four to eight fashion articles, with an average length of exactly five. In contrast to sentences, outfits do not have an inherent order. To account for that we remove the positional encoding from BERT so it treats its input as a set.

Table 1 shows the results of evaluating the four different methods. We compare cross-entropy and recall@rank (r@r for short) on a randomly selected validation dataset consisting of 17k outfits that are held-out during training. The r@r is defined as the percentage of cases in which the masked-out item is among the top-r most probable items, according to the model. Model parameters are counted without embedding spaces for customer features and the last dense layer.

The empirical evaluation reveals the effectiveness of using a context for making predictions. The model's ability to replicate the stylist behavior better, i.e., achieve a higher r@r, improves substantially with the addition of a context. On r@1 we see a relative improvement of $+43\%$ by using the [GSU] method for conditioning over using no customer context at all ([None]) and $+16\%$ compared to [NP] (the best method without global state).

A comparison of the four different conditioning methods shows [GSU] to be most effective, followed by [GS], [NP], and [C]. The methods [C] and [NP] do not have any bias towards treating the context vector specially. They attend to other positions in the sequence the same way they attend to the context. The superiority of [GS] and [GSU] can presumably be explained by their explicit architectural ability to retrieve information from the global state and therefore effectively utilize the context for their prediction.

We acknowledge the differences between our outfits dataset and typical NLP benchmarks. Nonetheless we hypothesize that the effectiveness of our method translates to NLP. In particular when applied to use-cases in which the modality of context and sequence differ, e.g., for contexts comprised of numerical or categorical meta data about the text. That is because the model's freedom to read from the context separately allows it to process the different modalities of context and input sequence adequately.

5 Conclusions and Future Work

With Contextual BERT, we presented novel ways of conditioning the BERT model. The strong performance on a real-world use-case provides evidence for the superiority of using a global state to inject context into the Transformer-based architecture. Our proposal enables the effective conditioning of BERT, potentially leading to improvements in a range of applications where contextual information is relevant.

A promising idea for follow-up work is to allow for information to flow from the sequence to the global state. Further, it would be desirable to establish a contextual NLP benchmark for the research community to compete on. This benchmark would task competitors with contextualized NLP problems, e.g., social media platform-dependent text generation or named entity recognition for multiple domains.

References

Peter W. Battaglia, Jessica B. Hamrick, Victor Bapst, Alvaro Sanchez-Gonzalez, Vinícius Flores Zambaldi, Mateusz Malinowski, Andrea Tacchetti, David Raposo, Adam Santoro, Ryan Faulkner, Çaglar Gülçehre, H. Francis Song, Andrew J. Ballard, Justin Gilmer, George E. Dahl, Ashish Vaswani, Kelsey R. Allen, Charles Nash, Victoria Langston, Chris Dyer, Nicolas Heess, Daan Wierstra, Pushmeet Kohli, Matthew Botvinick, Oriol Vinyals, Yujia Li, and Razvan Pascanu. 2018. Relational inductive biases, deep learning, and graph networks. *CoRR*, abs/1806.01261.

Wen Chen, Pipei Huang, Jiaming Xu, Xin Guo, Cheng Guo, Fei Sun, Chao Li, Andreas Pfadler, Huan Zhao, and Binqiang Zhao. 2019. POG: personalized outfit generation for fashion recommendation at alibaba ifashion. In Ankur Teredesai, Vipin Kumar, Ying Li, Rómer Rosales, Evimaria Terzi, and George Karypis, editors, *Proceedings of the 25th ACM SIGKDD International Conference on Knowledge Discovery & Data Mining, KDD 2019, Anchorage, AK, USA, August 4-8, 2019*, pages 2662–2670. ACM.

Kevin Clark, Urvashi Khandelwal, Omer Levy, and Christopher D. Manning. 2019. What does BERT look at? an analysis of bert's attention. *CoRR*, abs/1906.04341.

Jacob Devlin, Ming-Wei Chang, Kenton Lee, and Kristina Toutanova. 2019. BERT: pre-training of deep bidirectional transformers for language understanding. In Jill Burstein, Christy Doran, and Thamar Solorio, editors, *2019 Conference of the North American Chapter of the Association for Computational Linguistics: Human Language Technologies*. Association for Computational Linguistics.

Chaitanya Joshi. 2020. Transformers are graph neural networks. *The Gradient*.

Guolin Ke, Di He, and Tie-Yan Liu. 2020. Rethinking positional encoding in language pre-training. *ArXiv*, abs/2006.15595.

Xinlong Li, Xingyu Fu, Guangluan Xu, Yang Yang, Jiuniu Wang, Li Jin, Qing Liu, and Tianyuan Xiang. 2020. Enhancing BERT representation with context-aware embedding for aspect-based sentiment analysis. *IEEE Access*, 8:46868–46876.

Alec Radford, Jeffrey Wu, Rewon Child, David Luan, Dario Amodei, and Ilya Sutskever. 2019. Language models are unsupervised multitask learners. *OpenAI Blog*, 1(8):9.

Ashish Vaswani, Noam Shazeer, Niki Parmar, Jakob Uszkoreit, Llion Jones, Aidan N. Gomez, Lukasz Kaiser, and Illia Polosukhin. 2017. Attention is all you need. In Isabelle Guyon, Ulrike von Luxburg, Samy Bengio, Hanna M. Wallach, Rob Fergus, S. V. N. Vishwanathan, and Roman Garnett, editors, *Advances in Neural Information Processing Systems 30: Annual Conference on Neural Information Processing Systems 2017, 4-9 December 2017, Long Beach, CA, USA*, pages 5998–6008.

Xing Wu, Shangwen Lv, Liangjun Zang, Jizhong Han, and Songlin Hu. 2018. Conditional BERT contextual augmentation. *CoRR*, abs/1812.06705.

Liwei Wu, Shuqing Li, Cho-Jui Hsieh, and James Sharpnack. 2020. SSE-PT: Sequential recommendation via personalized transformer.

Congying Xia, Chenwei Zhang, Hoang Nguyen, Jiawei Zhang, and Philip S. Yu. 2020. CG-BERT: conditional text generation with BERT for generalized few-shot intent detection. *CoRR*, abs/2004.01881.

Manzil Zaheer, Guru Guruganesh, Avinava Dubey, Joshua Ainslie, Chris Alberti, Santiago Ontañón, Philip Pham, Anirudh Ravula, Qifan Wang, Li Yang, and Amr Ahmed. 2020. Big bird: Transformers for longer sequences. *CoRR*, abs/2007.14062.

Semi-supervised Word Sense Disambiguation
Using Example Similarity Graph

Rie Yatabe, Minoru Sasaki
Ibaraki University
`{19nm732r, minoru.sasaki.01}@vc.ibaraki.ac.jp`

Abstract

Word Sense Disambiguation (WSD) is a well-known problem in the natural language processing. In recent years, there has been increasing interest in applying neural networks and machine learning techniques to solve WSD problems. However, these previous supervised approaches often suffer from the lack of manually sense-tagged examples. In this paper, to solve these problems, we propose a semi-supervised WSD method using graph embeddings based learning method in order to make effective use of labeled and unlabeled examples. The results of the experiments show that the proposed method performs better than the previous semi-supervised WSD method. Moreover, the graph structure between examples is effective for WSD and it is effective to utilize a graph structure obtained by fine-tuning BERT in the proposed method.

1 Introduction

In human languages, many words have multiple meanings, depending on the context in which they are used. Identifying the sense of a polysemous word within a given context is a fundamental problem in natural language processing. For example, the English word "bank" has different meanings as "a commercial bank" or "a land along the edge of a river," etc. Word sense disambiguation (WSD) is the task of deciding the appropriate meaning of a target ambiguous word in its context (Navigli, 2009).

Among various approaches to the WSD task used over the past two decades, a supervised learning approach has been the most successful. However, it is quite expensive in both time and cost to annotate a large amount of reliable training data because supervised WSD requires a large amount of manually labeled training examples to achieve good performance. Unsupervised learning approach does not need labeled examples and uses large amount of unlabeled examples to find word clusters which discriminates the senses of the words in different clusters. Unsupervised learning algorithms are typically less accurate than supervised algorithms because examples may not be assigned the correct sense. For these reasons, we focus on a semi-supervised learning method that uses both sense-labeled and unlabeled examples in different proportions.

In this paper, we propose a semi-supervised WSD method using graph embeddings based learning method. In this method, we extract features from the context around the target word for each labelled and unlabeled example and construct a graph structure between labelled and unlabeled examples to obtain classifiers for every polysemous word. Then, we construct classifiers for each polysemous word using Planetoid (Yang et al., 2016), which is a multi-task framework for graph-based semi-supervised learning. By using the proposed method, it is possible to incorporate information obtained from unlabeled examples without assigning a sense label to unlabeled examples. Moreover, by learning graph embeddings, it is possible to distinguish between two similar examples with different sense labels to construct a better classifier for WSD. To evaluate the efficiency of the proposed WSD method, we design some experiments using the Semeval-2010 Japanese WSD task data set and the Senseval-2 English lexical sample task data set.

The three contributions of this work can be summarized as follows:

1.   We employ a graph embeddings based learning method for a semi-supervised WSD system to incorporate information obtained from unlabeled examples.

This work is licensed under a Creative Commons Attribution 4.0 International License. License details: http://creativecommons.org/licenses/by/4.0/.

Proceedings of the Graph-based Methods for Natural Language Processing (TextGraphs), pages 51–59
Barcelona, Spain (Online), December 13, 2020

2.   We show that the graph structure between examples, which is constructed by the relation between the training data and the unlabeled data, is effective for WSD. The graph constructed by determining if the example sentences are the same usage with BERT is more effective than the graph constructed by two major similarities, cosine similarity and Jaccard coefficient.

3.   We show that the proposed method performs better than the previous semi-supervised WSD method on the Semeval-2010 Japanese WSD task and the SENSEVAL-2 English lexical sample task.

The rest of this paper is organized as follows. Section 2 is devoted to presenting related works in the literature. Section 3 describes the proposed semi-supervised WSD method. In Section 4, we describe an outline of our experiments. In Section 5, we present experimental results. Finally, we conclude the paper in Section 6.

2   Related Works

This section is a literature review of previous work on semi-supervised WSD and various related methods using a neural network.

In recent years, there has been increasing interest in applying neural networks and machine learning techniques to solve WSD problems. (Kågebäck and Salomonsson, 2016) employed a Bidirectional Long Short-Term Memory (Bi-LSTM) to encode information of both preceding and succeeding words within the context of a target word. (Yuan et al., 2016) used an LSTM language model to obtain a context representation from a context layer for the whole sentence containing a target word. The context representations were compared to the possible sense embeddings for the target word. Then, the word sense whose embedding had maximal cosine similarity was assigned to classify a target word. (Raganato et al., 2017) considered WSD as a neural sequence labelling task and constructed a sequence learning model for all-words WSD. These approaches are characterized by their high performance, simplicity, and ability to extract a lot of information from raw text.

In recent years, semi-supervised learning has been used in WSD tasks. Semi-supervised learning is a technique that makes use of a small number of sense-labelled examples with a large amount of unlabeled examples. (Yarowsky, 1995) proposed a bootstrapping model that only has a small set of sense-labelled examples that gradually assigns appropriate senses to unlabeled examples. (Taghipour and Ng, 2015) and (Yuan et al., 2016) proposed a semi-supervised WSD method to use word embeddings of surrounding words of the target word and showed that the performance of WSD could be increased by taking advantage of word embeddings. (Fujita et al. 2011) proposed a semi-supervised WSD method that automatically obtains reliable sense labelled examples using example sentences from the Iwanami Japanese dictionary to expand the labelled training data. Then, this method employs a maximum entropy model to construct a WSD classifier for each target word using common morphological features (surrounding words and POS tags) and topic features. Finally, the classifier for each target word predicts the sense of the test examples. They showed that this method is effective for the SemEval-2010 Japanese WSD task. (Sousa et al., 2020) proposed a graph-based semi-supervised WSD method using word embeddings and distance measures. Although this method fixes the graph structure and trains only the classification model, our method trains the classification model and the graph jointly.

Some research in the field of WSD has taken advantage of graph-based approaches. (Niu et al., 2005) proposed a label propagation-based semi-supervised learning algorithm for WSD, which combines labelled and unlabelled examples in the learning process. (Yuan et al., 2016) also introduced a label propagation (LP) for semi-supervised classification and LSTM language model. An LP graph consists of vertices of examples and edges that represent semantic similarity. In this graph, label propagation algorithms can be efficiently used to apply sense labels to examples based on the annotation of their neighbours. In this paper, we use a semi-supervised learning method that incorporates knowledge from unlabeled examples by using graph embeddings based learning method.

Besides the semi-supervised learning, several recent methods have shown that combining supervised neural WSD systems with external knowledge base information improves the WSD performance. Gloss-BERT (Huang et al., 2019) and BEM (Blevins and Zettlemoyer, 2020) combine supervised learning with knowledge from gloss information to make better performance. EWISE (Kumar et al., 2019) incorporates both gloss embeddings and Knowledge Graph Embeddings. EWISER (Bevilacqua and Navigli, 2020) incorporates both synset embeddings and WordNet relations instead of leveraging sense glosses.

These methods represent the relationships between words as a graph structure, which means that words are represented as nodes and the relationships between words are represented as edges. In this study, we use a graph structure where the nodes are examples and the edges are semantic similarity between examples, which is different from the structure of these previous methods.

3   WSD Method Using Graph-based Semi-supervised Learning

In this section, we describe the details of the proposed semi-supervised WSD method using graph embeddings based learning method.

3.1   Overview of the Proposed Method

Our WSD method is used to select the appropriate sense for a target polysemous word in context. WSD can be viewed as a classification task in which each target word should be classified into one of the predefined existing senses. Word senses were annotated in a corpus in accordance with "Iwanami's Japanese Dictionary (The Iwanami Kokugo Jiten)" (Nishio et al. 1994). It has three levels for sense Ids, and the middle-level sense is used in this task.

The proposed semi-supervised WSD method requires a corpus of manually labelled training data to construct classifiers for every polysemous word and a graph between labelled and unlabeled examples. For each labelled and unlabeled example, features are extracted from a context around the target word, and the feature vector is constructed. Given a graph structure and feature vectors obtained from training data, we learn an embedding space, for example, set to jointly predict the sense label and neighborhood similarity in the graph using Planetoid (Yang et al., 2016). When the WSD classifier is obtained, we input test examples only to the WSD model and predict one sense for each test example.

3.2   Features

3.2.1   Lexical and Syntactic Features

To implement the proposed WSD system, we extracted features from training data and test data of a target word, unlabeled examples from the Balanced Corpus of Contemporary Written Japanese (BCCWJ) corpus (Maekawa, 2014), and example sentences extracted from Iwanami Japanese Dictionary. To segment a sentence into words, we use popular Japanese morphological analyzer MeCab with the morphological dictionary UniDic.

In this paper, we extract the target word and the two words on either side of the target word and then use the following twenty features (BF) for the target word w_i, which is the i-th word in the example sentence.

    e1: the word w_{i-2}
    e2: part-of-speech of the word w_{i-2}
    e3: subcategory of the e2
    e4: the word w_{i-1}
    e5: part-of-speech of the word w_{i-1}
    e6: subcategory of the e5
    e7: the word w_i
    e8: part-of-speech of the word w_i
    e9: subcategory of the e8
    e10: the word w_{i+1}
    e11: part-of-speech of the word w_{i+1}
    e12: subcategory of the e11
    e13: the word w_{i+2}
    e14: part-of-speech of the word w_{i+2}
    e15: subcategory of the e14
    e16: word that contains dependency relation with the w_i
    e17: thesaurus ID number of the word w_{i-2}
    e18: thesaurus ID number of the word w_{i-1}

e19: thesaurus ID number of the word w_{i+1}

e20: thesaurus ID number of the word w_{i+2}

To obtain the thesaurus ID number of each word, we use five-digit semantic classes obtained from a Japanese thesaurus "Bunrui Goi Hyo" (NIJL, 2004). When a word has multiple thesaurus IDs, e17, e18, e19, and e20 contain multiple thesaurus IDs for each context word. As additional local collocation (LC) features, we use bi-gram, tri-gram, and skip-bigram patterns in the three words on either side of the target word like IMS (Zhong and Ng., 2010). Skip-bigram is any pair of words in an example order with arbitrary gaps. Then, we can represent a context of word w_i as a vector of these features, where the value of each feature indicates the number of times the feature occurs.

3.2.2 Contextual Word Embeddings Using ELMo

Next, considering the context of the input sentence, we apply contextual word representations derived from pre-trained bi-directional language models (biLMs) as features. We use a pre-trained ELMo model to obtain a word embeddings for input sentences containing the target word. This pre-trained ELMo model is a two-layer bidirectional LSTM structure to learn the contextual information from text. We use only the output of the last layer of the pre-trained model. The target word and the two words on either side of the target word are extracted and the word embeddings of these five words is obtained. Then, we generate a 5120 dimensional vector that concatenates the word embeddings of these five words. Word embeddings are generated for each word in an input sentence depending on the context so that different embeddings tend to be generated for each word sense. We consider that the word embeddings of these five words allows us to capture the context of the target word.

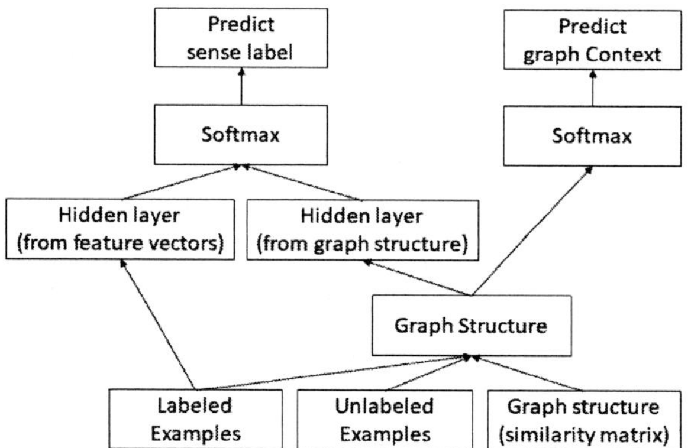

Figure 1. WSD model using graph embeddings based learning

3.3 Graph-based Semi-supervised Learning

We employ Planetoid, which is a graph-based semi-supervised learning framework, for the WSD model and predicts the sense of target word. The planetoid has two versions, transductive and inductive models. In this study, we use the inductive model which can predict labels for instances that are not observed in the graph. In the inductive model, as shown in Figure 1, we use a set of training examples, unlabeled examples and a graph structure representing the relationship between examples as input and learn a WSD classifier and graph context simultaneously. The classifier predicts the sense of the target word for unknown example.

The training examples and unlabeled examples are represented by feature vectors. The graph structure is constructed from the similarity between the obtained vectors. We learn a WSD model from the training data vector and the graph structure. Finally, we predict the appropriate sense label of the target word for the unknown examples using the optimized WSD model.

3.4 Input Graph Structure

3.4.1 Graph Using Jaccard Coefficient and Cosine Similarity

The input graph structure is constructed by the relation between the training data and the unlabeled data. In the graph structure, each node is an example and an edge is the similarity between nodes. The similarity between nodes is calculated by using the following calculation method between two vectors of examples. In the proposed method, nodes with the highest similarity and nodes that have a similarity not less than the threshold value 0.9 are connected by edge. Figure 2 shows how the nodes are connected.

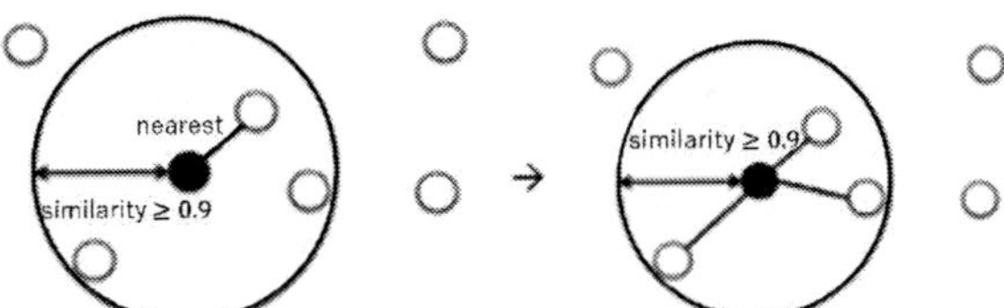

Figure 2. Edge connection between examples

The similarity calculation method between nodes uses Jaccard similarity J or cosine similarity. Jaccard similarity J is the ratio of the number of words in common between the two sets. Given a set of word vectors A and B, the similarity J is represented as follows:

$$J(A, B) = |A \cap B| / |A \cup B|, \qquad (0 \leq J(A, B) \leq 1)$$

Moreover, we use a mutual k-nearest neighbour graph to construct a graph structure. The mutual k-nearest neighbour graph is defined as a graph that connects edge between two nodes if each of the nodes belongs to the k-nearest neighbours of the other. In this method, the edges with the highest similarity between nodes are also added to the graph structure obtained by the mutual k-nearest neighbour graph. In our experiments, we use k=3 for the number of neighbours that have been provided by the user.

3.4.2 Graph Using Sentence Pair Classification by Fine-tuning BERT

To create a suitable graph structure, we use BERT to identify if two examples of the target word are used in the same sense. BERT is a ground-breaking natural language processing model for pre-training language representations. The pre-trained BERT model is built on a huge text data sets and is fine-tuned with just one additional output layer to create state-of-the-art models for various tasks. In our experiment, we use NWJC-BERT as a Japanese BERT pre-trained model published by the National Institute for Japanese Language and Linguistics (NINJAL) to compute BERT features. This model is trained on NINJAL Web Japanese Corpus (NWJC) pre-tokenized by MeCab with UniDic. Also, we use BERT-large-cased as an English pre-trained model and freeze the weights of parameters of BERT layers. We feed the output of these pre-training models into a three fully connected layer with ReLU activation function and softmax outputs to identify whether two examples are used in the same sense or not.

For each target word, we train a model to determine if usage is the same by entering example sentence pairs $s1$ and $s2$ in the training data. For all sentence pairs in the training data, pairs of seven words consisting of the target word and three words on either side of the target word $(w_{s1}^1, w_{s1}^2, \cdots, w_{s1}^7)$ and $(w_{s2}^1, w_{s2}^2, \cdots, w_{s2}^7)$ are extracted by performing morphological analysis. Then, we concatenate these sequences and feed the pair to BERT to get their contextualized representation:

$$\{'[CLS]', w_{s1}^1, w_{s1}^2, \cdots, w_{s1}^7, ' [SEP]', w_{s2}^1, w_{s2}^2, \cdots, w_{s2}^7, ' [SEP]' \},$$

where a special token '[CLS]' denotes the beginning of the input sequence and a token '[SEP]' is used for separating examples or denoting the end of the sequence. We add an untrained layer with two hidden layers of 64 units on the end to the pre-trained BERT model and train the model using all the example pairs obtained from the training data for 20 epochs. This model is applied to every unlabeled sentence pair to obtain semantically equivalent sentence pairs. The obtained equivalent sentence pairs are used to generate a graph structure.

4 Experiments

To evaluate the efficiency of the proposed WSD method using graph embeddings based learning, we conducted some experiments to compare the results to the baseline system. In this section, we describe an outline of the experiments.

4.1 Data Set

For our experiments, we relied on the lexical-sample datasets of both SemEval-2010 Japanese WSD (Okumura, 2010) and Senseval-2 Lexical Sample (Kilgarriff, 2001).

The SemEval-2010 Japanese WSD task data set includes 50 target words comprising 22 nouns, 23 verbs, and 5 adjectives. In this data set, there are 50 training and 50 test instances for each target word (there is no development set). As unlabeled example data for the construction of a graph structure, we used the BCCWJ developed by the National Institute for Japanese Language and Linguistics. The BCCWJ corpus comprises 104.3 million words covering various genres.

The Senseval-2 English Lexical Sample data consists of 8,611 training and 4,328 test examples of 73 words. These examples were extracted from the British National Corpus. This task uses WordNet 1.7 sense inventory as gold standard, which has fine-grained sense distinctions. As unlabeled example data for the construction of a graph structure, we used the SemCor corpus. The SemCor corpus is a subset of the Brown corpus that contains 362 texts comprising about 234,000 words.

4.2 Settings

In our experiments, to construct a graph for all examples, two nodes that represent two examples are linked if they are nearest and if their similarity (based on the Jaccard coefficient) is not less than a specified threshold value of 0.9. The basic idea behind this is that two nodes tend to have a high similarity if the corresponding contexts of the target word are similar.

For learning the graph-based neural network, we use default parameter settings from the existing implementation[1]. For the initialized embeddings, optimization of the loss function of class label prediction is repeated for 10,000 iterations, and optimization of the loss function of graph context prediction is repeated for 1,000 iterations. Then, Joint training of classification and graph context prediction is repeated for 1,000 iterations. The obtained model is used to classify new examples of the target word into semantic classes.

5 Experimental Results

Table 1 shows the results of the experiments using lexical features with various graph structures on the SemEval-2010 Japanese WSD task. The reported WSD task results in precision are averaged over three runs. As shown in Table 1, the average precision of the proposed method is 78.11%. Statistical significance is obtained using the Student's t-test, †P<0.05 in comparison to the WSD model without the graph embeddings. The proposed method obtains higher precision than the WSD model without the graph embeddings, with statistical significance. Therefore, experimental results show that the graph structure between examples is effective for WSD. However, the model with randomly connected graph obtains a lower precision than the model without graph embeddings. This shows that it is not effective for WSD to use the graph structure simply in the model, but that it is more effective to use a graph structures that takes into account the similarity between examples.

Among the WSD models using the graph structure based on the similarity between examples, the model using sentence pair classification by fine-tuning BERT obtains the highest precision. Therefore, it is effective for WSD to utilize a graph structure obtained by fine-tuning BERT in the proposed method.

In the Table 2, we show the experimental results using word embeddings with various graph structures. Statistical significance is obtained using the Student's t-test, ††P<0.01 in comparison to the WSD model using ELMo without the graph embeddings. In these experiments, we use the WSD models using a graph structure obtained by fine-tuning BERT. By using contextual word embeddings using ELMo as features, the average precision of the proposed WSD model is 80.93%. As a result, the proposed method outperformed the existing method in the semi-supervised learning method on the SemEval-2010 Japanese

---

[1] https://github.com/kimiyoung/planetoid

WSD task data. The average precision of the proposed method was improved by 2.7% in comparison with the model without graph embeddings so that we show that the graph structure is effective for WSD even when word embeddings are used as features.

	Precision (%)
No Graph (MLP only)	76.92
Random Connection Graph	76.72
Cosine Similarity	77.24
Jaccard Coefficient	77.76†
Pair Classification with BERT (no fine-tuning)	77.40
Pair Classification with BERT (proposed)	**78.11†**

Table 1: Experimental results using lexical features with various graph structures

	Precision (%)
(Fujita et al., 2011) (baseline)	79.20
No Graph (word2vec, MLP only)	70.65
No Graph (ELMo, MLP only)	77.23
Pair Classification with BERT (word2vec)	79.29
Cosine Similarity	80.64††
Jaccard Coefficient	80.90††
Pair Classification with BERT (ELMo) (proposed)	**80.93††**

Table 2: Experimental results using word embeddings with various graph structures

To demonstrate the effectiveness of the proposed method, we compared it with a WSD model using word2vec embeddings as features. We obtain word embeddings of word2vec using nwjc2vec (Asahara, 2018) and perform experiments using the WSD model with 1000 dimensional vectors concatenated with 200-dimensional word embeddings for 5 words. Experimental results showed that the average precision of the WSD model using word2vec is 79.6%. These results show that the proposed WSD model using contextual word embeddings with ELMo is more effective than the model using word2vec. In the WSD model with word2vec, the average precision of the model with graph is 7.36% higher than that without graph. This indicates that the graph structure is also effective for the WSD method using word2vec.

Table 3 shows the results of the experiments of the proposed method on the SENSEVAL-2 English lexical sample task. As shown in Table 3, the average precision of the proposed method is 73.09%. The proposed method achieves higher precision than the existing WSD model such as (Taghipour and Ng, 2015), (Kågebäck and Salomonsson, 2016). However, the average precision of the proposed method is slightly better than the model without a graph. One of the reasons for this is that the number of SemCor documents used as unlabeled examples is quite small. Therefore, it is necessary to extract enough examples of the target words by using a large corpus such as OMSTI in addition to SemCor.

	Precision (%)
(Taghipour and Ng, 2015) (baseline)	66.2
(Kågebäck and Salomonsson, 2016) (baseline)	66.90
No Graph (ELMo, MLP only)	73.01
Pair Classification with BERT (ELMo) (proposed)	**73.09**

Table 3: Experimental results using contextual word embeddings on SENSEVAL-2 lexical sample task

6   Conclusion

In this paper, we proposed a semi-supervised graph embeddings based learning method for the WSD task. The efficiency of the proposed method was evaluated on the Semeval-2010 Japanese WSD task and the SENSEVAL-2 English lexical sample task. Experimental results show that the proposed method performs better than the previous semi-supervised WSD method. Moreover, the graph structure between examples is effective for WSD and it is effective to utilize a graph structure obtained by fine-tuning BERT in the proposed method.

In the future, we would like to explore methods to construct an effective graph structure by using paraphrase information, and the dependency analysis technique, the effective filtering method for unlabeled data. In addition, we would like to develop a method to use the examples of the Iwanami's Japanese dictionary effectively.

Acknowledgements

This work was supported by JSPS KAKENHI Grant Number 18K11422.

Reference

Asahara, M. (2018). NWJC2Vec: Word embedding dataset from 'NINJAL Web Japanese Corpus'. Terminology, 24, pp. 7-22.

Bevilacqua M. and Navigli R. (2020). Breaking Through the 80% Glass Ceiling: Raising the State of the Art in Word Sense Disambiguation by Incorporating Knowledge Graph Information. Proceedings of the 58th Annual Meeting of the Association for Computational Linguistics (ACL2020), pp. 2854-2864.

Blevins, T. and Zettlemoyer, L. (2020). Moving Down the Long Tail of Word Sense Disambiguation with Gloss Informed Bi-encoders. Proceedings of the 58th Association for Computational Linguistics (ACL2020), pp. 1006-1017.

Fujita, S., and Fujino, A. (2011). Word Sense Disambiguation by Combining Labeled Data Expansion and Semi-Supervised Learning Method. Proceedings of 5th International Joint Conference on Natural Language Processing, pp. 676-685.

Huang, L., Sun, C., Qiu, X. and Huang, X. (2019). GlossBERT: BERT for Word Sense Disambiguation with Gloss Knowledge. Proceedings of the 2019 Conference on Empirical Methods in Natural Language Processing and the 9th International Joint Conference on Natural Language Processing (EMNLP-IJCNLP), pp. 3509-3514.

Kågebäck, M., and Salomonsson, H. (2016). Word Sense Disambiguation using a Bidirectional LSTM. Proceedings of the 5th Workshop on Cognitive Aspects of the Lexicon (CogALex-V), pp.51-56.

Kumar, S., Jat, S., Saxena, K. and Talukdar, P. (2019). Zero-shot Word Sense Disambiguation using Sense Definition Embeddings. Proceedings of the 57th Annual Meeting of the Association for Computational Linguistics (ACL2019), pp. 5670-5681.

Maekawa, K., Yamazaki, M., Ogiso, T., Maruyama, T., Ogura, H., Kashino, W., Koiso, H., Yamaguchi, M., Tanaka, M., and Den, Y. (2014). Balanced Corpus of Contemporary Written Japanese. Language Resources and Evaluation (LREC2014), pp. 345-371.

National Institute for Japanese Language. (2004). Bunrui Goi Hyo (enlarged and revised version). Dainippon Tosho.

Navigli, R. (2009). Word sense disambiguation: A survey, ACM Computing Surveys, vol. 41, no. 2, pp. 10:1-10:69.

Nishio, M., Iwabuchi, E., and Mizutani, S. (1994). Iwanami Kokugo Jiten Dai Go Han, Iwanami Publisher (in Japanese).

Niu, Z., Ji, D., and Tan, C.L. (2005). Word Sense Disambiguation Using Label Propagation Based Semi-Supervised Learning. Proceedings of the 43rd Annual Meeting on Association for Computational Linguistics, pp. 395-402.

Okumura, M., Shirai, K., Komiya, K., and Yokono, H. (2010). Semeval-2010 task: Japanese WSD., Proceedings of the SemEval-2010, ACL 2010, pp. 69-74.

Raganato, A., Bovi, C.D., and Navigli, R. (2017). Neural Sequence Learning Models for Word Sense Disambiguation. Proceedings of the 2017 Conference on Empirical Methods in Natural Language Processing (EMNLP2017), pp. 1156-1167.

Shinnou, H., Murata, M., Shirai, K., Fukumoto, F., Fujita, S., Sasaki, M., Komiya, K. and Inui, T. (2015) Classification of Word Sense Disambiguation Errors Using a Clustering Method, Journal of Natural Language Processing vol. 22, no. 5,pp. 319-362.

Sousa, S., Milios, E. and Berton, L. (2020) Word sense disambiguation: an evaluation study of semi-supervised approaches with word embeddings. Proceedings of the 2020 International Joint Conference on Neural Networks (IJCNN), pp. 1-8

Taghipour, K., and Ng, H.T. (2015). Semi-Supervised Word Sense Disambiguation Using Word Embeddings in General and Specific Domains. Proceedings of the 2015 Conference of the North American Chapter of the Association for Computational Linguistics: Human Language Technologies (HLT-NAACL2015), pp. 314-323.

Yang, Z., Cohen, W.W., and Salakhutdinov, R. (2016). Revisiting Semi-Supervised Learning with Graph Embeddings. Proceedings of the 33rd International Conference on International Conference on Machine Learning - Volume 48 (ICML'16), pp. 40-48.

Yarowsky, D. (1995). Unsupervised Word Sense Disambiguation Rivaling Supervised Methods. Proceedings of the 33rd Annual Meeting of the Association for Computational Linguistics pp. 189-196.

Yuan, D., Richardson, J., Doherty, R., Evans, C., and Altendorf, E. (2016). Semi-supervised Word Sense Disambiguation with Neural Models. Proceedings of the 26th International Conference on Computational Linguistics (COLING2016), pp. 1374-1385.

Zhong, Z., and Ng, H.T. (2010). It Makes Sense: A Wide-Coverage Word Sense Disambiguation System for Free Text. Proceedings of the ACL 2010 System Demonstrations, pp.78-83.

Incorporating Temporal Information in Entailment Graph Mining

Liane Guillou[†*], **Sander Bijl De Vroe**[†*], **Mohammad Javad Hosseini**[†‡],
Mark Johnson[§], **and Mark Steedman**[†]
[†]University of Edinburgh, [‡] The Alan Turing Institute, UK, [§]Macquarie University
`liane.guillou@ed.ac.uk, sbdv@ed.ac.uk, javad.hosseini@ed.ac.uk`
`mark.johnson@mq.edu.au, steedman@inf.ed.ac.uk`

Abstract

We present a novel method for injecting temporality into entailment graphs to address the problem of spurious entailments, which may arise from similar but temporally distinct events involving the same pair of entities. We focus on the sports domain in which the same pairs of teams play on different occasions, with different outcomes. We present an unsupervised model that aims to learn entailments such as win/lose → play, while avoiding the pitfall of learning non-entailments such as win ↛ lose. We evaluate our model on a manually constructed dataset, showing that incorporating time intervals and applying a temporal window around them, are effective strategies.

1 Introduction

Recognising textual entailment and paraphrases is core to many downstream NLP applications such as question answering and semantic parsing. In the case of open-domain question answering over unstructured data, the answer to a question may not be explicitly stated in the text, but may be recovered via paraphrases and/or entailment rules.

Entailment graphs (Berant et al., 2011; Berant et al., 2015; Hosseini et al., 2018), in which nodes represent predicates and edges are entailment relations, have been proposed as a means to answer such questions. They can be mined using unsupervised methods applied over large collections of text, by keeping track of which entity pairs occur with which predicates. One common error made by these graphs, however, is that they assert spurious associations between similar but temporally distinct events that occur with the same entity pairs. For example, both the predicates *beat* and *lost against* will apply to sports team entity pairs such as (**Arsenal**, **Man United**). This is likely to mislead the current methods into incorrectly assigning an entailment relation between these two predicates.

In this paper we extend the framework of Hosseini et al. (2018) to incorporate the temporal location of events, with the aim of mitigating these spurious entailments. Temporal information can be used to disentangle these groups of highly correlated predicates, because although they will share entity pairs, they will never occur at the same time. For example, in Figure 1 Arsenal and Man United played each other three times in 2019, with three different outcomes: **win** (*beat*), **lose** (*lost against*), **tie** (*tied with*).

In previous methods, the context in which the predicates occur appears to be the same, because they only consider entity pairs as context. Therefore they mistakenly take the examples in Figure 1 as evidence of entailments or paraphrases between the three outcome predicates (win, lose, and tie), depending on the distributions found in the data. Our method enriches this context to include time interval information, thereby filtering out combinations that are not temporally near each other. Thus we hope to avoid learning that *beat* → *lost against*, while still learning that *beat* → *play*.

As an initial test domain, we focus on the sports news genre, using extracted relations that involve two sports teams. We evaluate on a manually constructed dataset of 1,312 entailment pairs based on paraphrases of the predicates in the graph on the right hand side of Figure 1. Our goal is to recover the structure of this graph in an unsupervised way, separating each of the highly correlated outcome predicates while predicting that they all entail *play*.

This work is licensed under a Creative Commons Attribution 4.0 International Licence. Licence details: `http://creativecommons.org/licenses/by/4.0/`.

---

[*]The first two authors contributed equally to this work

Proceedings of the Graph-based Methods for Natural Language Processing (TextGraphs), pages 60–71
Barcelona, Spain (Online), December 13, 2020

Arsenal-*played* and *lost against*-**Man United** 1-3 (25/01/2019)
Arsenal-*played* and *beat*-**Man United** 2-0 (10/03/2018)
Arsenal-*played* and *tied with*-**Man United** 1-1 (30/09/2019)

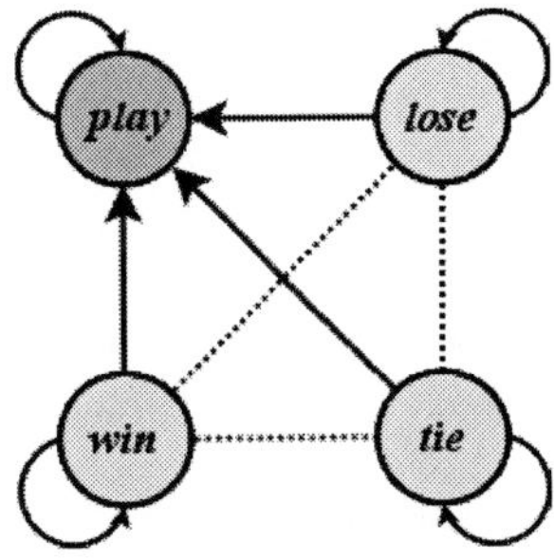

Figure 1: Example sentences (left) and their resulting (collapsed) entailment/non-entailment graph (right)

The contributions of this work are: 1) a model for incorporating relation-level time intervals into an entailment graph mining procedure, outperforming non-temporal models, and 2) a manually constructed evaluation dataset of sports domain predicates. To our knowledge this is the first attempt to incorporate temporal information for learning entailment graphs.

2 Related Work

2.1 Entailment Graphs

Entailment graphs have been constructed for a range of domains, including newswire (Hosseini et al., 2018), health (Levy et al., 2014), and commonsense (Yu et al., 2020). In order to leverage temporal information, our work focuses on the news domain, in which each article has a known publication date and temporal expressions are commonly used.

A range of node representations have been explored, including Open-IE propositions (Levy et al., 2014), typed predicates (Berant et al., 2011; Hosseini et al., 2018), and eventualities (Yu et al., 2020). In this work we use typed predicates, leveraging the second level in the FIGER hierarchy (Ling and Weld, 2012), to enable a close examination of events that take place between two sports teams.

Whether predicates in the graph entail each other may be determined using a variety of similarity measures. These are inspired by the Distributional Inclusion Hypothesis, which states that a predicate p entails another predicate q if for any context in which p can be used, q may be used in its place (Dagan et al., 1999; Geffet and Dagan, 2005). They include the symmetric Lin's similarity measure (Lin, 1998), the directional Weeds' precision and recall measures (Weeds and Weir, 2003), and the Balanced Inclusion score (BInc) (Szpektor and Dagan, 2008). BInc, the geometric mean of Lin's similarity and Weed's precision, combines the desirable behaviors of symmetric and directional measures. We adapt and examine each of these similarity measures using our evaluation dataset.

Alternatively, Hosseini et al. (2019) performed link prediction on the set of relation triples extracted from the text, and showed improvements over BInc by augmenting the data with additional predicted triples. We consider this link prediction model to be beyond the scope of this work.

2.2 Evaluating Entailment Graphs

The construction of entailment datasets has been framed as a number of manual annotation tasks including image captioning (Bowman et al., 2015) and question answering (Levy and Dagan, 2016).

The dataset creation method used by Levy and Dagan (2016) aims to address the bias towards real world knowledge. They ask human annotators to mark possible answers to questions as True/False (entailment/non-entailment), with entities in the answer replaced using tokens representing their type (e.g. *London* becomes *city*). The method also aims to address the bias of other datasets such as Zeichner's dataset (Zeichner et al., 2012) and the SherLIic dataset (Schmitt and Schütze, 2019), in which candidate entailments were automatically pre-selected for manual annotation according to a similarity measure. Entailments that exist, but are not captured by these similarity measures will therefore be excluded.

There has been very little work on the specific problem of evaluating entailment of a temporal nature. The FraCas test suite (Cooper et al., 1996) contains a small section of which only a few examples are entailments between predicates. The TEA dataset (Kober et al., 2019) consists of pairs of sentences in which temporally ordered predicates have varying tense and aspect, such as *is visiting* → *has arrived*, but does not include non-entailments that can be learned through the temporal separation of events (such as the outcome predicates *win* and *lose* that we are interested in). Since there is no dataset to evaluate this phenomenon, we construct our own (Section 4.1). Our method for dataset construction is similar to that of Berant et al. (2011). They manually annotated all edges in 10 typed entailment graphs, resulting in 3,427 edges (entailments) and 35,585 non-edges (non-entailments).

3 Method

3.1 Relation Extraction

We use a pipeline based on a Combinatory Categorial Grammar (CCG, (Steedman, 2000)) parser to extract binary relations with time intervals. These relations are used to construct typed entailment graphs using the unsupervised method of Hosseini et al. (2018), adapted to compare only pairs of relations that are temporally near each other. We extract binary relations of the form **arg1**-*predicate*-**arg2** (e.g. **Arsenal**-*beat*-**Man United**), following the example of Lewis and Steedman (2013) and Berant et al. (2015). We use a pipeline approach similar to that described by Hosseini et al. (2018), which allows us to extract open-domain relations. Relations are extracted from the NewsSpike corpus (Zhang and Weld, 2013) of news articles collected from multiple sources over a period of approximately six weeks.

We traverse dependency graphs generated over the output of the Rotating CCG parser (Stanojević and Steedman, 2019), starting from verb and preposition nodes, until we reach an argument leaf node. The traversed nodes are used to form (lemmatised) predicate strings, and arguments are classified as either a Named Entity (extracted by the CoreNLP Named Entity recogniser), or a general entity (all other nouns and noun phrases). Predicate strings may include (non-auxiliary) verbs, verb particles, adjectives, and prepositions. Negation nodes are detected via string match ("not", "n't", and "never"), and are included in the predicate if there is a path between the negation node and a node in the predicate. We map passive predicates to active ones. Modifiers such as "managed to" as in the example "Arsenal managed to beat Man United" are also extracted and included in the predicate. As the modifiers may be rather sparse, we extract the relation both with and without the modifier.

We extract and resolve time expressions in the document text, using SUTime (Chang and Manning, 2012), available via CoreNLP. If there is a path in the CCG dependency graph between the time expression and a node in the predicate, the relation is assigned a time interval. Entities are mapped to types by linking to their Freebase (Bollacker et al., 2008) IDs using AIDA-Light (Nguyen et al., 2014), and subsequently mapping these IDs to their fine-grained FIGER types (Ling and Weld, 2012).

To restrict the data to the sports domain we filter the set of output relations, accepting only those involving two entities of the fine-grained FIGER type *organization/sports_team*. This results in a set of 78,439 binary relations extracted from 24,147 articles, of which 14,664 (approximately 19%) have time intervals derived from SUTime. The sports domain has the advantage that events are similar and should be easily separable in time, and it provides the straightforward *win-lose-tie* outcome set. Sports data is common in NewsSpike, and sports teams have reliable Named Entity linking, making it suitable for an initial investigation. In the future we will apply this method to other entity type pairs.

3.2 Graph Construction

The input to the graph construction step is the set of typed binary relations paired with their time intervals. As we focus on events that involve two sports teams, the output is a single **organization-organization** graph, rather than the typical set of graphs (one for every pair of types). Note that these graphs contain only locally learned entailments, and that global inference across graphs is not performed. This is sufficient to demonstrate the benefit of incorporating time intervals.

In the original method for computing local entailment scores, Hosseini et al. (2018) extract a feature vector for each typed predicate (e.g. *play* with type pair organization-organization). The entity pairs from the binary relations (e.g. **Arsenal**, **Man United**) are used as the feature types, and the pointwise mutual information (PMI) between the predicate and the entity pair is the value. These feature vectors are then used to compute local similarity scores.

We extend this method to consider the time intervals for each of the binary relations, with the goal of comparing only those events that are temporally near each other. To achieve this, we filter the counts of predicate q according to whether each event's time interval overlaps with any of p's. In other words, an event in q is retained if it is close enough to any event in p. We consider new local similarity scores based on both the filtered counts, and scaled PMI scores.

Algorithm 1 describes the process of filtering counts using time intervals. The process uses a set of edges $\mathcal{E}$ between predicate nodes to store filtered count information. We loop through each entity pair ep and get the list of predicates that occur with that entity pair (line 4). Then, for each pair of predicates, we instantiate *edgeObjects* (line 7) between predicates p and q (in both directions), to store the filtered count information. We also retrieve p and q's *timeObjects*, containing a list of the time intervals at which the predicate and entity pair co-occurred (lines 8–9). For each pair of time intervals we compute whether there is an overlap (lines 12–19). The filtered count is the total number of events in predicate p that temporally overlap with any event in predicate q.

The count is stored in the *edgeObject* $edge_{p,q}$. Once all counts have been collected, they are used to compute the similarity measures. The computation of temporal measures is identical to that of the non-temporal counterparts, but they use the filtered counts as input instead of the regular counts. Each *edgeObject* populates a cell in $\mathbf{W}$, the sparse matrix of all similarity scores between predicates p and q, as presented by Hosseini et al. (2018). The filtered counts are also used to scale the PMI scores (see section 4.2).

Consider the following minimal worked example: Two matches between Arsenal and Man United, one where Arsenal wins (on 10/03/2018), and one where they lose (on 25/01/2019). This initially results in the following extracted predicates and counts: *play* (2), *win* (1), *lose* (1). After filtering, we add a count of 1 to both the *win* $\rightarrow$ *play* and *lose* $\rightarrow$ *play* edges, and a count of 0 to the *win* $\rightarrow$ *lose* edge (and its reverse).

We consider three possible sources of time intervals: 1) the resolved time expressions extracted from raw text using SUTime, 2) the document creation date (provided as metadata in the NewsSpike corpus), and 3) a combination of the two – using resolved time expressions where these are available, and backing off to the document creation date where they are not. The intuition behind using time expressions extracted from the article text is that these ought to more accurately pinpoint the time interval of the events. However, as such expressions may be sparse, we also investigate the use of the document creation date, under the assumption that sports news is likely to be reported very close the day of the event.

We also consider a temporal window to extend the time intervals by N days either side. This would mitigate the problem of sports events being reported several days after the event, especially when we fall back to the document creation date. For sports matches we would expect to see a benefit in using a small window of a few days, and a detrimental effect as that window grows increasingly larger. Specifically, we expect that larger windows would render temporal information useless, preventing our model from being able to distinguish between two different matches involving the same pair of teams. Time interval source and window size are event-specific parameters that we experiment with in Section 5.1.

4 Evaluation

4.1 Dataset Construction

We propose a semi-automatic method to construct a small evaluation dataset based on manually constructed paraphrase clusters. We start with a small set of predicates for which we know the entailment pattern, in our case $\{win, play, lose$ and $tie\}$. We restrict the dataset to include only those binary relations that involve two sports teams, by filtering on the fine-grained FIGER (Ling and Weld, 2012) type *organization/sports_team*. We then order the predicates by their frequency in the corpus, and manually select paraphrases of our small set with a count of at least 20 (the 235 most frequent predicates). This results in four clusters of paraphrases, with sizes of 26, 8, 3 and 5 respectively for *win*, *lose*, *tie* and *play*. We then automatically generate entailment pairs (1,312 in total), labelling them according to the pattern

---

Algorithm 1 Temporal filtering in local graph computation

```
 1: procedure TEMPORALFILTER(entity_pairs, predicates)
 2:     E ← initialiseAllEdgeObjects(predicates)                          ▷ Initialise set of edges
 3:     for ep in entity_pairs do
 4:         predicates_ep ← getPredicatesForEntityPair(predicates, ep)
 5:         for p ← 0 to length(predicates_ep) do
 6:             for q ← p + 1 to length(predicates_ep) do
 7:                 edge_{p,q}, edge_{q,p} ← getEdgeObjects(E, p, q)
 8:                 time_objects_{ep,p} ← getTimeObjects(ep, p)
 9:                 time_objects_{ep,q} ← getTimeObjects(ep, q)
10:                 overlap_p ← initialiseVectorOfZeros(length(time_objects_{ep,p}))
11:                 overlap_q ← initialiseVectorOfZeros(length(time_objects_{ep,q}))
12:                 for i ← 0 to length(time_objects_{ep,p}) do
13:                     for j ← 0 to length(time_objects_{ep,q}) do
14:                         if compareIntervals(time_objects_{ep,p}[i], time_objects_{ep,q}[j]) = 1 then
15:                             overlap_p.set(i, 1)
16:                             overlap_q.set(j, 1)
17:                         end if
18:                     end for
19:                 end for
20:                 edge_{p,q}.addEdgeCounts(sum(overlap_p))          ▷ Events in p that temporally overlap with any q
21:                 edge_{q,p}.addEdgeCounts(sum(overlap_q))
22:             end for
23:             E.update(edge_{p,q}, edge_{q,p})
24:         end for
25:     end for
26:     return E
27: end procedure
```

---

in Table 1, with premises in the rows and hypotheses in the columns.

We include the *paraphrase* category for completeness, although we are more interested in the effect of separating temporally disjoint sports match outcomes. The paraphrase category contains predicates of varying gradation, such as *crush* suggesting a strong victory or *eliminate* indicating that a team is knocked out of a tournament. We wish to avoid specific predicates such as *eliminate* entailing non-specific predicates like *beat*. To avoid this issue we manually annotated the predicates for specificity, and for the *paraphrase* entailments subset we only generate pairs for non-specific predicates. More generally, a set of paraphrase clusters with a total of n predicates yields $n^2 - n$ pairs (not taking into account the paraphrase subsets reduction).[1] The dataset of 1,312 entailment pairs is available here.

(a) 1 = entailment, 0 = non-entailment. Blue = base (entailments, and non-entailments from temporally disjoint outcomes), orange = directional non-entailment, green = paraphrases

	win	lose	tie	play
win	1	0	0	1
lose	0	1	0	1
tie	0	0	1	1
play	0	0	0	1

(b) Examples from the evaluation dataset

Category	Examples	Size
entailment 1	defeat → vs crush → face	272
outcome 0	beat → fall to outscore → lose	446
directional 0	play → win go against → tie	272
paraphrase 1	top → knock off defeat → outplay	322

Table 1: Entailment pairs evaluation dataset

4.2 Similarity Measures

We compute both symmetric and directional similarity measures to learn entailments, making use of the temporally filtered counts and PMI scores described in Section 3.2. Specifically, we adapted Lin's

---

[1] The subtracted term comes from duplicate pairs like *defeat-defeat*

similarity measure (Lin, 1998), Weeds' precision and recall measures (Weeds and Weir, 2003), and BInc (Szpektor and Dagan, 2008). The adaptations of these measures are:

Temporal count-based measures using the temporally filtered counts: Weeds' precision, recall, and similarity (harmonic average of precision and recall); Lin's similarity; BInc using Weed's precision and count-based Lin's similarity.

Temporal PMI-based measures: As a proxy to computing Conditional PMI between an entity pair, predicate p, and predicate q, which would be computationally expensive (if not infeasible) given the existing graph construction framework, we scale the original PMI scores. We apply two strategies: 1) *Ratio:* scale the original PMI scores according to the ratio of filtered counts to regular counts, 2) *Binary:* use the original PMI score if any of the events in predicate p overlap with any event in predicate q, otherwise set the score to zero. The following measures use the Ratio and Binary PMI strategies: Weeds' precision, recall, and similarity; Lin's similarity; BInc using Weed's PMI precision and Lin's similarity.

Temporal hybrid BInc measures: Computed using count-based Weeds' precision and PMI-based Lin's similarity, using the temporally filtered counts. We do this for both Ratio and Binary PMI.

We also ensure that for every temporal measure, its non-temporal counterpart is also included, and we include cosine similarity as a symmetric baseline. In total, we experiment with 29 similarity measures.

5   Experiments, Results and Analysis

5.1   Experimental Settings

As described in Section 3.1 we extract all possible relations from the NewsSpike corpus and map their entities to types using the FIGER hierarchy. We construct a typed entailment graph for the organization/organization type pair using the subset of these relations where both entities are sports teams. We compute entailment scores using the set of 29 similarity measures described in Section 4.2. Due to space constraints we highlight results for eight of these measures: BInc and cosine similarity baselines, and the best performing temporal measures and their non-temporal counterparts.

We experimented with different values for the event-specific time information source and temporal window described in Section 3.2. We constructed typed entailment graphs using only time expressions (timexOnly), only the document creation date (docDateOnly), and using time expressions where available, otherwise backing off to the document creation date (timexAndDocDate). For each of the time interval sources, we also applied windows of 1, 2, 3, 4, 5, 6, 7, 30 and 3,650 days, as well as *no window*.

We used the evaluation dataset described in Section 4.1 and Table 1 to evaluate entailments captured under each of these experimental settings. We evaluate on three different configurations of the dataset: **Base** (entailment 1 and outcome 0), **Directional** (entailment 1 and directional 0), and **All** (entailment 1, outcome 0, directional 0, paraphrase 1). When we introduce parameter tuning in future work, we plan to assign a development/test split to the dataset.

5.2   Temporal Information Source

See Table 2 for area under the curve (AUC) scores for each of the three temporal information sources, for a range of temporal (T) and non-temporal similarity measures. To evaluate the similarity measures fairly we calculate AUC under a recall threshold (a recall of 0.75 is reached by all non-timexOnly measures). The *timexOnly* source has the weakest performance, since it has access to a sparser set of time intervals (with only 19% of relations linked to a time expression in the text). When we focus on the low recall range (< 0.15), however, we find that the temporal measures outperform the non-temporal ones. This is especially promising as it highlights the benefit of using the more accurate time intervals resolved from time expressions in the text; these give temporal measures a larger increase than the document date. When using only the document creation date (*docDateOnly*), we find that temporal and non temporal measures perform similarly. Results for the *timexAndDocDate* source show that leveraging both time expression and document time information together leads to the most effective model.

Similarity measure	timexOnly		docDateOnly	timexAndDocDate
	rec < 0.15	rec < 0.75	rec < 0.75	rec < 0.75
T. BInc (Count)	0.111	0.127	**0.467**	**0.469**
BInc (Count)	0.106	**0.467**	**0.467**	0.467
T. BInc (Ratio PMI)	0.108	0.108	0.446	0.449
T. BInc (Binary PMI)	**0.114**	0.114	0.446	0.448
BInc	0.093	0.444	0.444	0.444
T. Weed's Pr (Count)	0.113	0.129	0.436	0.436
Weed's Pr (Count)	0.087	0.436	0.436	0.436
Cosine Sim	0.100	0.420	0.420	0.420

Table 2: Temporal information source: AUC scores for the base evaluation dataset, and a temporal window size of 4 days

5.3 Temporal Window Size

In Figure 2 we can see that there is a sharp improvement in AUC score for all of the temporally-informed similarity measures when a window of one day is applied[2]. This is likely due to data sparsity and because sports articles report on the same event on different days. The horizontal lines represent the non-temporally-informed similarity measures. We can also see that the choice of window size depends on the similarity measure. For the majority of the temporally-informed similarity measures, a window size between one and four days works well. For this class of predicates a window size of 4 seems suitable, as it avoids conflating games that happen on consecutive weekends, while giving some leeway. We discuss the possibility of using a dynamic window in Section 6.

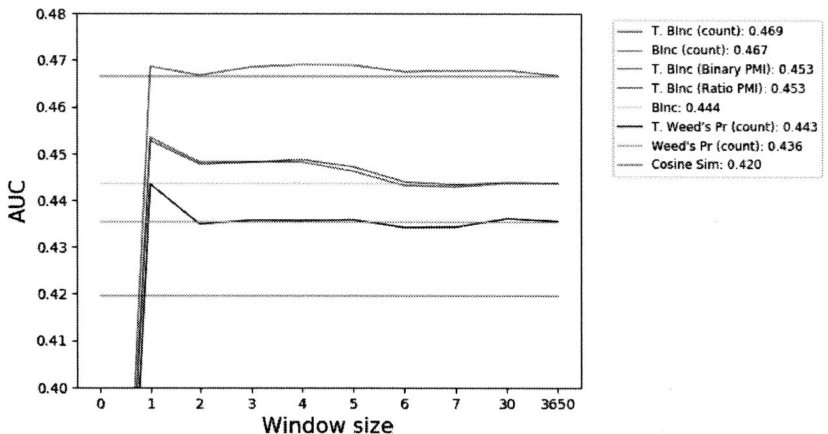

Figure 2: Effects of window size for the *timexAndDocDate* temporal information source

5.4 Comparing Similarity Measures

We can see from Figure 3 that *BInc*, a state-of-the-art measure for relation entailment, does not perform well within the temporal setting and is outperformed by a number of the temporal measures. Of those, *T. BInc count sims*, the version of BInc that uses the temporally filtered counts, produces the best results on the *base* subset of the evaluation dataset. The two temporally informed measures that use scaled PMI scores (*T. Ratio BInc sims* and *T. Binary BInc sims*) also outperform *BInc* but to a lesser degree. This may be due to sparsity in the set of binary relations making it difficult to estimate accurate scaled PMI scores. We hope to alleviate this problem by moving to a larger corpus in future work[3]. In more general terms, for each similarity measure, the temporal version performs better (with the exception of Weed's probabilistic precision, for which there is no change).

---

[2]With no window, the temporally informed similarity measures perform poorly (between 0.24 and 0.26)

[3]We have already compiled a dataset of 10 years worth of news data from multiple sources

5.5 Performance on Data Subsets

Our main interest is in performance on the *base* dataset, but for completeness and comparison to previous work, which tests directionality more, we also evaluated on the *all* and *directional* subsets (see Table 3).

To investigate the challenge of directionality in entailment we consider the set of entailments and their reverse, e.g. play $\rightarrow$ win ("entailment 1" and "directional 0" in Table 1(b)). We find that in general the temporal similarity measures still perform strongly. *T. Weeds' precision*, the only purely directional measure in the set, performs comparably to its non-temporal counterpart on the *directional* subset. The second best measure is *BInc* which is unsurprising given that it also captures directionality, and that the dataset no longer tests temporality.

We also evaluate on the complete dataset (*all*) which includes paraphrases ("paraphrase 1" in Table 1(b)). Here we find that *T. Weeds' precision* is again the best measure, closely followed by the PMI-based *T. BInc* scores (Binary and Ratio). We expect that the strong performance of *T. Weeds' precision* is due to correctly identifying the directional entailments in the dataset, and that the drop in performance between the *directional* and *all* subsets is due to the inclusion of paraphrases, which are challenging for all measures, but particularly for the Weed's precision measures which have no symmetric component. *BInc* also performs reasonably well on this subset, showing that temporally-uninformed measures remain competitive when multiple phenomena are tested. In general we find that at least one temporally-informed similarity measure still performs strongly for each of the subsets in the dataset.

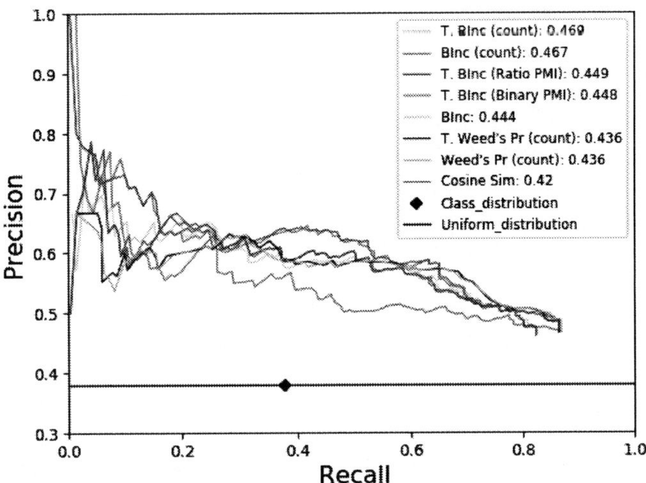

Figure 3: Best results on the base evaluation dataset: timexAndDocDate with a temporal window size of 4 days. For calculating AUC the recall threshold is set to < 0.75 for all similarity measures

5.6 Effects of Using Temporal Information

To see the benefits of including temporal information, we compare the AUC scores for the temporal and non-temporal similarity measures. We use the *timexAndDocDate* temporal information source, and a window size of four days (see Figure 3). The organization-organization graph has 46,899 nodes and between 7,888,372 and 8,256,182 edges depending on the similarity measure. We can see that the temporal similarity measure *T. BInc count* outperforms *BInc*, the state-of-the-art non-temporal similarity measure for relation entailment employed by Berant et al. (2011) and Hosseini et al. (2018). We conclude that incorporating temporal information is beneficial for accurately predicting entailments and non-entailments for highly correlated predicates that are part of distinct events.

Similarity measure	Base	Dir	All
T. BInc (Count)	**0.469**	0.433	0.433
BInc (Count)	0.467	0.433	0.434
T. BInc (Ratio PMI)	0.449	0.449	0.442
T. BInc (Binary PMI)	0.448	0.449	0.442
BInc	0.444	0.447	0.442
T. Weed's Pr (Count)	0.436	0.491	**0.448**
Weed's Pr (Count)	0.436	**0.492**	0.447
Cosine Sim	0.420	0.372	0.397

Table 3: AUC scores for different subsets of the evaluation dataset. Temporal information source is timexAndDocDate, temporal window size is 4 days

6   Discussion and Future Work

The NewsSpike corpus covers a period of approximately six weeks so the outcomes of two matches between two teams within this period may be fairly similar (as there will have been few changes to the teams management, players, etc.). In future work we plan to move to a corpus covering a larger time period, for which we would expect to observe a greater effect. Expanding beyond the sports team domain would also allow us to study events with longer duration, such as a president holding office, preceded by their campaign, and election.

Expanding the domain will also give us a collection of local graphs of types beyond just organization-organization, across which we can then learn globally consistent similarity scores (as in Hosseini et al. (2018)). We can then also collapse cliques in the graph into paraphrase clusters with a single relation identifier, which we hope will improve performance, especially on sparser predicates. Our dataset is perfectly suited to evaluating benefits from this addition due to its origin in paraphrase clusters.

Whilst we can observe a positive effect when using temporal information, the effect is modest. Upon closer inspection we found that this was due to relatively few events being filtered. An analysis of a subset of sentences revealed that relations were being extracted spuriously due to various linguistic phenomena. Issues are caused by conditionals (e.g. "if Arsenal win"), modals ("I still expect Arsenal…"), incorrect future predictions ("Arsenal will win") and counterfactuals ("had Arsenal won,…"). These types of predictions appear to be especially common in the sports domain. Another issue arose due to an incorrect application of passive to active conversion (**Arsenal**-*lost to*-**Man United** from "Man United lost to Arsenal") resulting from incorrect verb feature labels in the CCG parses. Finally, SUTime sometimes provides partial time information which can result in a whole year being used as an interval, creating spurious overlaps[4]. Addressing these issues should lead to a larger effect from using temporal information, because it would reduce overlaps and allow more filtering.

Our algorithm lends itself naturally to mining entailments with a temporal relation such as *visit* → *arrived*. We plan to achieve this by splitting the window into a before and after frame, producing separate entailment scores for different orderings. We also plan to investigate setting the window dynamically. In the current setup, events stay relevant for a similar amount of time, but different predicates should allow comparison for different granularities of time. For example, the window around a person *being president* should be larger than a person *visiting* a location. Initially we might aim to learn a different window size per predicate (for example by taking into account average predicate duration and granularity). Dynamic windowing could become particularly valuable with a broader domain.

More generally, our method could incorporate in its filtering any function of the contextualised events to determine whether their co-occurrence should contribute to an entailment score. Currently a binary decision is made based on time interval overlap, but one might use features such as (lexical) aspect, tense, the presence of other entities, etc. Previous work was limited to using the presence of two entities as a proxy for entailment relevance; with our refinements we could expand to involving not only time but also

---

[4]Focusing only on short time intervals failed to offset the other sources of spurious overlaps

other features of the contextualised events.

We will also explore the use of other temporal resolution systems and aim to develop more sophisticated ways of linking times to events, which currently only occurs through CCG dependencies. More time intervals might be propagated using the TempEval (UzZaman et al., 2013) ordering approach or through other means, for instance by reasoning about tense, Reichenbachian reference time (Reichenbach, 1947), or event coreference (within, or across documents).

7   Conclusions

We injected temporal information into the local entailment graph construction method of Hosseini et al. (2018), with the goal of comparing only those events that are temporally near each other. This is achieved by filtering the counts of predicate p according to whether its events' time intervals overlap with the those of predicate q. We considered a range of new local similarity scores based on both temporally filtered counts and scaled PMI scores, which we evaluate on a semi-automatically constructed dataset, based on manually constructed paraphrase clusters.

Our temporal similarity measures outperform their non-temporal counterparts, including BInc, the state-of-the-art measure for relation entailment. We also show that using a combination of time expressions recovered from the text and the document creation date performed better than using only one of these sources, and that adding a temporal window around the time intervals of the events is essential. The performance of the temporal similarity measures over the non-temporal measures is particularly strong at the low recall range when only time expressions from the text are used. This is especially promising as it suggests that there is much room for improvement in using more sophisticated temporal resolution systems and methods for linking times to events.

Acknowledgements

We thank Miloš Stanojević for assistance with the Rotating CCG parser, Nick McKenna and Ian Wood for helpful discussions, and the reviewers for their valuable feedback. This work was funded by the ERC H2020 Advanced Fellowship GA 742137 SEMANTAX, a grant from The University of Edinburgh and Huawei Technologies, and The Alan Turing Institute under EPSRC grant EP/N510129/1.

References

Jonathan Berant, Ido Dagan, and Jacob Goldberger. 2011. Global learning of typed entailment rules. In *Proceedings of the 49th Annual Meeting of the Association for Computational Linguistics: Human Language Technologies*, pages 610–619, Portland, Oregon, USA, June. Association for Computational Linguistics.

Jonathan Berant, Noga Alon, Ido Dagan, and Jacob Goldberger. 2015. Efficient global learning of entailment graphs. *Computational Linguistics*, 41(2):221–263, June.

Kurt Bollacker, Colin Evans, Praveen Paritosh, Tim Sturge, and Jamie Taylor. 2008. Freebase: A collaboratively created graph database for structuring human knowledge. In *Proceedings of the 2008 ACM SIGMOD International Conference on Management of Data*, SIGMOD '08, page 1247–1250, New York, NY, USA. Association for Computing Machinery.

Samuel R. Bowman, Gabor Angeli, Christopher Potts, and Christopher D. Manning. 2015. A large annotated corpus for learning natural language inference. In *Proceedings of the 2015 Conference on Empirical Methods in Natural Language Processing*, pages 632–642, Lisbon, Portugal, September. Association for Computational Linguistics.

Angel X. Chang and Christopher Manning. 2012. SUTime: A library for recognizing and normalizing time expressions. In *Proceedings of the Eighth International Conference on Language Resources and Evaluation (LREC'12)*, pages 3735–3740, Istanbul, Turkey, May. European Language Resources Association (ELRA).

Robin Cooper, Dick Crouch, Jan Van Eijck, Chris Fox, Josef Van Genabith, Jan Jaspars, Hans Kamp, David Milward, Manfred Pinkal, Massimo Poesio, Steve Pulman, Ted Briscoe, Holger Maier, and Karsten Konrad. 1996. Using the framework.

Ido Dagan, Lillian Lee, and Fernando C. N. Pereira. 1999. Similarity-based models of word cooccurrence probabilities. *Machine Learning*, 34:43–69.

Maayan Geffet and Ido Dagan. 2005. The distributional inclusion hypotheses and lexical entailment. In *Proceedings of the 43rd Annual Meeting of the Association for Computational Linguistics (ACL'05)*, pages 107–114, Ann Arbor, Michigan, June. Association for Computational Linguistics.

Mohammad Javad Hosseini, Nathanael Chambers, Siva Reddy, Xavier R. Holt, Shay B. Cohen, Mark Johnson, and Mark Steedman. 2018. Learning typed entailment graphs with global soft constraints. *Transactions of the Association for Computational Linguistics*, 6:703–717.

Mohammad Javad Hosseini, Shay B. Cohen, Mark Johnson, and Mark Steedman. 2019. Duality of link prediction and entailment graph induction. In *Proceedings of the 57th Annual Meeting of the Association for Computational Linguistics*, pages 4736–4746, Florence, Italy, July. Association for Computational Linguistics.

Thomas Kober, Sander Bijl de Vroe, and Mark Steedman. 2019. Temporal and aspectual entailment. In *Proceedings of the 13th International Conference on Computational Semantics - Long Papers*, pages 103–119, Gothenburg, Sweden, May. Association for Computational Linguistics.

Omer Levy and Ido Dagan. 2016. Annotating relation inference in context via question answering. In *Proceedings of the 54th Annual Meeting of the Association for Computational Linguistics (Volume 2: Short Papers)*, pages 249–255, Berlin, Germany, August. Association for Computational Linguistics.

Omer Levy, Ido Dagan, and Jacob Goldberger. 2014. Focused entailment graphs for open IE propositions. In *Proceedings of the Eighteenth Conference on Computational Natural Language Learning*, pages 87–97, Ann Arbor, Michigan, June. Association for Computational Linguistics.

Mike Lewis and Mark Steedman. 2013. Combined distributional and logical semantics. *Transactions of the Association for Computational Linguistics*, 1:179–192.

Dekang Lin. 1998. An information-theoretic definition of similarity. In *Proceedings of the Fifteenth International Conference on Machine Learning*, ICML '98, page 296–304, San Francisco, CA, USA. Morgan Kaufmann Publishers Inc.

Xiao Ling and Daniel S. Weld. 2012. Fine-grained entity recognition. In *Proceedings of the Twenty-Sixth AAAI Conference on Artificial Intelligence*, AAAI'12, page 94–100. AAAI Press.

Dat Ba Nguyen, Johannes Hoffart, Martin Theobald, and Gerhard Weikum. 2014. Aida-light: High-throughput named-entity disambiguation. *Workshop on Linked Data on the Web*, 1184:1–10.

Hans Reichenbach. 1947. The tenses of verbs. *Time: From Concept to Narrative Construct: a Reader*.

Martin Schmitt and Hinrich Schütze. 2019. SherLIiC: A typed event-focused lexical inference benchmark for evaluating natural language inference. In *Proceedings of the 57th Annual Meeting of the Association for Computational Linguistics*, pages 902–914, Florence, Italy, July. Association for Computational Linguistics.

Miloš Stanojević and Mark Steedman. 2019. CCG parsing algorithm with incremental tree rotation. In *Proceedings of the 2019 Conference of the North American Chapter of the Association for Computational Linguistics: Human Language Technologies, Volume 1 (Long and Short Papers)*, pages 228–239, Minneapolis, Minnesota, June. Association for Computational Linguistics.

Mark Steedman. 2000. *The Syntactic Process*. MIT Press, Cambridge, MA, USA.

Idan Szpektor and Ido Dagan. 2008. Learning entailment rules for unary templates. In *Proceedings of the 22nd International Conference on Computational Linguistics (Coling 2008)*, pages 849–856, Manchester, UK, August. Coling 2008 Organizing Committee.

Naushad UzZaman, Hector Llorens, Leon Derczynski, James Allen, Marc Verhagen, and James Pustejovsky. 2013. Semeval-2013 task 1: Tempeval-3: Evaluating time expressions, events, and temporal relations. In *Second Joint Conference on Lexical and Computational Semantics (* SEM), Volume 2: Proceedings of the Seventh International Workshop on Semantic Evaluation (SemEval 2013)*, volume 2, pages 1–9.

Julie Weeds and David Weir. 2003. A general framework for distributional similarity. In *Proceedings of the 2003 Conference on Empirical Methods in Natural Language Processing*, pages 81–88.

Changlong Yu, Hongming Zhang, Yangqiu Song, Wilfred Ng, and Lifeng Shang. 2020. Enriching large-scale eventuality knowledge graph with entailment relations. In *Automated Knowledge Base Construction*.

Naomi Zeichner, Jonathan Berant, and Ido Dagan. 2012. Crowdsourcing inference-rule evaluation. In *Proceedings of the 50th Annual Meeting of the Association for Computational Linguistics (Volume 2: Short Papers)*, pages 156–160, Jeju Island, Korea, July. Association for Computational Linguistics.

Congle Zhang and Daniel S Weld. 2013. Harvesting parallel news streams to generate paraphrases of event relations. In *Proceedings of the 2013 Conference on Empirical Methods in Natural Language Processing*, pages 1776–1786.

Graph-based Syntactic Word Embeddings

Ragheb Al-Ghezi
Aalto University
`ragheb.al-ghezi@aalto.fi`

Mikko Kurimo
Aalto University
`mikko.kurimo@aalto.fi`

Abstract

We propose a simple and efficient framework to learn syntactic embeddings based on information derived from constituency parse trees. Using biased random walk methods, our embeddings not only encode syntactic information about words, but they also capture contextual information. We also propose a method to train the embeddings on multiple constituency parse trees to ensure the encoding of global syntactic representation. Quantitative evaluation of the embeddings shows competitive performance on POS tagging task when compared to other types of embeddings, and qualitative evaluation reveals interesting facts about the syntactic typology learned by these embeddings.

1 Introduction

Distributional similarity methods have been the standard learning representation in NLP. Word representations methods such as Word2vec, GloVe, and FastText [1, 2, 3] aim to create vector representation to words from other words or characters that mutually appear in the same context. The underlying premise is that "a word can be defined by its company" [4]. For example, in the sentences, "I eat an apple every day" and "I eat an orange every day", the words 'orange' and 'apple' are similar as they share similar contexts.

Recent approaches have proposed a syntax-based extension to distributional word embeddings to include functional similarity in the word vectors by leveraging the power of dependency parsing[5] [6]. Syntactic word embeddings have been shown to be advantageous in specific NLP tasks such as question type classification[7], semantic role labeling[8], part-of-speech tagging[6], biomedical event trigger identification[9], and predicting brain activation patterns [10]. One limitation of these methods is that they do not encode the hierarchical syntactic structure of which a word is a part due to its reliance on non-constituency parsing such as dependency parsing. While the latter analyzes the grammatical structure of a sentence by establishing a directed binary head-dependent relation among its words, constituency parsing analyzes the syntactic structure of a sentence according to a phrase structure grammar.

Syntactic hierarchy has advantages in tasks such as grammar checking, question answering, and information extraction [11]. It has also been encoded in neural models such as Recursive Neural Tensor Network and has proved it can predict the compositional semantic effects of sentiment in language [12]. Moreover, it can uniquely disambiguate the functional role of some words and therefore the overall semantic meaning. Figure 1 shows the modal verb *should* in the following sentences: *(1) Let me know should you have any question.* and *(2) I should study harder for the next exam.* Even though the word *should* is a modal verb (MD) in both sentences, it exhibits two different grammatical functions: conditionality and necessity respectively. Similarly, the word *is* in *(3) The king is at home.* and *(4) Is the king at home?* has a similar semantic meaning in both sentences, yet it exhibits two different syntactic roles (statement-forming and question-forming). Traditional word embeddings methods give a contextual, semantic representation to words like *is* and *should*, but they make no distinction of their grammatical function due to the absence of information on syntactic hierarchy. On the other hand, constituency

This work is licensed under a Creative Commons Attribution 4.0 International License. License details: `http://creativecommons.org/licenses/by/4.0/`.

Proceedings of the Graph-based Methods for Natural Language Processing (TextGraphs), pages 72–78
Barcelona, Spain (Online), December 13, 2020

parse trees provide a syntactic representation that can easily capture such distinction. Figures (a) and (b) show constituency parse tree of sentences (1) and (2) respectively. The difference in the position of the modal verb *should* in both sentences indicates a difference in the grammatical function, especially if it is compared to words with similar grammatical function in other sentences such as the one in (figure (c)). Comparing figures (a) and (c), we can note that *should* hold the same sense of conditionality the word *if* has. To this end, we propose a simple, graph-based framework to build syntactic word embeddings that can be flexibly customized to capture syntactic as well as contextual information by leveraging information derived from either manually or automatically constituency-parsed trees.

While recent transformer-based models such as BERT [13] have proved to be more sophisticated than word embeddings, the latter remains a popular choice due to its simplicity and efficiency. Thus, the contribution of this work is two-fold: (1) bridge the research gap in the literature of word embedding by introducing hierarchical syntactic embeddings based on constituency parsing (2) propose a graph-theoretic training method that cluster words according to their syntactic and constituent role without sacrificing the original context in which a word appears.

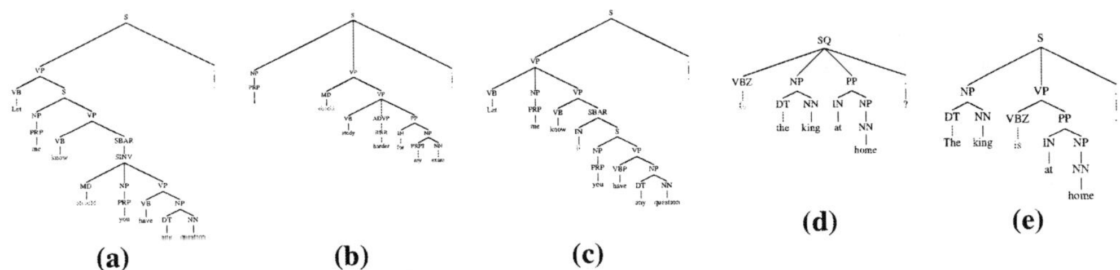

Figure 1: Trees (a), (b), (d) and (e) show different positions of the words *should* and *is* respectively indicating differences in syntactic functions. Tree (c) is analogous to (a) suggesting similarity in syntactic function between *should* and *if*.

2   Related Work

The NLP literature is rich with studies suggesting an improvement to original word embeddings models by incorporating external semantic resources like lexicons and ontologies [14, 15, 16, 17, 18]. However, very few studies were dedicated to syntactic embeddings. One of the earliest methods was dependency-based word embeddings [5], which generalizes the Skip-gram algorithm to include arbitrary word context. Instead of using bag-of-word context, they use context derived automatically from dependency parse trees. Specifically, for a word w with modifiers $m_1, ..., m_k$ and head h, the contexts $(m1, lbl_1), ..., (m_k, lbl_k), (h, lbl_h^1)$, where lbl is a type of dependency relation between the head. and the modifier (e.g. nsub, dobj, etc). For example, the context for the word *scientist* in *"Australian scientist discovers star with telescope"* is Australian/amod and discovers/$nsubj^1$.

Another modification to *word2vec* model was proposed by [6] to improve the word embeddings to syntax-based tasks by making it sensitive to the positioning of the words, and thereby accounting for its lack of order-dependence. The modification does not involve incorporating external parsing information, but it includes using 2 output predictors for every word in the window context each of which is dedicated to predicting position-specific value. Results on syntax-based tasks such as POS tagging and parsing show an improvement over classic word2vec embeddings.

More recently, a new approach, named SynGCN, for learning dependency-based syntactic embeddings is introduced by [19]. SynGCN builds syntactic word representation by using Graph Convolution Network (GCN). Using GCN allows SynGCN to capture global information from the graph on which it was trained while remaining efficient at training due to parallelization. Experiments show that SynGCN obtains improvement over state-of-the-art approaches when used with methods such as ELMo [20].

Most syntactic word embeddings methods rely on dependency parsing, and to the best of our knowledge that our work is the first utilizing constituency parsing to build syntactic representation.

3   Method

Our goal is to learn word embeddings that not only capture the sentence-level syntactic hierarchy encoded by the constituency parse tree, but also capture a global (suprasentential) syntactic representation, and because the constituency parse tree only provides sentence-level syntactic representations, we need a method to combine multiple constituency parse trees. We also need a flexible algorithm to learn the embeddings from those combined trees. In this section, we present a method of parse tree combination (namely graph unionization) as well as the Node2vec algorithm.

Graph Unionization Given a training dataset of constituency parse trees, we compose one graph (henceforth supergraph, Figure 2) by unionizing all the sentence trees in the training dataset. Formally, let $G(V, E)$ be a graph in the training corpus, where V represents a lexical or a non-lexical vertex in a constituency parse tree and E is the edge between them, and let H be $\bigcup_{i=1}^{n} G_i(V_i, E_i)$ where $\bigcup$ is a non-disjoint union operator and n is the number of sentences in the training corpus. The vertices and edges of the supergraph V_H and E_H are $\bigcup_{i=1}^{n} V_i$ and $\bigcup_{i=1}^{n} E_i$ respectively [21, 22].

Node2vec For learning syntactic embeddings from the supergraph, we use a variant of skip-gram algorithm, called node2vec algorithm[23]. Node2vec adapts Word2vec algorithm to graphs in which a node is defined by an arbitrary set of other nodes in the same graph sampled using a biased random walk. Using tunable parameters p and q, the biased random walk offers BFS and DFS search behavior in which more diverse neighborhoods are explored, and therefore richer representation may be learned[23].

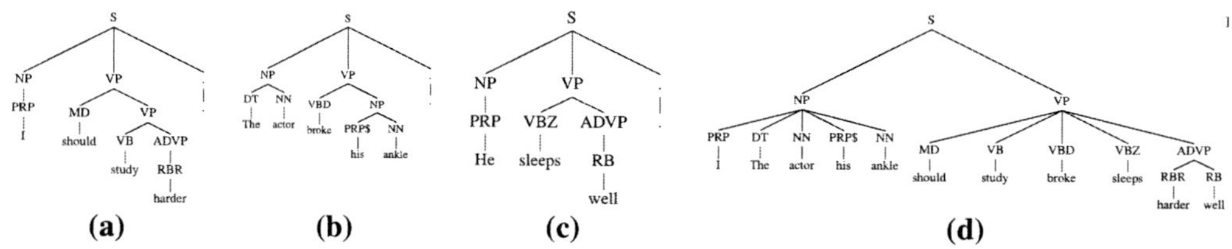

Figure 2: Trees (a), (b) and (c) are sample parse trees in the training corpus while (d) represents their unionized supergraph.

As shown in Figure 2, nodes tagged with certain labels, such as adjectives (JJ) or nouns (NN), will be linked together in the supergraph while remaining children of a noun phrase (NP). Similarly, sentences with similar grammatical structures such as interrogative sentences or questions (SQ) will be clustered together in the supergraph. It can be noted that the supergraph can cluster words of similar syntactic functions together while simultaneously enforcing/preserving the global syntactic hierarchy of the training corpus. The supergraph with the aid of the biased sampling strategy Node2vec offers the flexibility of learning customizable syntactic representation. A breadth-first search strategy, for instance, would favor the selection of words of similar POS tags and thereby yielding word-class-specific representation while a depth-first strategy would yield more hierarchical or contextual representation.

4   Data and Experiment

For the purposes of training the syntactic embeddings, we use the Penn Treebank corpus[24], which contains over 43,000 constituency parse trees to sentences collected from the Wall Street Journal (WSJ). Next, we unionize all the parses trees into one supergraph. The supergraph has 51071 vertices and 65895 edges, and it has an average degree of 2.5805 and a density of 5.05×10^{-5}. We chose to unionize all the trees in the training corpus for simplicity, but we certainly could have grouped the sentences into clusters of thematic or semantic identity prior to applying unionization. After that, we train the embeddings with node2vec algorithm using SGD of 10,000 epochs and a learning rate of 0.025 with a weight decay of 0.005. In terms of node2vec hyperparameters, we chose a random walk of length 200 and a batch size of 100, and the return parameter p and the in-out parameter q are both set to $10^{-}6$. Lower p values keep the walk close to the starting node, and lower q values encourage the walk to behave in a DFS manner [23]. The training took 51 seconds on 1 Tesla K80 GPU using the Graphvite Python package[25]. We initialize the word vectors randomly for simplicity, but initialization with other types of distributional embeddings such as word2vec or GloVe is possible. We decide to explore the latter in future work.

5 Results

We conduct two types of evaluations: qualitative and quantitative. In the qualitative evaluation, we examine the extent to which the learned embeddings can encode grammatical information about the words using words analogies and word arithmetics. In addition, we compare its performance against GloVe vectors [2] and SynGCN [19] on one stream task, POS tagging.

5.1 Qualitative Evaluation

One common method to evaluate word embeddings is examining word vectors by their top k nearest neighbors in the latent vector space. From table 5.1, we observe that the top 3 neighbors for the words *complicate, failed, earthquakes* are all of the similar syntactic category: a present verb attracts similar present verbs; a plural noun attracts plural nouns; and so on. Similarly, the adjective *responsible* and the adverb *handsomely* maintain a very close distance to words of the same part-of-speech. In contrast, neither GloVe vectors nor SynGCN exhibit similar neighborhood typology. This confirms that our constituency-based embeddings have consistently preserved syntactic information about words.

Another way to evaluate word embeddings is by explaining word analogies by the means of word vector arithmetics [26]. The famous example used in [1] is *woman is to queen as man is to king*, or $(w_q + w_k) - w_m \approx w_w$. When we apply the same method to our constituency-based syntactic vectors, we assert that the vector arithmetic sense strongly matches the syntactic analogies. For example, in table 5.1, if we subtract the sum of word vectors in the prepositional phrase (PP) *in an industrial* from the PP *of any clearly domestic*, the top 3 nearest neighbors in our embeddings are all adverbs (ADV) to compensate for the missing adverb in the second PP. We also note the case is not true for the other types of embeddings where the top nearest neighbors are affected by words in the PP. Similarly, applying the same arithmetic operations to the phrases *his state-of-the-art plan* and *her plan* would results in adjective vectors, unlike the other embeddings.

word	SynGCN (Cos Sim)		GloVe (Cos Sim)		Ours (Cos Sim)	
	complicates	0.60	complicating	0.90	**prune**	0.97
complicate	complicating	0.51	complicates	0.87	**ruin**	0.97
	simplify	0.43	**jeopardize**	0.83	**outpace**	0.97
	failing	0.61	failing	0.89	**reconstructed**	0.98
failed	unsuccessful	0.56	attempt	0.88	**slated**	0.98
	fail	0.54	attempts	0.86	**challenged**	0.98
	earthquake	0.65	**quakes**	0.90	**failures**	0.98
earthquakes	**tsunamis**	0.61	**aftershocks**	0.80	**sons**	0.98
	quakes	0.58	**tremors**	0.79	**bouts**	0.98
	generously	0.48	doled	0.71	**effectively**	0.97
handsomely	**ornately**	0.46	rewarded	0.70	**negligently**	0.97
	competently	0.45	gambled	0.68	**inexorably**	0.97
	accountable	0.52	**involved**	0.90	**extensive**	0.97
responsible	responsibility	0.41	responsibility	0.84	**fifth-biggest**	0.97
	tasked	0.39	planning	0.80	**one-woman**	0.97
([of]+[any]+[clearly]+[domestic]) -	none	0.28	ignore	0.76	**precariously**	0.88
([in] + [an] + [industrial])	all	0.27	acknowledge	0.76	**slightly**	0.87
	interestingly	0.26	**necessarily**	0.75	**equitably**	0.87
([his]+[state-of-the-art]+[plan]) -	plans	0.35	build	0.69	**government-held**	0.92
([her] + [assignment])	**cutting-edge**	0.34	renovation	0.66	**harder-line**	0.90
	planning	0.34	redevelopment	0.65	**front-page**	0.90
	will	0.52	we	0.91	**will**	0.92
([would] + [need])-[require]	**should**	0.59	come	0.90	**might**	0.91
	could	0.47	want	0.88	**can**	0.91

Table 1: Comparison of top 3 KNN with cosine similarity produced by SynGCN [19], GloVe [2], and our embeddings. Words in bold belong to the same POS tag/ grammatical category.

5.2 Intrinsic Evaluation

We also test the performance of our constituency-based embeddings on a mainstream task, parts-of-speech tagging. Our goal is not to achieve state-of-the-art results in POS tagging, but we want to demonstrate the grammatical potential of our embeddings. For this purpose, we treat POS tagging as

	SVM- F1 Score	CRF- F1 Score
Glove [2]	0.731	0.894
SynGCN [19]	**0.892**	0.898
Ours	0.881	**0.910**

Table 2: Evaluation on POS tagging using SVM and CRF classifiers. Scores represent a mean F1 score of 5-fold cross-validation.

an independent classification task (as opposed to structured prediction one) in which a non-sequential classifier support vector machine (SVM) is used to predict a POS tag for a word acontextually. The use of non-neural, non-sequential classifier ensures that the grammatical generalizability comes strictly from the embeddings and not from the neural network or the context. Nevertheless, we also treat POS tagging as a structured prediction task in which we use a sequential classifier like conditional random field (CRF) for the purposes of comparison. Performance is also reported for two other word embeddings: GloVe and SynGCN under the same settings.

We test the performance using the trained vectors on the first 2000 sentences of the Brown corpus [27]. In table 2, we report the mean F1 score of 5-fold cross-validation in which we can observe that our vectors are competitive in performance to SynGCN and far better than GloVe when used with SVM classifier. In addition, our embeddings outperform both of the competing embeddings when used with CRF.

Even though the performance of the constituency-based embeddings slightly lags behind SynGCN in the case of independent classification, the size of the corpus upon which our embeddings were trained (Penn Treebanks 1 million tokens) is much smaller compared to the one upon which SynGCN was trained (Wikipedia 1.1 billion tokens). In addition, the flexibility of learning customizable syntactic word embeddings as well as the training efficiency make constituency-based word embeddings a powerful and promising research direction that can be applied to other graph-based tasks.

6 Conclusion and Future Work

We presented a simple and efficient framework to learn syntactic embeddings from constituency parse trees using a combination of multiple graph unionization and biased random walk. Our framework can be flexibly customized to learn purely contextual and non-contextual syntactic embeddings, and it can be also used as a post-hoc method for other kinds of (distributional) word embeddings. Thus, for future studies, we would like to investigate training constituency-based vectors on a larger corpus and examine the effect of different initialization on more mainstream tasks such as machine translation and automatic speech recognition.

7 Acknowledgments

We would like to thank Sandeep Suntwal, Yaroslav Getman, and Katja Voskoboinik for their helpful discussion and insightful comments. We also thank the anonymous reviewers for their constructive comments. This work was funded by the Academy of Finland (grant number 322625).

References

[1] Tomas Mikolov, Ilya Sutskever, Kai Chen, Greg S Corrado, and Jeff Dean. Distributed representations of words and phrases and their compositionality. In *Advances in neural information processing systems*, pages 3111–3119, 2013.

[2] Jeffrey Pennington, Richard Socher, and Christopher D Manning. Glove: Global vectors for word representation. In *Proceedings of the 2014 conference on empirical methods in natural language processing (EMNLP)*, pages 1532–1543, 2014.

[3] Piotr Bojanowski, Edouard Grave, Armand Joulin, and Tomas Mikolov. Enriching word vectors

with subword information. *Transactions of the Association for Computational Linguistics*, 5:135–146, 2017.

[4] J.R. Firth and F.R. Palmer. *Selected Papers of J.R. Firth, 1952-1959*. Indiana University Studies in the History and Theory of Linguistics. Longmans, 1968.

[5] Omer Levy and Yoav Goldberg. Dependency-based word embeddings. In *Proceedings of the 52nd Annual Meeting of the Association for Computational Linguistics (Volume 2: Short Papers)*, pages 302–308, 2014.

[6] Wang Ling, Chris Dyer, Alan W Black, and Isabel Trancoso. Two/too simple adaptations of word2vec for syntax problems. In *Proceedings of the 2015 Conference of the North American Chapter of the Association for Computational Linguistics: Human Language Technologies*, pages 1299–1304, 2015.

[7] Alexandros Komninos and Suresh Manandhar. Dependency based embeddings for sentence classification tasks. In *Proceedings of the 2016 conference of the North American chapter of the association for computational linguistics: human language technologies*, pages 1490–1500, 2016.

[8] Michael Roth and Mirella Lapata. Neural semantic role labeling with dependency path embeddings. *arXiv preprint arXiv:1605.07515*, 2016.

[9] Jian Wang, Jianhai Zhang, Yuan An, Hongfei Lin, Zhihao Yang, Yijia Zhang, and Yuanyuan Sun. Biomedical event trigger detection by dependency-based word embedding. *BMC medical genomics*, 9(2):45, 2016.

[10] Samira Abnar, Rasyan Ahmed, Max Mijnheer, and Willem Zuidema. Experiential, distributional and dependency-based word embeddings have complementary roles in decoding brain activity. *arXiv preprint arXiv:1711.09285*, 2017.

[11] Dan Jurafsky and James H Martin. Speech and language processing. vol. 3, 2014.

[12] Richard Socher, Alex Perelygin, Jean Wu, Jason Chuang, Christopher D Manning, Andrew Y Ng, and Christopher Potts. Recursive deep models for semantic compositionality over a sentiment treebank. In *Proceedings of the 2013 conference on empirical methods in natural language processing*, pages 1631–1642, 2013.

[13] Jacob Devlin, Ming-Wei Chang, Kenton Lee, and Kristina Toutanova. Bert: Pre-training of deep bidirectional transformers for language understanding. *arXiv preprint arXiv:1810.04805*, 2018.

[14] Manaal Faruqui, Jesse Dodge, Sujay K Jauhar, Chris Dyer, Eduard Hovy, and Noah A Smith. Retrofitting word vectors to semantic lexicons. *arXiv preprint arXiv:1411.4166*, 2014.

[15] Douwe Kiela, Felix Hill, and Stephen Clark. Specializing word embeddings for similarity or relatedness. In *Proceedings of the 2015 Conference on Empirical Methods in Natural Language Processing*, pages 2044–2048, 2015.

[16] Julien Tissier, Christophe Gravier, and Amaury Habrard. Dict2vec: Learning word embeddings using lexical dictionaries. 2017.

[17] Chang Xu, Yalong Bai, Jiang Bian, Bin Gao, Gang Wang, Xiaoguang Liu, and Tie-Yan Liu. Rc-net: A general framework for incorporating knowledge into word representations. In *Proceedings of the 23rd ACM international conference on conference on information and knowledge management*, pages 1219–1228, 2014.

[18] Tom Bosc and Pascal Vincent. Auto-encoding dictionary definitions into consistent word embeddings. In *Proceedings of the 2018 Conference on Empirical Methods in Natural Language Processing*, pages 1522–1532, 2018.

[19] Shikhar Vashishth, Manik Bhandari, Prateek Yadav, Piyush Rai, Chiranjib Bhattacharyya, and Partha Talukdar. Incorporating syntactic and semantic information in word embeddings using graph convolutional networks. *arXiv preprint arXiv:1809.04283*, 2018.

[20] Matthew E Peters, Mark Neumann, Mohit Iyyer, Matt Gardner, Christopher Clark, Kenton Lee, and Luke Zettlemoyer. Deep contextualized word representations. *arXiv preprint arXiv:1802.05365*, 2018.

[21] Frank Harary. *Graph Theory. Addison Wesley Publishing Company.* 1969.

[22] Jonathan L Gross and Jay Yellen. *Graph theory and its applications.* CRC press, 2005.

[23] Aditya Grover and Jure Leskovec. node2vec: Scalable feature learning for networks. In *Proceedings of the 22nd ACM SIGKDD international conference on Knowledge discovery and data mining*, pages 855–864, 2016.

[24] Mitchell P Marcus, Beatrice Santorini, Mary Ann Marcinkiewicz, and Ann Taylor. Treebank-3. *Linguistic Data Consortium, Philadelphia*, 14, 1999.

[25] Zhaocheng Zhu, Shizhen Xu, Meng Qu, and Jian Tang. Graphvite: A high-performance cpu-gpu hybrid system for node embedding. In *The World Wide Web Conference*, pages 2494–2504. ACM, 2019.

[26] Carl Allen and Timothy Hospedales. Analogies explained: Towards understanding word embeddings. *arXiv preprint arXiv:1901.09813*, 2019.

[27] W Nelson Francis and Henry Kucera. Brown corpus manual. *Letters to the Editor*, 5(2):7, 1979.

A Appendices

A.1 Datasets

We train the closed-world and open-world models on the closed-world training sets (Table 3) and validate/test on the open-world triples. The missing entities in the open-world and closed-world datasets do not overlap.

Dataset	$|E|$	$|E^{open}|$	$|R|$	Number of Triples			Open World Triples	
				Train	Valid	Test	Valid	Test
FB20k	14,904	5,019	1,341	472,860	48,991	57,803	-	11,586
DBPedia50k	24,624	2,139	351	32,388	123	2,095	164	4,320
FB15k-237-OWE	12,324	13,857	235	242,489	12,806	-	9,424	22,393

Table 3: Datasets used for training closed- and open-world KGC models. $|E^{open}|$ is the number of open-world entities that are present in these datasets.

A.2 Hyperparameters

The ComplEx-RST and ComplEx-RCT models are trained on a workstation with Intel Core i7 6700k and a single Nvidia GTX1080 GPU for DBPedia50k and FB15k-237-OWE datasets. The models on FB20k dataset are trained on a Nvidia Quadro P6000. These models are trained in around 1-2 hours on average.

We provide all hyperparameters that are used for the experiments in Table 4. Additionally, we provide code, data and configs for the experiments at `https://github.com/haseebs/RST-OWE`. For all our experiments, we ran a hyperparameter sweep over batch size: {128, 256}, distance metric: {Euclidean, Cosine} (see Equation 4) and learning rate: {0.01, 0.001, 0.0001}. The final values were selected by tuning on the validation set with the value of *filtered MRR* as the criterion. For the clustering parameters η and S we conducted a grid search too. The resulting values were chosen to produce meaningful clusters based on a manual inspection in addition of achieving the greatest reduction in number of clusters at a negligible negative impact on accuracy.

Hyperparameter	DBPedia50k	FB15k-237-OWE	FB20k
Learning Rate	0.001	0.001	0.001
Optimizer	Adam	Adam	Adam
Embedding Dim	300	300	300
Batch Size	128	256	128
Distance Metric	Euclidean	Euclidean	Cosine
Number of Iterations (η)	6	6	6
Similarity factor (S)	0.8	0.8	0.8

Table 4: Hyperparameters used in the ComplEx-RCT and ComplEx-RST experiments.

Relation Specific Transformations
for Open World Knowledge Graph Completion

Haseeb Shah
Department of Computer Science
University of Alberta
hshah1@ualberta.ca

Johannes Villmow, Adrian Ulges
DCSM Department
RheinMain University of Applied Sciences
{johannes.villmow, adrian.ulges}@hs-rm.de

Abstract

We propose an open-world knowledge graph completion model that can be combined with common closed-world approaches (such as ComplEx) and enhance them to exploit text-based representations for entities unseen in training. Our model learns relation-specific transformation functions from text-based embedding space to graph-based embedding space, where the closed-world link prediction model can be applied. We demonstrate state-of-the-art results on common open-world benchmarks and show that our approach benefits from relation-specific transformation functions (RST), giving substantial improvements over a relation-agnostic approach.

1 Introduction

Knowledge graphs are an interesting source of information that can be exploited by retrieval (Dong et al., 2014) and question answering systems (Ferrucci et al., 2010). They are, however, known to be inherently sparse (Paulheim, 2017). To overcome this problem, *knowledge graph completion (KGC)* enriches graphs with new triples. While most existing approaches require all entities to be part of the training graph, for many applications it is of interest to infer knowledge about entities *not* present in the graph i.e. *open-world* entities. Here, approaches usually assume some text describing the target entity to be given, from which an entity representations can be inferred, for example via text embeddings (Mikolov et al., 2013; Devlin et al., 2018). To the best of our knowledge, only a few such *open-world* KGC approaches have been proposed so far (Xie et al., 2016; Shi and Weninger, 2017a; Shah et al., 2019).

We suggest a simple yet effective approach towards open-world KGC[1]: Similar to Shah et al. (2019)'s OWE model, our approach enables *existing* KGC models to perform open-world prediction: Given an open-world entity, its name and description are aggregated into a text-based entity representation, and a transformation from text-based embedding space to graph-based embedding space is learned, where the closed-world KGC model can be applied. However, while OWE's transformation only takes the open-world *entity* into account, our approach also utilizes the target triple's *relation*, such that specific mappings are learned for different relations such as *birthplace*, *spouse*, or *located_in* (see Figure 1). We demonstrate that this extension comes with strong improvements, yielding state-of-the-art results on common open-world datasets.

2 Related Work

Interest in KGC has increased recently, with most of the work focusing on embedding-based approaches. Earlier approaches (Nickel et al., 2016) have recently been complemented by other models such as DistMult (Yang et al., 2014), TransR (Lin et al., 2015), ComplEx (Trouillon et al., 2016), ProjE (Shi and Weninger, 2017b) and RotatE (Sun et al., 2019). The above models estimate the probability of triples $(head, rel, tail)$ using a scoring function $\phi(u_{head}, u_{rel}, u_{tail})$, where u_x denotes the embedding of entity/relation x and is a real-valued or complex-valued vector. ϕ depends on the model and varies from simple translation (Bordes et al., 2013) over bilinear forms (Yang et al., 2014) to complex-valued

---

[1] We make our code available under https://github.com/haseebs/RST-OWE

This work is licensed under a Creative Commons Attribution 4.0 International License. License details: http://creativecommons.org/licenses/by/4.0/.

Proceedings of the Graph-based Methods for Natural Language Processing (TextGraphs), pages 79–84
Barcelona, Spain (Online), December 13, 2020

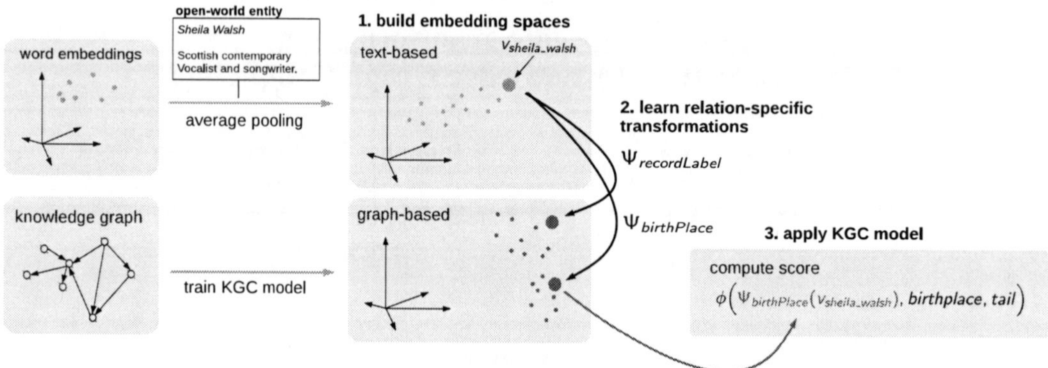

Figure 1: Our approach first trains a KGC model on the graph without using textual information (bottom left). For every annotated entity, we extract a text-based embedding v by aggregating the word embeddings for tokens in the entity's name and description (top left). A transformation Ψ is trained to map v to the space of graph-based embeddings (center). The learned mapping can then be applied to unknown entities, thus allowing the trained KGC model to be applied (right).

forms (Trouillon et al., 2016). Training happens by learning to discriminate real triples from perturbed ones, typically by negative sampling (Nickel et al., 2016).

While the knowledge graph completion models described above leverage only the structure of the graph, some approaches combine text with graph information, typically using embeddings that represent terms, sentences or documents (Goldberg, 2016). Embeddings are usually derived from language models, either in static form (Mikolov et al., 2013) or by contextualized models (Devlin et al., 2018). KGC models can employ such textual information for entities scarcely linked in the graph (Gesese et al., 2019). Most approaches combine a textual embedding with structural KGC approaches, either by initializing structural embeddings from text (Socher et al., 2013; Wang and Li, 2016), interpolating between textual and structural embeddings (Xu et al., 2017), sometimes with a joined loss (Toutanova and Chen, 2015) and gating mechanisms (Kristiadi et al., 2019). Others perform a fine-tuning for KGC based on textual labels of the entities and relations (Yao et al., 2019).

Only few other works have addressed *open-world KGC* so far. Xie et al. (2016) proposed DKRL with a joint training of graph-based embeddings (TransE) and text-based embeddings while regularizing both types of embeddings to be aligned using an additional loss. ConMask (Shi and Weninger, 2017a) is a text-centric approach where text-based embeddings for entities and relations are derived by an attention model over names and descriptions. Closest to our work is OWE (Shah et al., 2019), which trains graph and text embeddings independently and then learns a mapping between the two embedding spaces (more details are provided in Section 3). While OWE's mapping only take entities into account, our extended model's mapping is learned given both the entity *and relation* when predicting a triple. Orthogonal to our work, WOWE (Zhou et al., 2020) extends the OWE approach by replacing the averaging aggregator with a weighted attention mechanism and can be combined with our approach.

3 Approach

Given a knowledge graph $\mathcal{G} \subset E \times R \times E$ containing triples (h, r, t) (E and R denote finite sets of entities and relations), KGC models can perform tail prediction as follows: Given a pair of head and relation (h, r), the tail is estimated as

$$t^* = \arg\max_{t \in E} \quad \phi(u_h, u_r, u_t) \tag{1}$$

where u_h, u_r, u_t are entity/relation embeddings and ϕ is a model-specific scoring function. Note that this approach – and our extension – can be applied for head prediction accordingly.

We address an open-world setting, where the triple's head is not a part of the knowledge graph, i.e.

Test Entity v_h	Relation r	Nearest Neighbors to $\Psi_r(v_h)$	Test Entity v_h	Relation r	Nearest Neighbors to $\Psi_r(v_h)$
Sheila Walsh (Scottish contemporary vocalist and songwriter)	birthPlace	1. Nigel McGuiness (British) 2. Darren Burridge (British) 3. Kim Newman (British)	Ferlyn Wong (Singaporean singer, dancer and actress)	occupation	1. Park Ji-yeon (singer) 2. Kim Sae-ron (actress) 3. Park Shin-hye (actress)
	recordLabel	1. Picture this live (album) 2. Thick as a Brick (album) 3. Whiplash Smile (album)		genre	1. Tony An (singer) 2. Exodus (album) 3. S.E.S. (band)

Table 1: Relation-specific transformations map entities to corresponding regions in embedding space: When mapping *Sheila_Walsh* with the *birthplace* relation, the resulting embedding lies in a cluster of British people. When mapping with the *recordLabel* relation, the resulting embedding lies close to pop albums (which also have a recordLabel relation).

$h \notin E$. However, h is assumed to come with a textual description. Our approach (Figure 1) transforms this text into a token sequence $\mathcal{W}_h = (w_1, w_2, ..., w_n)$, from which a sequence of embeddings $(v_{w_1}, v_{w_2}, ..., v_{w_n})$ is derived using a textual embedding model pre-trained on a large text corpus. We experimented with BERT (Devlin et al., 2018) but did not achieve major improvements over static embeddings, likely because descriptions on KGC datasets tend to be short. Instead we use Wikipedia2Vec (Yamada et al., 2016), which contains phrase embeddings for entity names like "Sheila Walsh". If no phrase embedding is available, we use token-wise embeddings instead. If no embedding is available for a token, we use a vector of zeros as an "unknown" token. The resulting sequence of embeddings is aggregated by average pooling to obtain a single text-based embedding vector of the head entity $v_h \in \mathbb{R}^d$.

The key step of our approach is to learn transformation functions Ψ_r that align the text-based and graph-based embedding spaces such that $\Psi_r(v_h) \approx u_h$. When applying this mapping, the open-world entity's text-based embedding v_h is transformed into a graph-based proxy embedding $\Psi_r(v_h)$. Triples with h are scored by applying the KGC model from Equation 1 to $\Psi_r(v_h)$:

$$t^* = \arg\max_{t \in E} \ \phi\Big(\Psi_r(v_h), u_r, u_t\Big) \qquad (2)$$

Like OWE (Shah et al., 2019), we use an affine transformation $\Psi_r(v) = A_r \cdot v + b_r$. Our focus of this paper is to deal with relation specificity, for which we propose the following two strategies:

Relation Specific Transformation (RST) While the OWE model consists of a global transformation function (Ψ), our proposed RST approach trains a separate transformation function per relation (Ψ_r): Our hypothesis is that when predicting a tail $(h, r, ?)$, including information on the relation r may be beneficial. Have a look at Table 1, where the transformation $\Psi_{birthPlace}$ maps v_{Shiela_Walsh} to a completely different region in the graph embedding space than $\Psi_{recordLabel}$.

Therefore, we learn a separate transformation Ψ_r for each relation $r \in R$, containing a separate learnable matrix A_r and vector b_r. For a fair comparison with OWE, we use the ComplEx KGC model (Trouillon et al., 2016) in our experiments and use separate parameters for the real and imaginary parts.

Relation Clustering Transformation (RCT) Our second approach – Relation Clustering Transformation (RCT) – aggregates relations to clusters and then learns a separate transformation Ψ_C for each cluster C. We use an agglomerative clustering approach (pseudo-code in Figure 2), which first initializes each cluster with a single relation $r \in R$ and conducts η fusion steps, each joining "similar" clusters: Let $t(C)$ denote the set of tails attached to any relation r in C. Clusters C, C' are fused if the number of shared tails, divided by size of the smaller cluster, exceeds a threshold $\mathcal{S}$:

$$\frac{|t(C) \cap t(C')|}{min(|t(C)|, |t(C')|)} > \mathcal{S} \qquad (3)$$

3.1 Training

Our text embeddings v and graph embeddings u are based on pretrained models, such that the only parameters Θ to be learned are the relation matrices A_r and vectors b_r. First a KGC model is trained

Model	DBPedia50k				FB15k-237-OWE				FB20k			
	H@1	H@3	H@10	MRR	H@1	H@3	H@10	MRR	H@1	H@3	H@10	MRR
Target Filtering Baseline[†]	4.5	9.7	23.0	11.0	6.4	14.2	23.3	12.7	17.5	32.1	41.2	27.2
DKRL[†]	-	-	40.0	23.0	-	-	-	-	-	-	-	-
ConMask[†]	47.1	64.5	**81.0**	58.4	21.5	39.9	45.8	29.9	42.3	57.3	71.7	53.3
ComplEx-OWE-200[†]	49.0	62.3	73.6	57.7	29.1	41.0	52.7	37.3	44.2	55.9	68.2	52.3
ComplEx-OWE-300[†]	51.9	65.2	76.0	60.3	31.6	43.9	56.0	40.1	44.8	57.1	69.1	53.1
WOWE (Zhou et al., 2020)	52.7	66.5	76.9	61.2	31.9	44.1	56.4	40.4	45.2	58.3	70.0	54.1
ComplEx-RCT ($\eta : 6, \mathcal{S} : 0.8$)	54.2	68.6	79.1	63.1	33.0	45.7	58.2	41.7	46.4	59.4	71.0	55.0
ComplEx-RST	**55.7**	**69.1**	80.1	**64.3**	**33.2**	**46.0**	**58.8**	**42.0**	**49.8**	**63.5**	**75.5**	**58.7**

Table 2: Comparison with other open-world KGC models on tail prediction. The Relation Specific Transformation (ComplEx-RST) performs best, particularly on the DBPedia50K and FB20K datasets with long textual descriptions († results reported by Shah et al. (2019)).

on the full graph $\mathcal{G}$, obtaining graph-based entity embeddings $u_1, ..., u_n$. We then choose the subset E^t of all entities in the graph with textual descriptions, and define $\mathcal{G}^t := \mathcal{G} \cap (E^t \times R \times E)$ as all triplets containing heads with text. We then minimize the following loss:

$$L(\Theta) = \sum_{(h,r,t)\in\mathcal{G}^t} \text{dist}\Big(\Psi_r(v_h), u_h \Big) \tag{4}$$

with *dist()* referring either to Euclidean or cosine distance between the graph- and text-based head embeddings. As we use ComplEx, where embeddings u_h contain real and imaginary parts, the above loss is summed for both parts. Since the number of entities in the datasets used is limited and overfitting is expected to be an issue, we neither fine-tune into the graph nor the text-embeddings.

4 Evaluation

We evaluate our model on FB20k (Xie et al., 2016), DBPedia50k (Shi and Weninger, 2017a) and FB15k-237-OWE (Shah et al., 2019) and compare our model with the state of the art on the task in open-world tail prediction. Results are illustrated in Table 2. Due to the lack of an open-world validation set on FB20k, we remove random 10% of the test triples and use them as a validation set. Hyperparameters were optimized using a grid search (details in the appendix). We use the same evaluation criteria as Shah et al. (2019), and evaluate our results only on ComplEx to provide a fair comparison with the OWE models. For training the closed-world KGC models, we utilize OpenKE (Han et al., 2018). Additionally, we use the target filtering approach (Shi and Weninger, 2017a) on any results reported. The Target Filtering Baseline is evaluated by assigning random scores to all targets that pass the target filtering criterion.

Results We observe that the ComplEx-RST outperforms all other approaches – including OWE – by a margin on all metrics except Hits@10 on DBPedia50k. ComplEx-RCT (relation clusters) performs competitively with the ComplEx-RST (one mapping per relation), while the number of transformation functions is reduced from 351 to 279 in case of DBPedia50k, from 235 to 114 in case of FB15k-237-OWE and from 1341 to 522 in case of FB20k. The values of η and $\mathcal{S}$ were optimized to achieve the greatest reduction in number of clusters at a negligible negative impact on accuracy. We also note that the improvement achieved by utilizing the relation information is higher in DBPedia50k and FB20k, both of which use very long descriptions compared to FB15k-237-OWE. We believe that this is because the longer descriptions often have more pieces of information relevant to the relation, which the relation-specific transformations are able to extract and utilize.

Finally, in Figure 2 (right) we investigate which relations benefit strongest from relation-specific mappings: Each point represents a relation in FB15k-237-OWE. We observe that points to the left (rare relations) tend to benefit stronger from learning a transformation of their own (RST). Those scarce relations seem to be underrepresented in the training data and – accordingly – in the global mapping.

```
Input: Training set G, similarity factor
       S ∈ ℝ, iterations η ∈ ℤ
Output: Clusters C = {c₁, c₂, ..., cₘ}
for i ← 1...|R| do
    cᵢ ← {rᵢ}
Procedure make_clusters(C, η)
    if η = 0 then
        return C
    for i ← 1...|C| do
        t(cᵢ) ← get_tails(cᵢ, G)
        for j = i+1...|C| do
            t(cⱼ) ← get_tails(cⱼ, G)
            if |t(cᵢ)∩t(cⱼ)| / min(|t(cᵢ)|,|t(cⱼ)|) > S then
                cᵢ ← cᵢ ∪ cⱼ
                delete cⱼ from C
                break
        make_clusters(C, η − 1)
end
make_clusters({c₁...c_|R|}, η)
```

Figure 2: The algorithm (left) outlines our implementation of the RCT approach in pseudo code. The plot (right) visualizes the improvement in MRR of ComplEx-RST compared to ComplEx-OWE on the y-axis. Each point is a relation in FB15k-237-OWE. The size of the point represents the number of test triples containing the relation. The x-axis shows the number of training triples containing the relation. We see that this improvement tends to be higher for scarce relations (left on the x-axis).

5 Conclusion

We have proposed a simple approach to incorporate relation-specific information into open-world knowledge graph completion. Our approach achieves state-of-the-art results on common open-source benchmarks and offers strong improvements over relation-agnostic state-of-the-art methods. An interesting direction for future work will be to adapt our model to longer textual inputs, e.g. by using attention to enable the model to select relevant passages (similar to ConMask (Shi and Weninger, 2017a)).

Acknowledgements

This work was funded by German Federal Ministry of Education and Research (Program FHprofUnt, Project DeepCA (13FH011PX6)).

References

Antoine Bordes, Nicolas Usunier, Alberto Garcia-Duran, Jason Weston, and Oksana Yakhnenko. 2013. Translating Embeddings for Modeling Multi-relational Data. In *Adv. in Neural Information Processing Systems*, pages 2787–2795.

Jacob Devlin, Ming-Wei Chang, Kenton Lee, and Kristina Toutanova. 2018. Bert: Pre-training of deep bidirectional transformers for language understanding. *arXiv preprint arXiv:1810.04805*.

Xin Dong, Evgeniy Gabrilovich, Geremy Heitz, Wilko Horn, Ni Lao, Kevin Murphy, Thomas Strohmann, Shaohua Sun, and Wei Zhang. 2014. Knowledge vault: A web-scale approach to probabilistic knowledge fusion. In *Proceedings of the 20th ACM SIGKDD International Conference on Knowledge Discovery and Data Mining*, KDD '14, page 601–610, New York, NY, USA. Association for Computing Machinery.

David Ferrucci, Eric Brown, Jennifer Chu-Carroll, James Fan, David Gondek, Aditya A. Kalyanpur, Adam Lally, J. William Murdock, Eric Nyberg, John Prager, Nico Schlaefer, and Chris Welty. 2010. Building Watson: An Overview of the DeepQA Project. *AI Magazine*, 31(3):59–79.

Genet Asefa Gesese, Russa Biswas, Mehwish Alam, and Harald Sack. 2019. A survey on knowledge graph embeddings with literals: Which model links better literal-ly?

Yoav Goldberg. 2016. A Primer on Neural Network Models for Natural Language Processing. *J. Artif. Int. Res.*, 57(1):345–420, September.

Xu Han, Shulin Cao, Lv Xin, Yankai Lin, Zhiyuan Liu, Maosong Sun, and Juanzi Li. 2018. Openke: An open toolkit for knowledge embedding. In *Proceedings of EMNLP*.

Agustinus Kristiadi, Mohammad Asif Khan, Denis Lukovnikov, Jens Lehmann, and Asja Fischer. 2019. Incorporating literals into knowledge graph embeddings. In *The Semantic Web - ISWC 2019 - 18th International Semantic Web Conference, Auckland, New Zealand, October 26-30, 2019, Proceedings, Part I*, pages 347–363.

Yankai Lin, Zhiyuan Liu, Maosong Sun, Yang Liu, and Xuan Zhu. 2015. Learning entity and relation embeddings for knowledge graph completion. In *Twenty-ninth AAAI conference on artificial intelligence*.

Tomas Mikolov, Ilya Sutskever, Kai Chen, Greg Corrado, and Jeffrey Dean. 2013. Distributed representations of words and phrases and their compositionality. *CoRR*, abs/1310.4546.

Maximilian Nickel, Kevin Murphy, Volker Tresp, and Evgeniy Gabrilovich. 2016. A Review of Relational Machine Learning for Knowledge Graphs. *Proceedings of the IEEE*, 104(1):11–33.

Heiko Paulheim. 2017. Knowledge Graph Refinement: A Survey of Approaches and Evaluation Methods. *Semantic Web*, 8(3):489–508.

Haseeb Shah, Johannes Villmow, Adrian Ulges, Ulrich Schwanecke, and Faisal Shafait. 2019. An open-world extension to knowledge graph completion models. In *The Thirty-Third AAAI Conference on Artificial Intelligence*, pages 3044–3051.

Baoxu Shi and Tim Weninger. 2017a. Open-World Knowledge Graph Completion. *CoRR*, abs/1711.03438.

Baoxu Shi and Tim Weninger. 2017b. ProjE: Embedding Projection for Knowledge Graph Completion. In *Proc. AAAI*, pages 1236–1242.

Richard Socher, Danqi Chen, Christopher D. Manning, and Andrew Y. Ng. 2013. Reasoning with neural tensor networks for knowledge base completion. In *Proceedings of the 26th International Conference on Neural Information Processing Systems - Volume 1*, NIPS'13, pages 926–934, USA. Curran Associates Inc.

Zhiqing Sun, Zhi-Hong Deng, Jian-Yun Nie, and Jian Tang. 2019. Rotate: Knowledge graph embedding by relational rotation in complex space. *arXiv preprint arXiv:1902.10197*.

Kristina Toutanova and Danqi Chen. 2015. Observed Versus Latent Features for Knowledge Base and Text Inference. In *3rd Workshop on Continuous Vector Space Models and Their Compositionality*, July.

Théo Trouillon, Johannes Welbl, Sebastian Riedel, Éric Gaussier, and Guillaume Bouchard. 2016. Complex Embeddings for Simple Link Prediction. In *Int. Conference on Machine Learning*, pages 2071–2080.

Zhigang Wang and Juanzi Li. 2016. Text-enhanced Representation Learning for Knowledge Graph. In *Proc. International Joint Conference on Artificial Intelligence*, pages 1293–1299.

Ruobing Xie, Zhiyuan Liu, Jia Jia, Huanbo Luan, and Maosong Sun. 2016. Representation Learning of Knowledge Graphs with Entity Descriptions. In *Proc. AAAI*, pages 2659–2665.

Jiacheng Xu, Xipeng Qiu, Kan Chen, and Xuanjing Huang. 2017. Knowledge Graph Representation with Jointly Structural and Textual Encoding. In *Proc. Int. Joint Conference on Artificial Intelligence*, pages 1318–1324.

Ikuya Yamada, Hiroyuki Shindo, Hideaki Takeda, and Yoshiyasu Takefuji. 2016. Joint Learning of the Embedding of Words and Entities for Named Entity Disambiguation. In *Proc. SIGNLL Conference on Computational Natural Language Learning*, pages 250–259, Berlin, Germany, August.

Bishan Yang, Wen-tau Yih, Xiaodong He, Jianfeng Gao, and Li Deng. 2014. Embedding Entities and Relations for Learning and Inference in Knowledge Bases. *CoRR*, abs/1412.6575.

Liang Yao, Chengsheng Mao, and Yuan Luo. 2019. Kg-bert: Bert for knowledge graph completion.

Yueyang Zhou, Shumin Shi, and Heyan Huang. 2020. Weighted aggregator for the open-world knowledge graph completion. In *Data Science*, pages 283–291, Singapore. Springer Singapore.

TextGraphs 2020 Shared Task on Multi-Hop Inference for Explanation Regeneration[*]

Peter Jansen
School of Information
University of Arizona, USA
pajansen@email.arizona.edu

Dmitry Ustalov
Yandex
Saint Petersburg, Russia
dustalov@yandex-team.ru

Abstract

The 2020 Shared Task on Multi-Hop Inference for Explanation Regeneration tasks participants with regenerating large detailed multi-fact explanations for standardized science exam questions. Given a question, correct answer, and knowledge base, models must rank each fact in the knowledge base such that facts most likely to appear in the explanation are ranked highest. Explanations consist of an average of 6 (and as many as 16) facts that span both core scientific knowledge and world knowledge, and form an explicit lexically-connected "explanation graph" describing how the facts interrelate. In this second iteration of the explanation regeneration shared task, participants are supplied with more than double the training and evaluation data of the first shared task, as well as a knowledge base nearly double in size, both of which expand into more challenging scientific topics that increase the difficulty of the task. In total 10 teams participated, and 5 teams submitted system description papers. The best-performing teams significantly increased state-of-the-art performance both in terms of ranking (mean average precision) and inference speed on this challenge task.

1 Introduction

Multi-hop inference is the task of combining two or more facts to make an inference. In the context of natural language processing, this is often studied in terms of question answering tasks, where a model must combine multiple textual facts (typically retrieved from different books, web pages, or other documents) to answer a question correctly. With the recent field-wide push towards building machine learning models that are able to explain the reasons behind their inferences, multi-hop inference has garnered a renewed interest, as the set of connected facts used to perform the inference can be supplied to the user as a form of human-readable explanation for why the inference is correct.

Multi-hop inference can be extremely challenging, particularly as the number of facts required to perform an inference increases, which typically causes large drops in performance (Fried et al., 2015; Jansen et al., 2017) and places strong limits on inference capacity (Jansen, 2018; Khashabi et al., 2019). Moreover, a body of recent work suggests that, in spite of steadily increasing performance on multi-hop benchmarks, much of this performance may be due to strong retrieval baselines rather than methods that are explicitly performing compositional inference (Min et al., 2019; Chen and Durrett, 2019; Trivedi et al., 2020). The Shared Task on Multi-Hop Inference for Explanation Regeneration aims to address some of these contemporary challenges in multi-hop inference by asking participants to develop systems that can construct very large multi-fact explanations for science exam questions that contain up to 16 facts. The task simplifies the question answering problem, supplying both question and correct answer a given model, allowing that model to squarely focus on the explanation construction task. For a given question, a model must pick a complete set of explanatory facts from a knowledge base of approximately 10,000 semi-structured facts that span core scientific knowledge as well as detailed common sense or world knowledge. These model-generated explanations are then evaluated against hand-authored explanations

---

[*]The two authors contributed equally to this work.

This work is licensed under a Creative Commons Attribution 4.0 International License. License details: http://creativecommons.org/licenses/by/4.0/.

Proceedings of the Graph-based Methods for Natural Language Processing (TextGraphs), pages 85–97
Barcelona, Spain (Online), December 13, 2020

generated by skilled human annotators whose goals in authoring were both explanatory completeness and having a high level of explanatory depth. An example question, answer, and short explanation graph is shown in Figure 1.

In the context of contemporary datasets for multi-hop inference, the WorldTree V2 corpus (Xie et al., 2020) used in this shared task has both substantially larger multi-hop inference problems and substantially less training data than other multi-hop inference datasets, making this shared task extremely challenging. For example, the frequently used HotpotQA dataset (Yang et al., 2018) requires aggregating sentences from 2 paragraphs in Wikipedia, and has seen contemporary models reach nearly 90% performance on its analogous supporting-fact selection task[1]. Similarly, QASC (Khot et al., 2020), a science-domain dataset[2] similar to WorldTree that requires selecting two supporting facts from a corpus, has also seen accuracy reach 90% (Khashabi et al., 2020). In contrast, the best-performing model in this 2020 shared task was able to achieve a MAP of 0.60 on the 1-to-16 fact multi-hop inference problems in WorldTree V2, highlighting the difficulty of this challenge task, and showcasing that there is still plenty of room to grow. An example 13-fact explanation from this shared task is shown in Figure 2, illustrating the difference in difficulty between generating 2-fact explanations and many-fact explanations that include detailed world knowledge.

This is the second iteration of the Shared Task on Multi-Hop Inference for Explanation Regeneration, which keeps the task identical to the first iteration run in 2019 (Jansen and Ustalov, 2019), but more than doubles the available training data, evaluation data, and supporting knowledge base. This increase in size is largely due to expanding the explanation corpus to more advanced years of standardized science exams, causing the task to also become significantly more challenging. In this regard, baseline *tf.idf* performance decreased from *0.30 MAP* in 2019 to *0.23 MAP* in 2020, a drop of more than 20% in performance, highlighting the challenging nature of this additional data. Participating teams used a wide variety of approaches, typically with large language models featuring prominently, augmented with graph neural networks, integer linear programming, or iterative scoring methods for the multi-hop inference task. In spite of the dataset being substantially more challenging than the 2019 shared task, participants made substantial increases both in overall task performance as well as in the speed of training and inference.

Our shared task has been organized on the CodaLab platform.[3] We released train and development datasets along with the baseline solution in advance to allow one to get to know the task specifics. We ran the *practice* phase from March 1 till April 5, 2020. Then we released the test dataset without answers and ran the official *evaluation* phase from April 6 till September 21, 2020. After that we established *post-competition* phase to enable long-term evaluation of the methods beyond our competition.

In this shared task summary paper we first highlight some of the contemporary challenges in multi-hop inference. We then describe the explanation regeneration task (framed as a ranking problem), the details of the training and evaluation dataset used for the shared task, followed by competition details and system descriptions for participating teams.

2   Contemporary Challenges in Multi-Hop Inference

A number of contemporary challenges exist in performing multi-hop inference for question answering, with several highlighted below. For a more in-depth survey of contemporary challenges and methods for multi-hop inference, see Thayaparan et al. (2020).

Semantic Drift.   Semantic drift is the tendency for inference algorithms based on graph traversal to traverse from highly-relevant facts (nodes) towards irrelevant nodes based on noisy signals. For example, when answering a question about *popular varieties of orchard apples*, without mechanisms to control for semantic drift, a given algorithm might traverse to facts about *popular apple computers* because common signals for traversal (such as two facts having one or more of the same words) are often noisy and lack context. Semantic drift has been observed across a wide variety of representations and traversal methods

---

[1]HOTPOTQA leaderboard: `https://hotpotqa.github.io/`
[2]QASC leaderboard: `https://allenai.org/data/qasc`
[3]`https://competitions.codalab.org/competitions/23615`

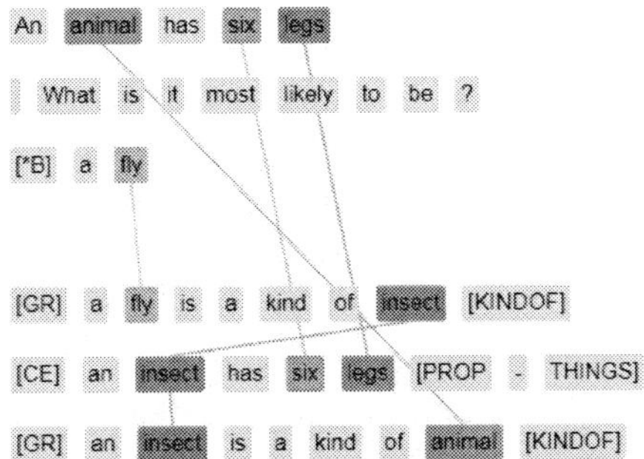

Figure 1: An example of the explanation regeneration task. A model is supplied with a question and correct answer *(top)*, and from this must construct an explanation from facts in the supporting knowledge base. An example 3-fact gold explanation is shown *(bottom)*. Facts are connected to question, answer, and/or other facts by explicit lexical overlap *(edges)*.

from word and dependency level (Fried et al., 2015; Pan et al., 2017) to sentence-level (Jansen et al., 2017) to paragraph-level (Clark and Gardner, 2018).

Many-hop multi-hop training data. Large, high-quality datasets for training multi-hop inference models generally were not available until recently (Yang et al., 2018; Jansen et al., 2018; Khot et al., 2020; Xie et al., 2020). Even as such, pragmatic challenges in dataset construction necessitate that each dataset will have limitations. The ideal dataset would be: (1) large in terms of the number of training and evaluation examples, (2) use natural rather than artificial questions, (3) use found (retrieved) rather than authored facts, (4) contain large many-fact multi-hop inference problems, (5) include explicit details of the inference required to be made, including any common sense or world knowledge that may otherwise be implicit and inaccessible to a model. In general, existing datasets tend to compromise on at least several of these (and other) desiderata for technical or pragmatic reasons (such as cost or scalability).

Relevance versus Completeness Judgements in Explanations. A given corpus will typically have facts that may have a spectrum of relevancies towards a given inference – some highly relevant, others completely irrelevant – and many of those facts may significantly overlap in the information they convey. Orthogonal to this is the idea of explanatory completeness – finding a set of facts that forms a complete inference chain, without holes or gaps, to arrive from question to correct answer. In dataset construction, it appears to be much easier to annotate relevance rather than make completeness judgements. Even still, human relevance judgements are typically provided for only a small subset of the facts in a corpus, as there are often multiple paths to building an explanation for a given question, and exhaustively constructing them all would be intractable. These are significant methodological limitations in training and evaluating contemporary multi-hop inference algorithms.

Chance performance on graph traversal. Intuitively, chance performance of "hopping" to relevant facts (nodes) in a knowledge graph can be very low – for example, if only 1% of the links from a given node are relevant to answering and explaining a given question, then chance performance on "hopping" to the correct facts in a 6-fact multi-hop explanation would be only 1 in 100 trillion. But, depending on the connection methodology used in graphs of natural language facts, it is possible for as many as 50% of the links from a given node to be relevant, dramatically increasing chance performance (Jansen, 2018), in some cases to be on the order of the effect sizes typically reported in the literature. This means that methods that appear to be increasing performance on multi-hop inference tasks may have significant proportions of their performance due to chance traversals.

Solving compositional questions with non-compositional methods. Similarly, while some correct multi-hop traversals may be due to chance, a recent body of work has shown that in other cases models may be using non-compositional methods (i.e. retrieving single facts) to correctly answer questions (Min

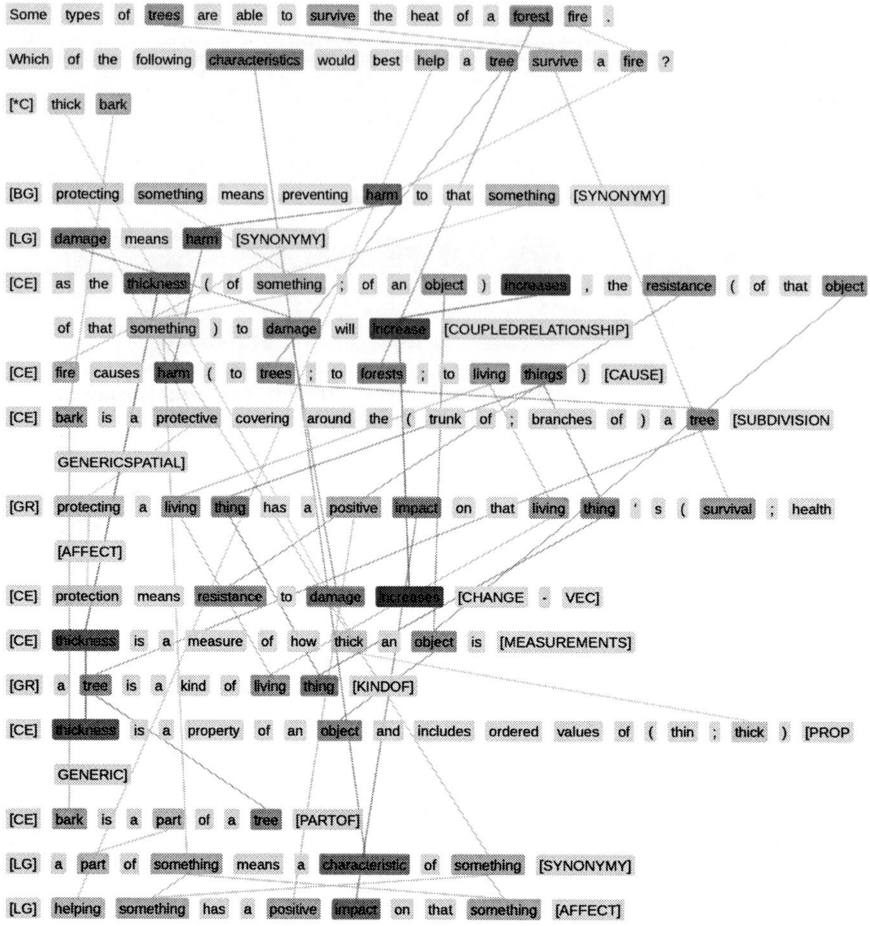

Figure 2: An example of a challenging explanation graph that contains 13 facts, including both core scientific knowledge as well as detailed common-sense or world knowledge.

et al., 2019; Chen and Durrett, 2019). Chen and Durrett (2019) found that simple baseline retrieval models could outperform state-of-the-art multi-hop methods on the HotpotQA dataset. Similarly, Trivedi et al. (2020) found that a large language model can appear to achieve above 70% performance on HotpotQA while only 18% of it's reasoning truly spans multiple facts. Trivedi et al. (2020) note that this is about the same amount of compositional inference a baseline RNN model, suggesting much of the contemporary performance on some multi-hop inference models may be due to better retrieval modules rather than advancing the science of explicitly combining multiple facts to support inferences.

Limited direct evaluations of multi-hop inference performance. An issue related to the above is that performance on multi-hop inference tasks is typically reported in terms of the performance on the downstream task (e.g. on question answering, or the ultimate performance in selecting a series of facts that support that inference). We have regularly argued (Fried et al., 2015; Jansen et al., 2017; Jansen, 2018; Jansen and Ustalov, 2019) that this is insufficient, and, when possible, models should explicitly report model performance as the number of facts being combined increases to allow teasing apart the contributions of a strong initial retrieval module with the performance of the mechanism that combines those facts to perform inference. Without this, from a methodological standpoint, it is difficult to measure

88

when we have truly made progress on the multi-hop inference task.[4]

3 Task Description

The task description follows the 2019 shared task (Jansen and Ustalov, 2019), and is described briefly here. The explanation regeneration task supplies models with questions, their correct answers, as well as a knowledge base of facts. From this, for a given question, the model must select a set of facts from the knowledge base that matches the gold explanation authored by a human annotator. An example of the explanation regeneration task is shown in Figure 3

While the task is natively a graph construction task, to encourage a wide variety of submissions, and enable evaluation between a wide variety of modeling choices, the explanation regeneration task is framed here as a ranking task, where a given model must selectively rank the facts it believes are in the gold explanation to the top of the list. This allows evaluating systems with standard ranking metrics, where here we make use of Mean Average Precision (MAP). Similarly, for this shared task, the knowledge base exists simultaneously as a semi-structured knowledge base of tables, as well as a large collection of free-text facts, allowing methods that operate over either structured or free text to be directly compared.

4 Training and Evaluation Dataset

This 2020 shared task on explanation regeneration transitions from Worldtree V1 (Jansen et al., 2018) to the new WorldTree V2 explanation corpus (Xie et al., 2020). Similar to the first WorldTree corpus, the second version contains large multi-hop inference problems that require models to construct large, detailed, multi-fact explanations for standardized science exam questions from the United States – but at a greater scale. WorldTree V1 consists of approximately 1.7k questions paired with explanations constructed from a knowledge base of approximately 5k facts, while V2 expands this to 4.4k questions and a knowledge base of 10k facts, more than doubling the amount of training and evaluation data available.

Questions. Questions consist of standardized science exam questions drawn from the Aristo Reasoning Challenge (ARC) corpus (Clark et al., 2018), a set of 4-choice multiple choice questions primarily drawn from 12 US states over the past two decades. Where the 2019 shared task consisted entirely of elementary science questions (intended for students typically between 9 to 10 years in age), the additional questions in the 2020 shared task primarily expand into middle school science (intended for students between 13 and 14 years of age). These questions typically require broader knowledge and more complex forms of reasoning than their elementary counterparts, increasing the overall difficulty of the task.

Explanations. Each question in WorldTree is paired with a detailed explanation for why the answer to that question is correct. Explanations take the form of a set of atomic facts that consist of both core scientific knowledge (e.g. *"cellular respiration is when a cell converts from oxygen and carbohydrates into carbon dioxide, water, and energy"*) as well as common-sense/world knowledge (e.g. *"if a container contains something, then that container touches that something"*), with the goal of authoring explanations at sufficient explanatory depth to meet the informal goal of making them *"meaningful to a 5 year old"*.

Each explanation ranges in length from 1 to over 16 facts (with the average explanation containing 6 facts). The explanations were authored such that key terms in the question, answer, and explanatory facts must be explicitly linked to each other to help make the inference process more explicit – and as such, while the set of facts for each explanation are unordered from the perspective of forming a narrative, they form a lexically-connected "explanation graph" describing how the knowledge interconnects.

Each fact in an explanation contains an additional rating describing that fact's "explanatory role" in the explanation, which can be either *CENTRAL, GROUNDING,* or *LEXICAL GLUE*:

1. *CENTRAL.* Central facts are the core facts required to address the scientific concept that the question is asking – for example, a question addressing what happens to a pot of water left outside in the

---

[4]Indeed, a particularly convincing example of strong multi-hop inference ability might be a model that combines a poor initial retrieval module (producing a long candidate list of facts) with a strong multi-hop module that successfully learns to meaningfully combine subsets of those facts into detailed explanations.

Question. A student placed an ice cube on a plate in the sun. Ten minutes later, only water was on the plate. Which process caused the ice cube to change to water?

Answer Candidates. (A) condensation   (B) evaporation   (C) freezing   (*D) melting

Gold Explanation from WorldTree Corpus.

Explanatory Role	Fact (Table Row)
CENTRAL	melting means changing from a solid into a liquid by adding heat energy
GROUNDING	an ice cube is a kind of solid
GROUNDING	water is a kind of liquid
CENTRAL	water is in the solid state, called ice, for temperatures between -273C and 0 C
LEXGLUE	heat means heat energy
LEXGLUE	adding heat means increasing temperature
CENTRAL	if an object absorbs solar energy then that object will increase in temperature
CENTRAL	if an object is in the sunlight then that object will absorb solar energy
CENTRAL	the sun is a source of (light ; light energy) called sunlight
LEXGLUE	to be in the sun means to be in the sunlight
CENTRAL	melting is a kind of process

Explanation Regeneration Task (Ranking).

Rank	Gold	Fact (Table Row)
1	⋆	melting is a kind of process
2		thawing is similar to melting
3		melting is a kind of phase change
4		melting is when solids are heated above their melting point
5		amount of water in a body of water increases by (storms ; rain ; ice melting)
6		an ice cube is a kind of object
7	⋆	an ice cube is a kind of solid
8		freezing point is similar to melting point
9		melting point is a property of a (substance ; material)
10		glaciers melting has a negative impact on the glaicial environment
11		plate tectonics is a kind of process
12		sometimes piles of rock are formed by melting glaciers depositing rocks
13		melting point can be used to identify a pure substance
14		ice crystals means ice
15		the (freezing point of water ; melting point of water) is 0C
16		the melting point of iron is 1538C
17		the melting point of oxygen is -218.8C
18	⋆	melting means changing from a solid into a liquid by adding heat energy
19		adding salt to a liquid decreases the melting point of that liquid
20		ice is a kind of food
...		

Ranks of gold rows: 1, 7, 18, 53, 102, 384, 408, 858, 860, 3778, 3956
Average precision of ranking: 0.149

Figure 3: The example of *explanation regeneration as ranking* provided to task participants. Models are provided with both a question and correct answer *(top)*. From this, they must selectively rank facts in a knowledge base such that facts most likely to be in the explanation are ranked higher *(bottom)*. This ranked list is then compared to the gold human-authored explanation *(middle)*, and evaluated using mean average precision. Example ranks are shown for the baseline *tf.idf* model.

arctic might contain a central fact such as *"freezing means a substance changes from a liquid to a solid by decreasing heat energy"*. On average, each explanation has 2.4 central facts.

2. *GROUNDING.* Grounding facts connect the core concept the question is addressing to specific examples that might be in the question or answer. In our water freezing example, two grounding facts might be *"water is a kind of substance"* and *"the freezing point of water is 0 C"*. On average, each explanation has 1.6 grounding facts.

3. *LEXICAL GLUE.* Lexical glue facts are an artifact of the requirement that the facts in each explanation must be "lexically connected" to each other – i.e. have shared important content lemmas in common. If an explanation contains one fact such as *"freezing means a substance changes from a liquid to a solid by decreasing heat energy"* and another that describes *"a fridge can be used for cooling*

Team	Performance (MAP)	Description
2020 Shared Task (WorldTree V2, 4.4k Elementary and Middle School Science Explanations)		
Baidu PGL	**0.603**	ERNIE Reranker + GNN
LIIR	0.584	Autoregressive Reasoning over Chains of Facts
aisys	0.523	
ChiSquareX	0.490 (0.506)	RoBERTa, BART, SciBERT, ELECTRA
Red Dragon AI	0.473 (0.561)	LSTM-Interleaved Transformer
Team IITian	0.452	
AG	0.346 (0.366)	BERT + Integer Linear Programming Reranking
mler	0.337	
dchandak99	0.325	
Baseline (tf.idf)	0.234	
2019 Shared Task (WorldTree V1, 1.6k Elementary School Science Explanations)		
ChainsOfReasoning	**0.563**	Exhaustive BERT + Chains
pbanerj6	0.413	BERT + XLNet Reranking
Red Dragon AI	0.402 (0.477)	Fine-tuned BERT + retrieval w/regression
jenlindadsouza	0.394	FrameNet + ConceptNET + and OpenIE
Baseline	0.296	

Table 1: Official leaderboard performance on the held out test set for the 2020 Shared Task on Multi-Hop Inference for Explanation Regeneration. Post-competition performance is shown in parentheses.

objects", because the critical link here (the concept of *cooling*) isn't described using the same words in both facts, the WorldTree explanation authoring procedure requires there to be an additional fact *"cooling means decreasing heat energy"* that makes this link explicit. These explicit linking facts are labeled as lexical glue, and would likely not be required for an explanation intended for adult humans, but help make the link between facts explicit for machine learning algorithms without this world knowledge. On average, each explanation has 1.3 lexical glue facts.

Knowledge Base. Each fact in WorldTree takes the form of a row in one of 80 semi-structured tables. Each table is centered around a particular kind of knowledge (e.g. taxonomic, part-of, properties, changes, causality, if-then relationships, coupled relationships, affordances, etc.), and contains between 2 and 16 content columns that allow each fact to form a semi-structured *n-ary* relation. The table topics and structure was empirically derived using prior studies in the science domain as a starting point (Khashabi et al., 2016; Jansen et al., 2016). Each fact in WorldTree can be used either in this semi-structured form, or read off directly as a plain text sentence, allowing both structured and free-text inference methods to use the same knowledge base, and be directly compared.

5 System Descriptions and Performance

The 2020 shared task received 10 submissions, nearly doubling submissions from the previous year. System performance is shown in Table 1. Five of the participating teams submitted system description papers, described below.

Baseline (tf.idf). A term frequency baseline. For a given question and answer pair, the model calculates the cosine similarity between a query vector (composed of term frequencies from either the question or correct answer) and document vectors (composed of term frequencies from a given fact in the knowledge base) for each fact in the knowledge base. This baseline uses the *tf.idf* weighting scheme when calculating cosine similarity (e.g. see Manning et al. (2008, Ch. 6)). For each (question, answer, fact) tuple, two cosines are calculated – one between question and fact, the other between answer and fact, and these two scores are combined into a linear model using the SVM^{rank} ranking classifier (Joachims, 2006),[5] to exhaustively rank each fact in the knowledge base for a given (question, answer) pair.

Baidu PGL. This best-performing system by Li et al. (2020) at Baidu combines language models and graph neural networks in a reranking framework. First, the ERNIE 2.0 language model (Sun et al., 2020), which achieves over 90% performance on the GLUE benchmark (Wang et al., 2018), is used to provide

---

[5]`http://svmlight.joachims.org/`

an initial ranking of facts in the knowledge base. The team notes that this nearly doubles oracle ceiling performance compared to a *tf.idf* model, ranking an average of 92% of gold facts within the top 100, while the initial ranking itself provides a comparatively strong 0.48 MAP on explanation reconstruction as a stand-alone retrieval model. A second ERNIE 2.0-based module then reranks the shortlist from the initial ranker, dramatically increasing performance to 0.59 MAP. A GNN based on GraphSage (Hamilton et al., 2017) is then used to help learn to aggregate facts in a multi-hop fashion, which increases performance by approximately 0.01 MAP. Finally, an ensemble model of the full model is constructed, raising performance 0.02 MAP to reach 0.62 on the development set, while evaluating at 0.60 MAP on the unseen test set.

LIIR. The LIIR team at KU Leuven (Cartuyvels et al., 2020) approach the explanation regeneration task as an autoregressive re-ranking problem. First, a dynamically-sized shortlist called a "neighbourhood of visible facts" is constructed based on pairwise *tf.idf* distances between questions and all facts in the knowledge base. The model then autoregressively ranks facts by iteratively selecting a top-ranked fact then then re-evaluating the scores of unpicked facts by conditioning them on the set of facts already determined to be within the explanation. As the team notes, "the role of many facts in explaining a question is not immediately apparent when they are looked at in isolation, and only becomes more evident when they are considered as a part of a larger explanation". This intuition arguably allows the LIIR model to incorporate both relevance and explanatory completeness (relative to other facts) into their iteratively constructed explanations. LIIR compare their model to the TextGraphs 2019 Shared Task winner *(Chains of Reasoning, Das et al. (2019))*, and note that their autoregressive model significantly outperforms *Chains of Reasoning* on both 2019 and 2020 datasets while taking approximately one-tenth the training time and one-half the inference time of the winning 2019 model.

ChiSquaredX. Large pre-trained language models serving as retrieval modules are the dominant contributor to performance in many approaches to the explanation regeneration task. While *Chains of Reasoning* previously showed that a BERT baseline can achieve state-of-the-art performance if exhaustively used to evaluate all candidates (Das et al., 2019), this is computationally expensive (particularly as the knowledge base size increases), and typically participants have chosen to use a language model to rerank the *top-k* ranked items from a less expensive retretrieval model, such as a *tf.idf* retriever. The number of available pre-trained language models has dramatically increased in the past year, and the ChiSquareX team (Pawate et al., 2020) examine explanation regeneration performance for a large subset of popular classic and newer language models when reranking the *top-100* facts from a *tf.idf* model, particularly in contexts where training time is limited. The ChiSquaredX team examine ALBERT (Lan et al., 2019), BART (Lewis et al., 2019), BERT (Devlin et al., 2019), DistilBERT (Sanh et al., 2019), ELECTRA (Clark et al., 2020), SciBERT (Beltagy et al., 2019), and RoBERTa (Liu et al., 2019). ChiSquaredX report that, for the *top-100* ranked facts, reraning performance can vary by several points depending on which model is chosen, while increasing the *top-k* can further increase performance by several points. Their top-performing RoBERTa model achieves a MAP of 0.51 when reranking the *top-500* facts retrieved by their *tf.idf* model.

Red Dragon AI. The Red Dragon AI team (Chia et al., 2020) present three model components for explanation regeneration. The first, an updated iterative-BM25 (I-BM25) module from the 2019 shared task (Chia et al., 2019), iteratively constructs a query vector by aggregating the closest N facts in the knowledge base, and is able to independently achieve a MAP of 0.47. The shortlisted results from the I-BM25 module are then reranked by one of two models: a transformer followed by an LSTM, or an LSTM-Interleaved Transformer (LIT), both of which were constructed to enable cross-document (here, cross-fact) interactions to help compose explanations jointly instead of one fact at a time. Their best performing I-BM25 + LIT model achieves a MAP of 0.56, nearly ten points higher than the I-BM25 alone. The team further investigate how several loss functions can affect performance, and empirically demonstrate that Binary Crossentropy outperforms other methods in their model.

AG. The AG team (Gupta and Srinivasaraghavan, 2020) more directly build explanation graphs by framing explanation regeneration as an Integer Linear Programming (ILP) graph-traversal problem, implemented as a set of constraints for the SemanticILP Solver (Khashabi et al., 2018). In contrast to

Metric	Q's N	Baseline tf.idf	AG	RDAI	Team CSX	LIIR	BPGL
Evaluating overlap considering only nouns, verbs, adjectives, and adverbs.							
(1-hop) Rows with 2 or more shared words with Q/A	1667	0.32	0.47	0.65	0.59	0.66	**0.69**
(1-hop) Rows with 1 shared word with Q/A	657	0.07	0.25	0.40	0.35	**0.49**	0.48
(2+ hop) Rows without shared words with Q/A	172	0.01	0.19	0.16	0.07	**0.31**	0.29
Evaluating overlap without filtering (all words considered).							
(1-hop) Rows with 2 or more shared words with Q/A	1667	0.26	0.41	0.59	0.53	0.61	**0.63**
(1-hop) Rows with 1 shared word with Q/A	657	0.09	0.32	0.45	0.39	**0.54**	0.52
(2+ hop) Rows without shared words with Q/A	172	0.00	0.23	0.20	0.06	**0.34**	0.33

Table 2: Explanation regeneration performance broken down by the proportion of lexical overlap a given explanatory fact has with the question or answer. *N* refers to the number of questions that have at least one explanatory fact meeting that criterion.

previous approaches towards using ILP on the science exam question set (Khashabi et al., 2016), to increase tractability, AG select only a shortlist of 30 most-relevant facts ranked from a BERT language model as input to their system, which are then reranked using their ILP model paired with a linear regression module. The total ILP plus regression pipeline achieves a MAP of 0.37.

6 Extended Evaluation and Analysis

The WorldTree corpus is designed to instrument various aspects of the multi-hop inference process, and here as in the first shared task we provide an extended analyses of shared task participant performance beyond the final measure of explanation regeneration quality. As these analyses are identical to those in the 2019 shared task, please see Jansen and Ustalov (2019) for a full description of the analysis metrics and procedures.

6.1 Performance by Lexical Overlap / Multiple Hops

One of the core methodological criticisms of current multi-hop inference models is that it is possible to achieve strong downstream performance on the multi-hop inference task without using multi-hop (or "compositional") methods (Min et al., 2019; Chen and Durrett, 2019; Trivedi et al., 2020), and we have argued that performance on compositional inference should be evaluated and reported more directly (Fried et al., 2015; Jansen, 2018; Jansen and Ustalov, 2019). As part of this, Table 2 shows performance of each model relative to the difficulty of accessing specific facts in an explanation. Some facts in an explanation share many of the same words as the question or answer, and are easier for models to locate than facts that share no words with the question or answer, that (arguably) must be accessed using other means – such as compositional methods that traverse to these challenging facts from other easier-to-locate facts that are "closer" to the question.

This year, Table 2 illustrates this methodological concern – while the winning *BPGL* team has higher overall downstream task performance, this appears due to slightly better performance at locating facts with a large amount of lexical overlap with either the question or answer. Similarly, the second-place model demonstrates slightly better performance at finding the most challenging facts that do not have lexical overlap with the question or answer, potentially due to the iterative nature of its collect-then-finish algorithm. That being said, it's important to note that both models have strong relative performance in both these measures, and further analysis would be required to tease apart the relative contributions of each model's retrieval module versus its aggregation module. It's also important to note that all submissions make improvements over the baseline model in accessing the most challenging multi-hop facts, most by substantial margins.

6.2 Additional Performance Evaluation

In addition to multi-hop inference performance, models can have a spectrum of performance characteristics that can be instrumented either to improve the model, or assessing its suitability for particular tasks. Table 3 breaks down model performance characteristics by explanatory role, knowledge type, and ranking

| | Questions | Baseline | | | Team | | |
Metric	N	tf.idf	AG	RDAI	CSX	LIIR	BPGL
Mean Average Precision (MAP)							
MAP	1670	0.23	0.37	0.55	0.50	0.57	**0.60**
MAP by Explanatory Role							
CENTRAL rows	1619	0.27	0.42	0.59	0.54	0.57	**0.65**
GROUNDING rows	1150	0.15	0.21	0.40	0.36	**0.44**	**0.44**
LEXICALGLUE rows	987	0.05	0.12	0.27	0.24	**0.39**	0.30
MAP by Table Knowledge Types							
Retrieval tables	1670	0.22	0.37	0.49	0.44	0.51	**0.53**
Inference-supporting tables	1670	0.11	0.19	0.21	0.18	0.22	**0.23**
Complex inference tables	1670	0.12	0.22	0.28	0.25	0.29	**0.32**
Precision@K							
Precision@1	1670	0.38	0.45	0.76	0.70	0.73	**0.78**
Precision@2	1670	0.30	0.38	0.65	0.60	0.65	**0.68**
Precision@3	1670	0.25	0.34	0.56	0.52	0.58	**0.61**
Precision@4	1670	0.22	0.30	0.51	0.46	0.52	**0.54**
Precision@5	1670	0.19	0.28	0.46	0.42	0.47	**0.48**
Precision@10	1670	0.13	0.21	0.30	0.29	0.32	**0.33**
Precision@20	1670	0.08	0.15	0.18	0.17	0.19	**0.20**

Table 3: Explanation regeneration performance broken down by explanatory role, knowledge types, and ranking precision profile *(Precision@K)*. Note that small (third decimal) differences in performance relative to Table 1 are possible due to slight differences in how truncated lists are handled during scoring.

performance profile. Of particular note is that while the *BPGL* and *LIIR* models perform similarly overall, the *BPGL* model appears to be accessing significant more central explanatory knowledge to reach its performance, while conversely the *LIIR* model accesses significantly more lexical glue explanatory knowledge. This is likely due to the difference in methods between the two systems – *BPGL* leverage a large state-of-the-art language model that is likely able to retrieve many core facts more directly, where as the iterative nature of the *LIIR* algorithm may require the linking-nature of the lexical-glue facts to enable its multi-hop process and access facts more distant from the question. Both hypotheses are (of course) speculative and based on the narrative of the system descriptions, and would require empirical confirmation, but highlight that different models with very similar overall performance can have different performance profiles and strengths when investigated in more depth.

7   Conclusion

The 2020 Shared Task on Multi-Hop Inference for Explanation Regeneration successfully achieved a new state-of-the-art performance on the explanation regeneration task using the benchmark WorldTree V2 dataset. Participating teams used a wide variety of methods, typically combining large pre-trained language models with task-specific modules for performing the multi-hop inference task, and improved both explanation regeneration accuracy and speed. Additional analyses show that models with similar downstream performance can show different performance profiles on specific aspects of the task in general, and on multi-hop performance in particular, emphasizing the need to report detailed performance profiles when working on multi-hop inference tasks.

8   Acknowledgements

The organizers wish to express their thanks to all shared task teams for their participation. We thank Zhengnan Xie, Jaycie Ryrholm Martin, Elizabeth Wainwright, and Steven Marmorstein for contributions to the WorldTree explanation corpus, who were funded by the Allen Institute for Artificial Intelligence (AI2). Peter Jansen's work on the explanation corpus and shared task was supported by National Science Foundation (NSF Award #1815948, "Explainable Natural Language Inference").

References

Iz Beltagy, Kyle Lo, and Arman Cohan. 2019. SciBERT: A Pretrained Language Model for Scientific Text. In *Proceedings of the 2019 Conference on Empirical Methods in Natural Language Processing and the 9th International Joint Conference on Natural Language Processing (EMNLP-IJCNLP)*, pages 3615–3620, Hong Kong. Association for Computational Linguistics.

Ruben Cartuyvels, Graham Spinks, and Marie-Francine Moens. 2020. Autoregressive Reasoning over Chains of Facts with Transformers. In *Proceedings of the 28th International Conference on Computational Linguistics*. Association for Computational Linguistics. In press.

Jifan Chen and Greg Durrett. 2019. Understanding Dataset Design Choices for Multi-hop Reasoning. In *Proceedings of the 2019 Conference of the North American Chapter of the Association for Computational Linguistics: Human Language Technologies, Volume 1 (Long and Short Papers)*, NAACL-HLT 2019, pages 4026–4032, Minneapolis, MN, USA. Association for Computational Linguistics.

Yew Ken Chia, Sam Witteveen, and Martin Andrews. 2019. Red Dragon AI at TextGraphs 2019 Shared Task: Language Model Assisted Explanation Generation. In *Proceedings of the Thirteenth Workshop on Graph-Based Methods for Natural Language Processing (TextGraphs-13)*, pages 85–89, Hong Kong. Association for Computational Linguistics.

Yew Ken Chia, Sam Witteveen, and Martin Andrews. 2020. Red Dragon AI at TextGraphs 2020 Shared Task : LIT : LSTM-Interleaved Transformer for Multi-Hop Explanation Ranking. In *Proceedings of the Graph-based Methods for Natural Language Processing (TextGraphs)*. Association for Computational Linguistics.

Christopher Clark and Matt Gardner. 2018. Simple and Effective Multi-Paragraph Reading Comprehension. In *Proceedings of the 56th Annual Meeting of the Association for Computational Linguistics (Volume 1: Long Papers)*, ACL 2018, pages 845–855, Melbourne, VIC, Australia. Association for Computational Linguistics.

Peter Clark, Isaac Cowhey, Oren Etzioni, Tushar Khot, Ashish Sabharwal, Carissa Schoenick, and Oyvind Tafjord. 2018. Think you have Solved Question Answering? Try ARC, the AI2 Reasoning Challenge. arXiv:1803.05457 [cs.AI].

Kevin Clark, Minh-Thang Luong, Quoc V. Le, and Christopher D. Manning. 2020. ELECTRA: Pre-training Text Encoders as Discriminators Rather Than Generators. In *International Conference on Learning Representations*.

Rajarshi Das, Ameya Godbole, Manzil Zaheer, Shehzaad Dhuliawala, and Andrew McCallum. 2019. Chains-of-Reasoning at TextGraphs 2019 Shared Task: Reasoning over Chains of Facts for Explainable Multi-hop Inference. In *Proceedings of the Thirteenth Workshop on Graph-Based Methods for Natural Language Processing (TextGraphs-13)*, pages 101–117, Hong Kong. Association for Computational Linguistics.

Jacob Devlin, Ming-Wei Chang, Kenton Lee, and Kristina Toutanova. 2019. BERT: Pre-training of Deep Bidirectional Transformers for Language Understanding. In *Proceedings of the 2019 Conference of the North American Chapter of the Association for Computational Linguistics: Human Language Technologies, Volume 1 (Long and Short Papers)*, NAACL-HLT 2019, pages 4171–4186, Minneapolis, MN, USA. Association for Computational Linguistics.

Daniel Fried, Peter Jansen, Gustave Hahn-Powell, Mihai Surdeanu, and Peter Clark. 2015. Higher-order Lexical Semantic Models for Non-factoid Answer Reranking. *Transactions of the Association for Computational Linguistics*, 3:197–210.

Aayushee Gupta and Gopalakrishnan Srinivasaraghavan. 2020. Explanation Regeneration via Multi-Hop ILP Inference over Knowledge Base. In *Proceedings of the Graph-based Methods for Natural Language Processing (TextGraphs)*. Association for Computational Linguistics.

William L. Hamilton, Rex Ying, and Jure Leskovec. 2017. Inductive Representation Learning on Large Graphs. In *Proceedings of the 31st International Conference on Neural Information Processing Systems*, NIPS '17, pages 1025–1035, Long Beach, CA, USA. Curran Associates Inc.

Peter Jansen and Dmitry Ustalov. 2019. TextGraphs 2019 Shared Task on Multi-Hop Inference for Explanation Regeneration. In *Proceedings of the Thirteenth Workshop on Graph-Based Methods for Natural Language Processing (TextGraphs-13)*, pages 63–77, Hong Kong. Association for Computational Linguistics.

Peter Jansen, Niranjan Balasubramanian, Mihai Surdeanu, and Peter Clark. 2016. What's in an Explanation? Characterizing Knowledge and Inference Requirements for Elementary Science Exams. In *Proceedings of COLING 2016, the 26th International Conference on Computational Linguistics: Technical Papers*, COLING 2016, pages 2956–2965, Osaka, Japan. The COLING 2016 Organizing Committee.

Peter Jansen, Rebecca Sharp, Mihai Surdeanu, and Peter Clark. 2017. Framing QA as Building and Ranking Intersentence Answer Justifications. *Computational Linguistics*, 43(2):407–449.

Peter Jansen, Elizabeth Wainwright, Steven Marmorstein, and Clayton Morrison. 2018. WorldTree: A Corpus of Explanation Graphs for Elementary Science Questions supporting Multi-hop Inference. In *Proceedings of the Eleventh International Conference on Language Resources and Evaluation*, LREC 2018, pages 2732–2740, Miyazaki, Japan. European Language Resources Association (ELRA).

Peter Jansen. 2018. Multi-hop Inference for Sentence-level TextGraphs: How Challenging is Meaningfully Combining Information for Science Question Answering? In *Proceedings of the Twelfth Workshop on Graph-Based Methods for Natural Language Processing*, TextGraphs-12, pages 12–17, New Orleans, LA, USA. Association for Computational Linguistics.

Thorsten Joachims. 2006. Training Linear SVMs in Linear Time. In *Proceedings of the 12th ACM SIGKDD International Conference on Knowledge Discovery and Data Mining*, KDD '06, pages 217–226, New York, NY, USA. ACM.

Daniel Khashabi, Tushar Khot, Ashish Sabharwal, Peter Clark, Oren Etzioni, and Dan Roth. 2016. Question Answering via Integer Programming over Semi-Structured Knowledge. In *Proceedings of the Twenty-Fifth International Joint Conference on Artificial Intelligence (IJCAI-16)*, pages 1145–1152, New York, NY, USA.

Daniel Khashabi, Tushar Khot, Ashish Sabharwal, and Dan Roth. 2018. Question Answering as Global Reasoning over Semantic Abstractions. In *The Thirty-Second AAAI Conference on Artificial Intelligence (AAAI-18)*, pages 1905–1914, New Orleans, LA, USA.

Daniel Khashabi, Erfan Sadeqi Azer, Tushar Khot, Ashish Sabharwal, and Dan Roth. 2019. On the Capabilities and Limitations of Reasoning for Natural Language Understanding. arXiv:1901.02522 [cs.CL].

Daniel Khashabi, Tushar Khot, Ashish Sabharwal, Oyvind Tafjord, Peter Clark, and Hannaneh Hajishirzi. 2020. UNIFIEDQA: Crossing Format Boundaries With a Single QA System. arXiv:2005.00700 [cs.CL].

Tushar Khot, Peter Clark, Michal Guerquin, Peter Jansen, and Ashish Sabharwal. 2020. QASC: A Dataset for Question Answering via Sentence Composition. In *The Thirty-Fourth AAAI Conference on Artificial Intelligence (AAAI-20)*, pages 8082–8090, New York, NY, USA.

Zhenzhong Lan, Mingda Chen, Sebastian Goodman, Kevin Gimpel, Piyush Sharma, and Radu Soricut. 2019. ALBERT: A Lite BERT for Self-supervised Learning of Language Representations. arXiv:1909.11942 [cs.CL].

Mike Lewis, Yinhan Liu, Naman Goyal, Marjan Ghazvininejad, Abdelrahman Mohamed, Omer Levy, Ves Stoyanov, and Luke Zettlemoyer. 2019. BART: Denoising Sequence-to-Sequence Pre-training for Natural Language Generation, Translation, and Comprehension. arXiv:1910.13461 [cs.CL].

Weibin Li, Yuxiang Lu, Zhengjie Huang, Weiyue Su, Jiaxiang Liu, Shikun Feng, and Yu Sun. 2020. PGL at TextGraphs 2020 Shared Task: Explanation Regeneration using Language and Graph Learning Methods. In *Proceedings of the Graph-based Methods for Natural Language Processing (TextGraphs)*. Association for Computational Linguistics.

Yinhan Liu, Myle Ott, Naman Goyal, Jingfei Du, Mandar Joshi, Danqi Chen, Omer Levy, Mike Lewis, Luke Zettlemoyer, and Veselin Stoyanov. 2019. RoBERTa: A Robustly Optimized BERT Pretraining Approach. arXiv:1907.11692 [cs.CL].

Christopher D. Manning, Prabhakar Raghavan, and Hinrich Schütze. 2008. *Introduction to Information Retrieval*. Cambridge University Press, New York, NY, USA.

Sewon Min, Eric Wallace, Sameer Singh, Matt Gardner, Hannaneh Hajishirzi, and Luke Zettlemoyer. 2019. Compositional Questions Do Not Necessitate Multi-hop Reasoning. In *Proceedings of the 57th Annual Meeting of the Association for Computational Linguistics*, ACL 2019, pages 4249–4257, Florence, Italy. Association for Computational Linguistics.

Boyuan Pan, Hao Li, Zhou Zhao, Bin Cao, Deng Cai, and Xiaofei He. 2017. MEMEN: Multi-layer Embedding with Memory Networks for Machine Comprehension. arXiv:1707.09098 [cs.AI].

Aditya Girish Pawate, Varun Madhavan, and Devansh Chandak. 2020. ChiSquareX at TextGraphs 2020 Shared Task: Leveraging Pretrained Language Models for Explanation Regeneration. In *Proceedings of the Graph-based Methods for Natural Language Processing (TextGraphs)*. Association for Computational Linguistics.

Victor Sanh, Lysandre Debut, Julien Chaumond, and Thomas Wolf. 2019. DistilBERT, a distilled version of BERT: smaller, faster, cheaper and lighter. arXiv:1910.01108 [cs.CL].

Yu Sun, Shuohuan Wang, Yu-Kun Li, Shikun Feng, Hao Tian, Hua Wu, and Haifeng Wang. 2020. ERNIE 2.0: A Continual Pre-Training Framework for Language Understanding. In *The Thirty-Fourth AAAI Conference on Artificial Intelligence (AAAI-20)*, pages 8968–8975, New York, NY, USA.

Mokanarangan Thayaparan, Marco Valentino, and André Freitas. 2020. A Survey on Explainability in Machine Reading Comprehension. arXiv:2010.00389 [cs.CL].

Harsh Trivedi, Niranjan Balasubramanian, Tushar Khot, and Ashish Sabharwal. 2020. Is Multihop QA in DiRe Condition? Measuring and Reducing Disconnected Reasoning. arXiv:2005.00789 [cs.CL].

Alex Wang, Amanpreet Singh, Julian Michael, Felix Hill, Omer Levy, and Samuel Bowman. 2018. GLUE: A Multi-Task Benchmark and Analysis Platform for Natural Language Understanding. In *Proceedings of the 2018 EMNLP Workshop BlackboxNLP: Analyzing and Interpreting Neural Networks for NLP*, pages 353–355, Brussels, Belgium. Association for Computational Linguistics.

Zhengnan Xie, Sebastian Thiem, Jaycie Martin, Elizabeth Wainwright, Steven Marmorstein, and Peter Jansen. 2020. WorldTree V2: A Corpus of Science-Domain Structured Explanations and Inference Patterns supporting Multi-Hop Inference. In *Proceedings of the 12th Conference on Language Resources and Evaluation (LREC 2020)*, pages 5456–5473, Marseille, France. European Language Resources Association (ELRA).

Zhilin Yang, Peng Qi, Saizheng Zhang, Yoshua Bengio, William Cohen, Ruslan Salakhutdinov, and Christopher D. Manning. 2018. HotpotQA: A Dataset for Diverse, Explainable Multi-hop Question Answering. In *Proceedings of the 2018 Conference on Empirical Methods in Natural Language Processing*, EMNLP 2018, pages 2369–2380, Brussels, Belgium. Association for Computational Linguistics.

PGL at TextGraphs 2020 Shared Task: Explanation Regeneration using Language and Graph Learning Methods

Weibin Li, Yuxiang Lu, Zhengjie Huang, Jiaxiang Liu
Weiyue Su, Shikun Feng, Yu Sun
Baidu Inc., China
{liweibin02,luyuxiang,huangzhengjie,liujiaxiang}@baidu.com
{suweiyue,fengshikun01,sunyu02}@baidu.com

Abstract

This paper describes the system designed by the Baidu PGL Team which achieved the first place in the TextGraphs 2020 Shared Task. The task focuses on generating explanations for elementary science questions. Given a question and its corresponding correct answer, we are asked to select the facts that can explain why the answer is correct for that question and answering (QA) from a large knowledge base. To address this problem, we use a pre-trained language model to recall the top-K relevant explanations for each question. Then, we adopt a re-ranking approach based on a pre-trained language model to rank the candidate explanations. To further improve the rankings, we also develop an architecture consisting both powerful pre-trained transformers and GNNs to tackle the multi-hop inference problem. The official evaluation shows that, our system can outperform the second best system by 1.91 points.

1 Introduction

The TextGraphs 2020 Shared Task on Explanation Regeneration (Jansen and Ustalov, 2020) asks participants to develop methods to reconstruct gold explanations for elementary science questions. Concretely, given an elementary science question and its corresponding correct answer, the system need to perform the multi-hop inference and rank a set of explanatory facts that are expected to explain why the answer is correct from a large knowledge base.

Multi-hop inference is the task of combining more than one piece of information to solve a reasoning task, such as question answering. Multi-hop inference or information aggregation has been shown to be extremely challenging (Jansen, 2018), especially for the case here, where current estimates suggest that an average of 4 to 6 sentences are required to answer and explain a given question. An example is shown in Figure 1.

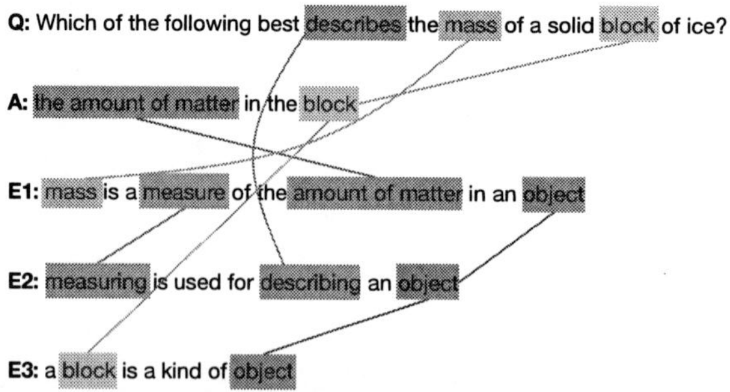

Figure 1: A subgraph of explanation sentences that explains why the answer is correct for the question.

In the TextGraphs 2020 Shared Task, we not only need to consider extracting the semantic information between the question and each explanation, but also need to take the structural relationship between the

This work is licensed under a Creative Commons Attribution 4.0 International License. License details: http://creativecommons.org/licenses/by/4.0/.

98

explanations into account. Therefore, we adopt a pipeline architecture to address the problem. First, we use a pre-trained language model to recall the top-K relevant explanations for each question. Then, we adopt a re-ranking approach based on another pre-trained language model to rank the candidate explanations. Finally, to further improve the rankings, we also develop an architecture utilizing the power of pre-trained transformers (Vaswani et al., 2017) and graph neural networks (GNNs) (Kipf and Welling, 2016) to tackle the multi-hop inference problem. We also adopt a Virtual Adversarial Training (Takeru et al., 2018) method to train our model and got a slight improvement.

The rest of the paper is organized as follows. In Section 2, we will briefly describe the task, the dataset and the evaluation metrics of the task. Section 3 shows the details of our approach. Our experiments will be shown in Section 4.

2 Task

Task. As described in Section 1, the TextGraphs 2020 Shared Task focuses on selecting a set of explanation sentences that can explain the answer of a question, which can be regarded as a ranking task. Concretely, given an elementary science question, its corresponding correct answer and a set of explanation sentences, the goal is to determine whether an explanation sentence is the reason for the QA.

Corpus. The data used in this shared task comes from the WorldTree V2 corpus (Xie et al., 2020). The dataset includes approximately 4400 standardized elementary and middle school science exam questions (3rd through 9th grade). Each example in the WorldTree V2 corpus contains detailed annotation stating whether a fact is a part of the explanation for that question. For each explanation, the WorldTree V2 corpus also includes annotation for how important each fact is towards the explanation.

Evaluation. Explanation reconstruction performance is evaluated in terms of mean average precision (MAP) by comparing the ranked list of facts with the gold explanation. Therefore, it is intuitive for us to regard the task as a ranking problem.

3 Approach

Our system consists of two major components. The first part is an information retrieval (IR) system based on the pre-trained language model to retrieve the top-K relevant explanation sentences from the whole knowledge base. The second part consists of two modules, including a pointwise ranking module to rank candidate facts and a graph-based module to counter the problem of multi-hop inference.

3.1 Retrieval

Recently, pre-trained language models (Devlin et al., 2018; Liu et al., 2019; Lan et al., 2019; Sun et al., 2020) have achieved state-of-the-art results in various language understanding tasks such as question answering (Rajpurkar et al., 2016; Khashabi et al., 2018). For our IR system, we use ERNIE 2.0 (Sun et al., 2020), the world's first model to score over 90 in terms of the macro-average score on GLUE benchmark (Wang et al., 2018), as our retriever. We concatenate the question, the correct answer and the explanation sentence as input of the retriever which will return a score to determine whether an explanation sentence is relevant to that question. Then for each question, we can get the top-K ranked facts from the corpus. Although a simple tf-idf based retriever can obtain the top-K ranked facts in a shorter time, its result is not very effective compared with the pre-trained model, as shown in Table 1. Since the pre-trained model already has strong semantic representation capabilities, it can achieve an excellent result on 5000 steps fine-tuning within two hours. Details can be found in Section 4.1.

Retriever	MAP@top100	Oracle MAP@top100
TF-IDF	25.49%	50.78%
Ours	48.80%	92.03%

Table 1: The recall result of different retrievers on the development set. The **Oracle MAP@top100** is the upper bound MAP score where all the relevant facts in these 100 candidate facts are ranked first.

3.2 Ranking

Our re-ranking component consists of two modules. Since we only fine-tune the retriever for 5000 steps, it can be still improved by the pre-trained model. Therefore, we use another pre-trained model based on ERNIE 2.0 (Sun et al., 2020) to re-rank the candidate explanation sentences from the retrieval stage. We significantly improve the performance on the task, outperforming the retriever by more than 10% of MAP. However, we found that there are many facts that have lexical overlap with the question, but they are not the reason for the QA. On the contrary, some key facts that have no lexical overlap with the question are ranked low. This kind of key facts are usually the explanation of other relevant facts, rather than the direct explanation of the question. Since each sample is only composed of a question, a correct answer and an explanation sentence, it is difficult for the retriever to learn the correlation between the candidate facts.

To address this problem, we utilize the graph neural networks (GNNs) to learn the correlation between the candidate facts. Graph neural networks (GNNs) are recursive neural networks for modeling the graph structure. Concretely, the graph structure here is the correlation between the candidate facts. As shown in Figure 1, **E1** explains the word *mass* for the question directly. **E2** explains the word *measure* for the **E1**. Therefore, **E2** can be regarded as a second order neighbor of the question, and we want to learn such relation with help of GNNs. Modern GNNs follow a neighborhood aggregation strategy, where we iteratively update the representation of a node by aggregating representations of its neighbors. In an attempt to integrate the powerful language understanding ability into graph learning, we present a graph aggregator with pre-trained transformers. Figure 2 shows the details of the architecture.

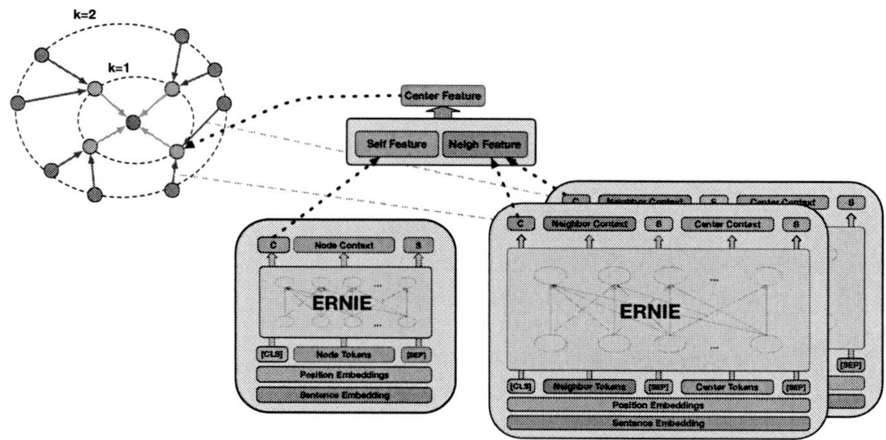

Figure 2: The overview of the architecture that integrates the powerful language understanding ability into graph learning.

As GraphSAGE-like (Hamilton et al., 2017) aggregation function only aggregate neighbors using simple operators, such as sum, mean or max. There's no direct interaction between the center node and each neighbor. In a text graph, node (sentence) interaction should not be limited in node-level (sentence-level) embedding. It should take the token-level (word-level) interaction between two nodes into account. In an attempt to make token-level interaction possible, we apply ERNIE on the edges of the graph by concatenating raw text tokens of the node pairs on the sampled edges (PGL, 2020). As shown in Figure 2, instead of obtaining the neigh feature directly from the neighbor sentence, we get the neighbor features by the interaction between the center tokens and the neighbor tokens. Then, the **[CLS]** embedding will be taken as the neigh feature.

To train the model we described above, we need to construct the edges between explanation facts. The K candidate explanation sentences for a question and a answer are regarded as nodes to form a graph. Here, edges can be a result of lexical overlap between explanation sentences. But we find that using this method will result in a very dense graph, and hence, each node in the graph is linked with many neighbors and most of them are irrelevant to the QA.

To alleviate this problem, we adopt a pairwise binary classification system, to score the explanation fact pairs in the candidate set for each question. We use the pre-trained language model to judge whether the explanation fact pair is relevant to the question and the answer. If both the two explanation sentences are relevant to the question and the answer, the label is 1, otherwise the label is 0. Then we rank all the explanation fact pairs by the score and select the top-M pairs as the edges of the text graph for each question. We then feed them to the text graph model we described above, and regard it as a node classification task.

4 Experiments

4.1 Model Configuration

In this work, the pre-trained language model we used to encode the text is ERNIE 2.0 (Sun et al., 2020), which is considered to be an expressive powerful model. For all experiments, the learning rate of the ERNIE encoder was initialized to $1e^{-4}$, batch size is 64 and the maximum sequence length is 128. We used the Adam optimizer with linear learning rate decay. In the retrieval phase, we fine-tuned the model for 5000 steps on a NVIDIA Tesla V100 (32GB GPU) machine. In the ranking phase, the pre-trained model was fine-tuned for 1 epoch with virtual adversarial training. To generate the edges for applying GNNs with the pre-trained language model to tackle multi-hop inference problem, we fine-tuned the ERNIE model for 5000 steps and selected the top 20 explanation sentence pairs as the edges for each question.

For evaluation, we select the top 100 ranked facts from the retrieval phase, and we found that the oracle MAP score can reach 92.03% with top 100 ranked facts, as shown in Table 1. We concatenate the correct answer choice with the question, because we found that adding the wrong options can mislead the model and leads to a lower MAP score. It is intuitive since the wrong options are not necessary to answer the question.

4.2 Experiment Results

We report the tf-idf based ranking scores as the baseline. From the Table 2 we can see that, though the tf-idf method can quickly score all the facts, its MAP score is very low compared with the ERNIE retriever. The ERNIE Re-ranker can significantly improve the performance on the task, which outperforms the retriever for more than 10% points of MAP score. The ERNIE graphsage model can also improve the performance of the Re-ranker. To further improve the performance on the leaderboard, we run our ERNIE Re-ranker model for three times and then ensemble them to get a better performance.

The performance of hidden test set of our final model is shown in Table 3. Our submission achieved the first place in TextGraphs 2020 Shared Task.

Model	MAP@top50	MAP@top100
TF-IDF	25.16%	25.49%
ERNIE Retriever	48.17%	48.80%
ERNIE Re-ranker	58.73%	59.16%
+ ERNIE Graphsage	59.53%	59.99%
ensemble ranking	61.58%	61.98%

Table 2: MAP score on the development set.

Model/participant	MAP
Our model	60.33%
alvysinger	58.43%
aisys	52.33%

Table 3: MAP score on the test set.

5 Conclusion

We proposed our approach to the shared task on "Multi-hop Inference Explanation Regeneration". Our system consists of a pre-trained model-based retriever and a graph-based pre-trained model for the re-ranking phase, and achieved the first place in TextGraphs 2020 Shared Task.

References

Jacob Devlin, Ming-Wei Chang, Kenton Lee, and Kristina Toutanova. 2018. Bert: Pre-training of deep bidirectional transformers for language understanding. *arXiv preprint arXiv:1810.04805*.

Will Hamilton, Zhitao Ying, and Jure Leskovec. 2017. Inductive representation learning on large graphs. In *Advances in neural information processing systems*, pages 1024–1034.

Peter Jansen and Dmitry Ustalov. 2020. TextGraphs 2020 Shared Task on Multi-Hop Inference for Explanation Regeneration. In *Proceedings of the Graph-based Methods for Natural Language Processing (TextGraphs)*. Association for Computational Linguistics.

Peter Jansen. 2018. Multi-hop inference for sentence-level textgraphs: How challenging is meaningfully combining information for science question answering? *arXiv preprint arXiv:1805.11267*.

Daniel Khashabi, Snigdha Chaturvedi, Michael Roth, Shyam Upadhyay, and Dan Roth. 2018. Looking beyond the surface: A challenge set for reading comprehension over multiple sentences. In *Proceedings of the 2018 Conference of the North American Chapter of the Association for Computational Linguistics: Human Language Technologies, Volume 1 (Long Papers)*, pages 252–262.

Thomas N Kipf and Max Welling. 2016. Semi-supervised classification with graph convolutional networks. *arXiv preprint arXiv:1609.02907*.

Zhenzhong Lan, Mingda Chen, Sebastian Goodman, Kevin Gimpel, Piyush Sharma, and Radu Soricut. 2019. Albert: A lite bert for self-supervised learning of language representations. In *International Conference on Learning Representations*.

Yinhan Liu, Myle Ott, Naman Goyal, Jingfei Du, Mandar Joshi, Danqi Chen, Omer Levy, Mike Lewis, Luke Zettlemoyer, and Veselin Stoyanov. 2019. Roberta: A robustly optimized bert pretraining approach. *arXiv preprint arXiv:1907.11692*.

Team PGL. 2020. Erniesage: Ernie sample aggregate. `https://github.com/PaddlePaddle/PGL/tree/master/examples/erniesage`.

Pranav Rajpurkar, Jian Zhang, Konstantin Lopyrev, and Percy Liang. 2016. Squad: 100,000+ questions for machine comprehension of text. In *Proceedings of the 2016 Conference on Empirical Methods in Natural Language Processing*, pages 2383–2392.

Yu Sun, Shuohuan Wang, Yu-Kun Li, Shikun Feng, Hao Tian, Hua Wu, and Haifeng Wang. 2020. Ernie 2.0: A continual pre-training framework for language understanding. In *AAAI*, pages 8968–8975.

Miyato Takeru, Maeda Shin-Ichi, Ishii Shin, and Koyama Masanori. 2018. Virtual adversarial training: A regularization method for supervised and semi-supervised learning. *IEEE Transactions on Pattern Analysis and Machine Intelligence*, pages 1–1.

Ashish Vaswani, Noam Shazeer, Niki Parmar, Jakob Uszkoreit, Llion Jones, Aidan N Gomez, Łukasz Kaiser, and Illia Polosukhin. 2017. Attention is all you need. In *Advances in neural information processing systems*, pages 5998–6008.

Alex Wang, Amanpreet Singh, Julian Michael, Felix Hill, Omer Levy, and Samuel Bowman. 2018. Glue: A multi-task benchmark and analysis platform for natural language understanding. In *Proceedings of the 2018 EMNLP Workshop BlackboxNLP: Analyzing and Interpreting Neural Networks for NLP*, pages 353–355.

Zhengnan Xie, Sebastian Thiem, Jaycie Martin, Elizabeth Wainwright, Steven Marmorstein, and Peter Jansen. 2020. WorldTree v2: A corpus of science-domain structured explanations and inference patterns supporting multi-hop inference. In *Proceedings of the 12th Language Resources and Evaluation Conference*, pages 5456–5473, Marseille, France, May. European Language Resources Association.

ChiSquareX at TextGraphs 2020 Shared Task: Leveraging Pre-trained Language Models for Explanation Regeneration[*]

Aditya Girish Pawate
IIT Kharagpur
adityagirish
pawate@gmail.com

Devansh Chandak
IIT Bombay
dchandak99@gmail.com

Varun Madhavan
IIT Kharagpur
varun.m.iitkgp
@gmail.com

Abstract

In this work, we describe the system developed by a group of undergraduates from the Indian Institutes of Technology, for the Shared Task at TextGraphs-14 on Multi-Hop Inference Explanation Regeneration (Jansen and Ustalov, 2020). The shared task required participants to develop methods to reconstruct gold explanations for elementary science questions from the WorldTree Corpus (Xie et al., 2020). Although our research was not funded by any organization and all the models were trained on freely available tools like Google Colab which restricted our computational capabilities, we have managed to achieve noteworthy results placing ourselves in the 4th place with a MAP score of 0.4902[1] in the evaluation leaderboard and 0.5062 MAP score on the post-evaluation-phase leaderboard using RoBERTa. We incorporated some of the methods proposed in the previous edition of Textgraphs-13 (Chia et al., 2019), which proved to be very effective, improved upon them, and built a model on top of it using powerful state-of-the-art pre-trained language models like RoBERTa (Liu et al., 2019), BART (Lewis et al., 2020), SciBERT (Beltagy et al., 2019) among others. Further optimization of our work can be done with the availability of better computational resources.

1 Introduction

The Shared Task is aimed at Multi-hop Inference for Explanation Regeneration. Participants are required to develop new and improve existing methods to reconstruct gold explanations for the WorldTree Corpus (Xie et al., 2020) of elementary science questions, their answers, and explanations.

Question: Which of the following is an example of an organism taking in nutrients? (A) a dog burying a bone (B) a girl eating an apple (C) an insect crawling on a leaf (D) a boy planting tomatoes
Answer: (B) a girl eating an apple
Gold Explanation Facts: 1) A girl means a human girl: Grounding 2) Humans are living organisms: Grounding 3) Eating is when an organism takes in nutrients in the form of food: Central 4) Fruits are kinds of foods: Grounding 5) An apple is a kind of fruit: Grounding
Irrelevant Explanation Facts: 1) Some flowers become fruits. 2) Fruit contains seeds. 3) living things live in their habitat. 4) Consumers eat other organisms

Table 1: An Example for Explanation Regeneration

The example highlights an instance for this task, where systems need to perform multi-hop inference to combine diverse information and identify relevant explanation sentences required to answer the specific question. The task provides a new and more challenging corpus of 9029 explanations and a set of gold explanations for each question and correct answer pair.

---

[1]Full, replicable code is available on Github for all methods described here, at https://github.com/dchandak99/TextGraphs-2020

This work is licensed under a Creative Commons Attribution 4.0 International Licence. Licence details: http://creativecommons.org/licenses/by/4.0/.

Proceedings of the Graph-based Methods for Natural Language Processing (TextGraphs), pages 103–108
Barcelona, Spain (Online), December 13, 2020

Team	MAP on leaderboard
Baidu PGL	0.6033
alvysinger	0.5843
aisys	0.5233
ChiSquareX	**0.4902**
Red Dragon	0.4793
mler	0.3367
dustalov (Baseline)	0.2344

Table 2: Final Leaderboard

Attributes	TG 2019	TG 2020
Questions	1680	4367
Explanations	4950	9029
Tables	62	81

Table 3: Dataset Comparison

2 Dataset

The dataset is the WorldTree Corpus V2.1(Xie et al., 2020) of Explanation Graphs and Inference Patterns supporting Multi-hop Inference (Februrary 2020 snapshot). It is a newer version of the dataset used in the TextGraphs-2019 (Jansen and Ustalov, 2019). The comparison between the two datasets is shown in Table 3.

3 Problem Review

The problem statement requires participants to build a system that, given a question and its answer choices, can identify the sentences that explain the answer given the question. This is a challenging task due to the presence of other irrelevant sentences in the corpora for the given question, which have equally significant lexical and semantic overlap as the correct ones (Fried et al., 2015). When a more classical graph theory approach using the semantic overlap of explanations and questions is tried, it leads to the problem of semantic drift (Jansen, 2018). More classic graph methods were attempted in (Kwon et al., 2018), where the challenge of semantic drift in multi-hop inference was analyzed, and the effectiveness of information extraction methods was demonstrated. Also, approaching the question as a language generation task is not effective and the current state-of-the-art models (Dušek et al., 2020) are not capable of generating the exact explanations as required by this task. So this task can easily be transformed into a sentence ranking problem in which we need to rank the relevant facts over all other given facts present in the corpus. The evaluation metric used for the task is the widely used and robust mean average precision (MAP) metric.

We have explained a few initial experiments that were undertaken in Section 4.1, followed by the pre-processing methods we incorporated in Section 4.2. We have then discussed our models in Sections 4.3 through 4.6. We have finally shown all our results and discussions in Section 5 followed by the conclusion and acknowledgments.

4 Model

4.1 Initial Experiments

We used the pure textual form of each explanation, problem and correct answer, rather than using a semi-structured form given in the column-oriented files provided in the dataset. Initially, we just reduced the original text of the questions that included all the answer choices. This was done by removing the incorrect answers, which thereby resulted in an improvement in performance. This is similar to what was seen in the previous edition of the task. Taking the TFIDF baseline with the basic pre-processing we got a MAP score of 0.3065 on the hidden test set. Taking this as the starting point, we built a $Sentence BERT$ Model in which we converted all questions and explanations into contextual word embedding vectors and ranked the explanations in descending order of cosine similarity of the embedded vectors. We observed a drop in the model's performance with the MAP score of 0.2427 on the test dataset, which is worse than the simple TFIDF ranker. We realized that it was the semantic overlap between the question and the irrelevant explanations that caused such an unexpected performance drop on further inspection. So we noted that we should not use contextual word embeddings, but instead, we must improve the simple but effective information retrieval technique of TFIDF for the ranker. We then used the Sublinear TFIDF[2] and Binary TFIDF. The optimized Sublinear TFIDF vectorizer gave a boost in the score: 0.3254 MAP.

4.2 Preprocessing

It was seen that the TFIDF algorithm was very sensitive to keywords, so we applied the pre-processing and optimization techniques mentioned in (Chia et al., 2019). For each of these, we performed Penn-Treebank tokenization, followed by lemmatization using the lemmatization files provided with the dataset.[3] We used NLTK for tokenization to reduce the vocabulary size needed by combining the different forms of the same keyword. We also removed stopwords, which thereby removed noise in the texts. A simple TFIDF based ranker along with the above pre-processing returned a MAP score of 0.3850. Substituting Sublinear TFIDF, we noticed that the score increased to 0.4080 MAP. With some experimentation, we were able to further improve the MAP score to 0.426 using Binary TFIDF. Finally, we applied Recursive TFIDF as proposed in this paper (Chia et al., 2019), in which the authors treated the TFIDF vector as a representation of the current chain of reasoning, each successive iteration built on the representation to accumulate a sequence of explanations. We optimized all the other variables like $normalization, maxlen, hops, scale$. We found the MAP to be completely independent of the normalization used. For $maxlen = \{128, 125, 144\}$, we found $maxlen = 128$ to be most efficient. For number of hops $= \{1,2,3\}$, we found 1 to be best. This may be because semantic drift creeps in as we explore the nodes further away from the current node. A scaling factor was used in each successive explanation as it is added to the TFIDF vector. For the downscaling factors$= \{1.25, 1.3, 1.35\}$, we found 1.25 was optimum. We got a slight improvement in the score 0.4430 MAP when used along with Binary TFIDF. All these steps were done as a part of the pre-processing step.

4.3 Pure Language Model approach

After doing all the pre-processing steps, we tried to apply a simple pure language model based approach that has shown good performance in Text Classification tasks. We took each processed question and concatenated each of the 9029 explanations to it one by one. Then for each of these question + explanation pairs, we used a simple language model based BERT classifier ($BERTForSequenceClassification$) to predict whether the explanation was one of the gold explanations for that question. The result for this was 0.4116 MAP, which was lesser than we expected. We deduced that there are two major problems with this simplistic approach.

- **Class imbalance:** Most of the question-explanations would be labeled 0 (False), since out of the 9029 total explanations only a few would actually be gold explanations for the question. This causes the classifier to output the 0 label almost all the time and prevents it from learning the true relations between the gold explanations and the question. It is possible that the class imbalance could be mitigated by searching for better hyperparameter values; however, we weren't able to do that with the available resources, so we applied a different technique to address this.

- **Non-scalability:** This approach would require inferences equal to the number of explanations in the corpus for every question. While it's possible to do this for this relatively small corpus of 9029 explanations, as the number of explanations becomes larger, this approach would no longer be feasible; requiring too much time for training and, more importantly, for inference.

4.4 Using TFIDF to retrieve relevant explanations

To address the above problems, we applied the optimal TFIDF vectorizer (TFIDF_binary + recursive) obtained in the pre-processing step to first obtain the most relevant explanations for a given question based on the lexical overlap between the question and the explanations. The number of explanations retrieved by this initial ranker (top_k) was a tuned parameter. This technique was very effective at retrieving the gold explanations for a question. We have shown the fraction of gold explanations retrieved when we

---

[2] https://nlp.stanford.edu/IR-book/html/htmledition/sublinear-tf-scaling-1.html
[3] PTB tokenization and stopwords from the NLTK package

Method	MAP Score
TFIDF + preproc	0.3850
sublinear + preproc	0.4080
binary + preproc	0.4267
recursive	0.4429
sublinear + recursive	0.4429
binary + recursive	0.4430

Table 4: Inital scores using only pre-processing and TFIDF

top_k	Fraction Retrieved
10	0.484
30	0.676
50	0.767
80	0.837
100	0.865
300	0.965
500	0.987

Table 5: Value of parameter top_k vs Fraction of gold explanations retrieved

consider the top_k explanations in Table 5. We can see that almost 87% of the gold explanations are retrieved when we that top 100 explanations from TFIDF, and almost 99% of gold explanations are retrieved when we took the top 500 explanations. This saves our computation as we now need to only train the model for at max 500 explanations per question instead of 9029 explanations. Now top_k retrieved explanations are concatenated to the questions as in the previous approach, and the classifier model is trained to classify whether a given explanation among the top_k explanations is the right explanation for the question or not. The MAP score using the $BERTForSequenceClassification$ model was 0.4365 MAP. We inferred that the score was low because the model was predicting the 0 label for almost all inputs since there was still a significant imbalance in the training dataset (though significantly less than before).

4.5 Addressing class imbalance

To address the class imbalance in question explanation pairs, we applied a simple approach of over-sampling of the minority class (Positive or '1' label). We simply repeated the gold explanations during training such that for each question, the number of positive and negative labeled explanations would be equal (equal to top_k/2). Hence the explanations for a given question were the top_k/2 negatively labeled explanations plus the positively labeled explanations retrieved by TFIDF repeated top_k/2 times. This was only applied while training, not during inference in the validation and test datasets. Using this simple technique, we were able to get a significant boost in the performance for the baseline of BERT with 0.4506 MAP score.

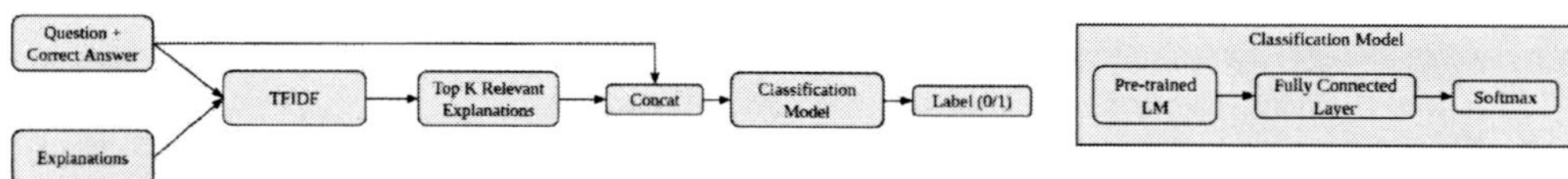

Figure 1: The Overall Flow of the Model

Figure 2: Inside the Classification Model

4.6 Pre-trained Language Models

We tried out all pre-trained language models available for sequence classification. We optimized the following hyperparameters: top_k, num_train_epochs, $batch\_size$, $learning\_rate$, $epsilon$, $gradient\_accumulation\_steps$, max_grad_norm, $weight\_decay$. The $batch\_size$ is dependent on the GPU RAM available. The parameters top_k and num_train_epochs are a function of training time. Since we needed to optimize the training time, we first trained all models with top_k as 100 with 3 epochs to get a preliminary model performance. Then we took the best models and trained it for a higher top_k (500 or 300 whichever was feasible) to get a boost in score. Our best performing model took close to 8 hours to complete the training. Further details of the models are given in the supplementary.

Parameter	Value
Optimizer	AdamW
Learning Rate	2e-5
Epsilon	1e-8
Max Grad Norm	1
Gradient Accumulation Steps	1

Table 6: Hyper Parameter Values

5 Results and discussion

We present the scores in the table given below. We got our best performance from RoBERTa. When we observe the results, we see that there is only a slight variation in the final scores of most pre-trained language models. We observe that the models overfit the given data. We could not perform a grid search to optimize all parameters due to computational constraints and had to manually search for the best hyperparameters due to which the performance of any given model may not be optimal. Further, we have trained only RoBERTa and BART for top_k 500 explanations and not other models because they had a long training time or a higher RAM requirement.

Model	Num Param	Batch Size	top_k	Train MAP	Dev MAP	Test MAP
RoBERTa (optimized)	355M	256	500	0.7210	0.5184	0.5061
RoBERTa	**355M**	**256**	**500**	**0.6708**	**0.5062**	**0.4902**
RoBERTa	355M	256	100	0.6182	0.4800	0.4798
BART	406M	128	300	0.7167	0.5036	0.4865
BART	406M	32	100	0.6708	0.4670	0.4769
SciBERT	110M	256	100	0.6544	0.4950	0.4855
ELECTRA	355M	128	100	0.6143	0.4943	0.4854
ALBERT	223M	32	100	0.6280	0.4813	0.4731
DistilBERT	134M	256	100	0.6049	0.4793	0.4641
BERT	110M	256	150	0.5776	0.4609	0.4506

Table 7: Final Results

6 Conclusion

We have given a system description of our team ChiSquareX which stood 4th place in the evaluation phase leaderboard with a MAP score of 0.4902. We have presented a system with optimized pre-processing of the dataset followed by an optimized TFIDF information retrieval scheme to obtain initial ranks, and then further pre-trained language model based re-ranker to rank the final explanations. Despite the computational constraints, just by leveraging Google Colab and other open-source tools, we have managed to fine-tune state-of-the-art pre-trained language models like RoBERTa, BART and ELECTRA on the (Xie et al., 2020) dataset and achieve a reasonable MAP score.

Acknowledgements

We would firstly like to thank the organizers Peter Jansen and Dmitry Ustalov for holding this shared task. It was a great learning experience for us. We would also like to thank the participants of TextGraphs-2019; their work was a great source of inspiration for us as to how to proceed with the task. (Chia et al., 2019) in particular, was a source of a number of simple but effective text pre-processing techniques to greatly improve performance. Additionally, we would like to extend a big thanks to the makers and maintainers of the excellent HuggingFace (Wolf et al., 2020) repository, without which most of our research would have been impossible.

References

Iz Beltagy, Kyle Lo, and Arman Cohan. 2019. Scibert: A pretrained language model for scientific text. In *EMNLP/IJCNLP*.

Yew Ken Chia, Sam Witteveen, and Martin Andrews. 2019. Red dragon AI at TextGraphs 2019 shared task: Language model assisted explanation generation. In *Proceedings of the Thirteenth Workshop on Graph-Based Methods for Natural Language Processing (TextGraphs-13)*, pages 85–89, Hong Kong, November. Association for Computational Linguistics.

Ondřej Dušek, Jekaterina Novikova, and Verena Rieser. 2020. Evaluating the State-of-the-Art of End-to-End Natural Language Generation: The E2E NLG Challenge. *Computer Speech & Language*, 59:123–156, January.

Daniel Fried, Peter Jansen, Gustave Hahn-Powell, Mihai Surdeanu, and Peter Clark. 2015. Higher-order lexical semantic models for non-factoid answer reranking. *Transactions of the Association for Computational Linguistics*, 3(0):197–210.

Peter Jansen and Dmitry Ustalov. 2019. TextGraphs 2019 Shared Task on Multi-Hop Inference for Explanation Regeneration. In *Proceedings of the Thirteenth Workshop on Graph-Based Methods for Natural Language Processing (TextGraphs-13)*, pages 63–77, Hong Kong. Association for Computational Linguistics.

Peter Jansen and Dmitry Ustalov. 2020. TextGraphs 2020 Shared Task on Multi-Hop Inference for Explanation Regeneration. In *Proceedings of the Graph-based Methods for Natural Language Processing (TextGraphs)*. Association for Computational Linguistics.

Peter Jansen. 2018. Multi-hop inference for sentence-level TextGraphs: How challenging is meaningfully combining information for science question answering? In *Proceedings of the Twelfth Workshop on Graph-Based Methods for Natural Language Processing (TextGraphs-12)*, pages 12–17, New Orleans, Louisiana, USA, June. Association for Computational Linguistics.

Heeyoung Kwon, Harsh Trivedi, Peter Jansen, Mihai Surdeanu, and Niranjan Balasubramanian. 2018. Controlling information aggregation for complex question answering. In Gabriella Pasi, Benjamin Piwowarski, Leif Azzopardi, and Allan Hanbury, editors, *Advances in Information Retrieval*, pages 750–757, Cham. Springer International Publishing.

Mike Lewis, Yinhan Liu, Naman Goyal, Marjan Ghazvininejad, Abdelrahman Mohamed, Omer Levy, Veselin Stoyanov, and Luke Zettlemoyer. 2020. BART: Denoising sequence-to-sequence pre-training for natural language generation, translation, and comprehension. In *Proceedings of the 58th Annual Meeting of the Association for Computational Linguistics*, pages 7871–7880, Online, July. Association for Computational Linguistics.

Y. Liu, Myle Ott, Naman Goyal, Jingfei Du, Mandar Joshi, Danqi Chen, Omer Levy, M. Lewis, Luke Zettlemoyer, and Veselin Stoyanov. 2019. Roberta: A robustly optimized bert pretraining approach. *ArXiv*, abs/1907.11692.

Thomas Wolf, Lysandre Debut, Victor Sanh, Julien Chaumond, Clement Delangue, Anthony Moi, Pierric Cistac, Tim Rault, Rémi Louf, Morgan Funtowicz, Joe Davison, Sam Shleifer, Patrick von Platen, Clara Ma, Yacine Jernite, Julien Plu, Canwen Xu, Teven Le Scao, Sylvain Gugger, Mariama Drame, Quentin Lhoest, and Alexander M. Rush. 2020. Huggingface's transformers: State-of-the-art natural language processing.

Zhengnan Xie, Sebastian Thiem, Jaycie Martin, Elizabeth Wainwright, Steven Marmorstein, and Peter Jansen. 2020. WorldTree v2: A corpus of science-domain structured explanations and inference patterns supporting multi-hop inference. In *Proceedings of the 12th Language Resources and Evaluation Conference*, pages 5456–5473, Marseille, France, May. European Language Resources Association.

Explanation Regeneration via Multi-Hop ILP Inference over Knowledge Base

Aayushee Gupta
International Institute of Information
Technology, Bangalore
aayushee.gupta1@iiitb.org

Gopalakrishnan Srinivasaraghavan
International Institute of Information
Technology, Bangalore
gsr@iiitb.ac.in

Abstract

Textgraphs 2020 Workshop organized a shared task on 'Explanation Regeneration'[1] that required reconstructing gold explanations for elementary science questions. This work describes our submission to the task which is based on multiple components: a BERT baseline ranking, an Integer Linear Program (ILP) based re-scoring and a regression model for re-ranking the explanation facts. Our system achieved a Mean Average Precision score of 0.3659[2].

1 Introduction

Question Answering (QA) has been a long standing challenge in the field of Natural Language Processing with considerable recent focus on machine reading comprehension(Welbl et al., 2018), complex question answering(Talmor and Berant, 2018), open domain and commonsense question answering(Mihaylov et al., 2018; Talmor et al., 2018) that require piecing together chunks of information in order to infer the correct answers - also known as Multi-Hop Inferencing. There has been a rapid rise in the development of such QA datasets as well as deep learning-based models for solving them but most of these models are ineffective in explaining why a model chooses a particular answer for a question.

Explanation regeneration is the task of generating simple sentence explanations for complex scientific phenomena related question answers. It is a multi-hop inference task wherein the gold explanation is formed by chaining together individual facts from a Knowledge Base (KB) ordered such that they form correct reasoning behind the answer to a question. It can be posed both as a Ranking problem where we iteratively rank relevant facts with respect to a question and as a Graph traversal problem, where we "hop" from some starting fact to other related facts until we have enough facts to infer the answer. To regenerate the correct chain of explanation facts, we have developed a system that can rank and score the facts in a KB by inferring over the graph of question, its correct answer and the relevant KB facts.

Integer Linear Programming has been used as an effective approach in answering questions over semi-structured tables(Clark et al., 2016), tuples from KB(Khot et al., 2017), and semantic abstractions of paragraphs of text(Khashabi et al., 2019). We use this approach to further rank and score relevant facts forming an explanation for a question answer pair. To find the relevant KB facts, we first rank each fact in the KB with respect to its bidirectional contextual representation with the question and its correct answer using a BERT baseline (Das et al., 2019). We then choose a set of top-K ranked facts forming a chain and create an Integer Linear Program with variables and constraints consisting of a graph of nodes and edges created from constituents of question, answer and the fact chain. The ILP maximizes the graph that has maximum alignment between the edges for re-scoring each fact in the chain. The fact scores from the ILP model are further combined with the help of a regression model to finally re-rank each fact in the top-K set of explanation facts.

The paper is organized as follows: Section 2 provides task description, followed by details of our system components in Section 3, detailed evaluation results in Section 4 and conclusion in Section 5.

---

[1] https://github.com/cognitiveailab/tg2020task

[2] Our code is available at: https://github.com/aayushee/Textgraphs

This work is licensed under a Creative Commons Attribution 4.0 International Licence. Licence details: http://creativecommons.org/licenses/by/4.0/.

Proceedings of the Graph-based Methods for Natural Language Processing (TextGraphs), pages 109–114
Barcelona, Spain (Online), December 13, 2020

The figure box (Figure 1) contains:

> Question: From Earth, the Sun appears brighter than any other star because the Sun is the
> Answer Options: [0]: newest star. [1]: largest star. [2]: hottest star. [3]: closest star.
> Correct Answer: closest star.
> Explanation:
> 1. the Sun is the star that is closest to Earth (ROLE: CENTRAL)
> 2. the sun is a source of (light ; light energy) called sunlight (ROLE: CENTRAL)
> 3. as a source of light becomes closer , the light will appear brighter (ROLE: CENTRAL)

Figure 1: An example of Question, Answer and Explanation from the dataset.

Dataset Type	Number of Examples
Train	2207
Dev	496
Test	1350

Table 1: Dataset statistics.

2 Task Description

The task of Explanation Regeneration(Jansen and Ustalov, 2020) is based on multiple choice elementary and middle school science exam question answers taken from ARC(Clark et al., 2018) dataset and supplemented with a set of curated explanation facts that explain the correct answer to each question. The explanation facts are atomic sentences from a KB and link a question and its correct answer in a chain-like manner that can be understood easily by a 5-year-old. To answer a question correctly, appropriate explanation facts must be retrieved from the KB and chained in the correct order.

2.1 Dataset Description

The WorldTree v2.1 dataset(Xie et al., 2020) consists of around 4400 natural language scientific questions with multiple choice answers along with their explanations created from curated scientific textual knowledge base of roughly 10000 facts. The facts are available in a semi-structured format and divided into 81 tables. An average explanation for a question is a combination of 5.6 facts which indicates the need for a multi-hop inferencing model to solve the task. The number of explanation facts for a question vary between 1 and 16. Each explanation fact is also labeled with the role it plays in an explanation (Central, Grounding, Lexical Glue, etc.) The dataset also comes with a set of common inference patterns which is a set of related facts required to solve specific scientific questions. A sample example from the dataset is shown in Figure 1 that has 3 facts in its explanation for the correct answer to the question. Data Statistics are also presented in Table 1.

3 System Description

The complete pipelined system in shown in Figure 2 that takes the input dataset, generates a baseline ranking of facts from which the top-K are given as input to the ILP program which generates scores for them, followed by generation of combined scores by the regression model and a final sorted list of scores for each question answer pair.

3.1 Baseline Ranking

We first obtain a baseline relevance ranking for each fact in the KB with respect to a question answer pair. For this, we combine each question with its correct answer and get its contextualized representation along with that of each fact in the KB by labeling a relevant explanation fact as 1 while irrelevant facts from KB as 0. We fine-tune BERT model for this individual fact ranking as suggested in (Das et al., 2019). This resulted in close to 21.5 million training samples corresponding to 9727 KB explanation facts for 2207 train questions. Due to computational constraints, we sampled a total of 500,000 positive

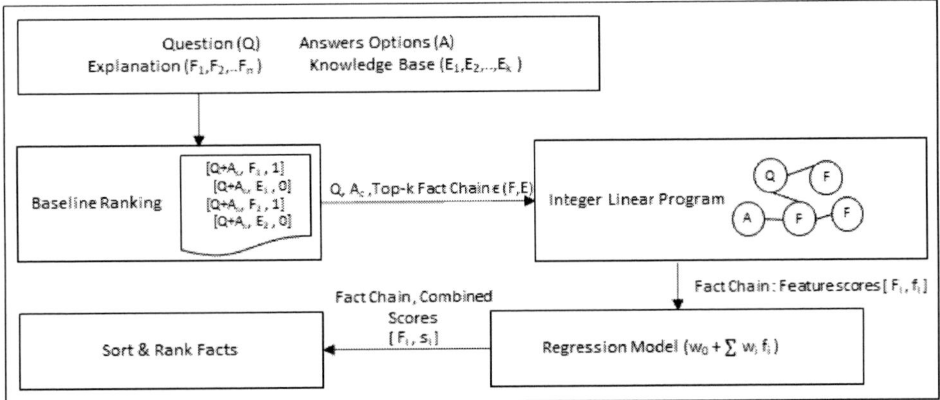

Figure 2: Components of our system. Here, $F_i \in F$ is the set of gold facts in an explanation, $E_i \in E$ is the set of facts in KB, $f_i \in$ set of alignment features, $s_i \in$ score for each fact.

and negative examples from the training dataset and fine-tuned BERT model for 3 epochs. This trained model was evaluated on the full test dataset to obtain initial ranks for each KB fact.

3.2 Sentence re-scoring via Integer Linear Program

The aim of this module is to find a relevant subgraph and score constituents of KB facts that are important with respect to question and its correct answer to re-score and re-rank such facts closer to the top while gathering the correct chain of facts that can explain the answer. This is done through an Integer Linear Program which takes as input a graph of nodes created from constituent parsing of question, correct answer, top-K ranked facts (fact chain) and edges that connect them to each other. An edge between two constituents is created if they are aligned to each other. Edges in the graph ensure that facts in a fact chain are connected to question, answer and other facts in the chain.

The variables of the ILP are all binary reflecting the presence or absence of a node or edge in the graph based on a minimum threshold alignment score value. The ILP maximizes a linear objective function which is the weight of the graph $G(V, E)$ with V vertices and E edges, subtracted by the weights of constraints C to find the best possible subgraph from all possible graphs $\mathcal{G}$:

$$\arg\max_{G \in \mathcal{G}} G(V, E) = \sum w(V) + \sum w(E) - \sum w(C) \tag{1}$$

The constraints are formulated such that G is a connected graph and has at least some connection with constituents from question, fact chain and correct answer. Variables are also created for each fact in a chain such that a maximum of 16 facts can be active in a fact chain. Some more constraints used can be found in the Supplementary material Table S1.

The edge weights between the graph nodes are calculated through multiple alignment scores:

- Question Fact Chain Alignments (QFA): Entailment scores between constituents of question and fact chain text.

- Fact Chain Answer Alignments (FAA): Entailment scores between constituents of fact chain and correct answer text.

- Intra-Fact Chain Alignments (IFA): Weighted scores between constituents of individual facts which have an edge in their dependency parse.

- Inter-Fact Chain Alignments (IFA2): Entailment scores between constituents of the fact chain.

The above alignment scores are obtained for all active nodes in the graph maximized by the ILP solution corresponding to each fact in a fact chain. We adapt the SemanticILP (Khashabi et al., 2019) solver to solve the constrained optimization problem that uses SCIP solver (Achterberg, 2009) for solving the ILP. The constituents from question, answer and fact chain are obtained through a shallow parse of sentences.[3] The entailment scores between phrases of words are calculated using a WordNet-based weighted alignment function which computes relevant word sense frequency of hypernyms and synonyms relations for all words(Khashabi et al., 2016).

3.3 Sentence re-ranking via Regression

Fact chain alignment scores obtained from the ILP for each QA pair are passed through a linear regression model that helps determine the correct coefficients for deriving a combined score and ranking for the facts in an explanation. The linear regression model minimizes the residual sum of squares between seen labels in the dataset and the labels predicted by linear approximation as follows:

$$\min_{w} ||Xw - y||_2^2 \tag{2}$$

where, X is the feature matrix of size $[N_s \times N_f]$, s is the number of samples, f is the number of features, w is the feature coefficient vector $[w_1, w_2...w_f]$ and y is the label vector. We consider the 4 alignment scores from ILP model (QFA, FAA, IFA, IFA2) as features for the regression model. For each fact in a chain, its score from the model is estimated as a linear combination of the alignment score features:

$$score = w_0 + w_1 \times QFA + w_2 \times FAA + w_3 \times IFA + w_4 \times IFA2 \tag{3}$$

The scores for each fact chain are then sorted in a descending order to re-rank facts in a chain leading to generation of the final explanation for each question.

To construct regression training data, we get scores from ILP for each question, its correct answer and a top-K fact chain from baseline TF-IDF model for which the correct explanation facts are labeled as 1 while the irrelevant ones as 0. For test data, we do the same, but the top-K fact chain is constructed from BERT baseline ranking. We scale the feature scores obtained from ILP model and downsample the negative class equivalent to the positive class samples while training the regression model since the class labels are imbalanced. The ILP solution was found to be infeasible for very few questions in the train and test dataset ($<$1%), which are skipped during regression phase. We train on 25000 samples (2200 questions) and test on all 40320 samples (1344 questions) corresponding to 30 facts in a chain for every question answer pair.

4 Evaluation Results

For evaluation, we consider following baseline models and compare their Mean Average Precision (MAP) scores on test data with our system:

1. **TF-IDF**: Treat each question and its correct answer as a query and rank each fact in the knowledge base based on its cosine similarity score with the query

2. **Fine-Tuned BERT Ranking**: Classify each fact in the KB based on its contextual representation with the question and its correct answer and create a ranked list based on classification score from a fine-tuned pre-trained BERT model (Wolf et al., 2019).

3. **Extractive Summarization**: Get an extractive summary of top-K ranked facts from fine-tuned BERT model using sentence similarity and weighted graph-based sentence ranking algorithm (Mihalcea and Tarau, 2004). The top-K BERT ranked facts are also prepended with question and its correct answer as a starting fact for summary extraction.

4. **Sentence Reranking with ILP and Regression**: Our system that uses top-K (K=30) ranked facts from BERT baseline ranking, obtains multiple alignment scores between these facts, question and its correct answer and then consider these scores as features to train a regression model that calculates scores for each fact chain. We augment these fact chains with remaining predictions from BERT baseline ranking for our final submission.

---

[3]https://github.com/CogComp/cogcomp-nlp

Evaluation Model	MAP
TF-IDF	0.30
Fine-tuned BERT Ranking	0.481
Top-K Fine-tuned BERT (K=30)	0.466
Top-K Fine-tuned BERT Summarization	0.347
ILP and Regression ReRanking (Ours)	0.365

Table 2: MAP scores on test data from our system and other baselines.

Features	MAP
QFA,FAA	0.3651
QFA,FAA,IFA	0.3659
QFA,FAA,IFA,IFA2	0.332

Table 3: MAP scores on test data from regression features.

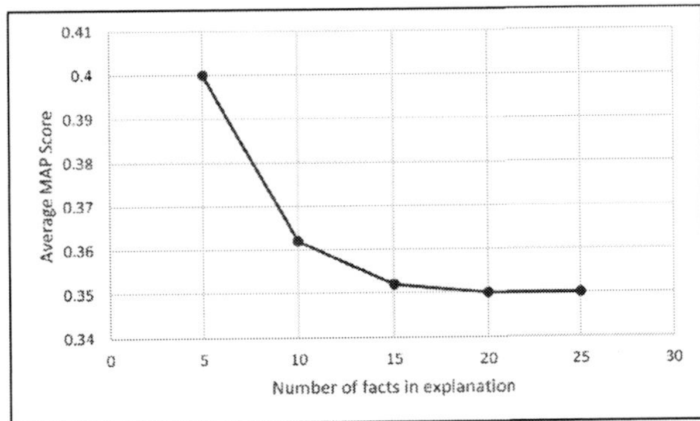

Figure 3: Line chart showing variation in Average MAP score of the model on test data with increasing number of facts in an explanation.

Table 2 presents test evaluation results having comparison of our system with other baselines and results with different features used in regression model are shown in Table 3. Results indicate that the baseline BERT ranking performs well while its summarized ranking has a reduced performance. Our system performs better than extractive summarization and TF-IDF ranking but does not beat the baseline ranking from BERT despite the BERT model ranking KB facts individually with respect to a question, correct answer pair while we consider ranking and scoring based on multiple hops between question, answer and the fact chain. The regression model performs best with QFA, FAA and IFA features. Our intuition that the addition of the Inter-Fact Chain Alignment feature would improve the ranking score did not turn out to be true probably because of the semantic drift among facts in an explanation indicating requirement of better ILP parameter tuning and phrasal entailment scoring methods. Figure 3 shows the decline in MAP score for our model with increase in number of gold explanations in the test data. This shows that performing multi-hop inference is indeed a difficult task when number of hops increases. An example of ranked outcomes from all the models is presented in Supplementary material Table S2.

5   Conclusion and Future Work

Explanation Regeneration is a multi-hop inferencing task that requires chaining together KB facts which can form an explanation for the correct answer to a question. Ranking each fact individually in the KB is not enough to solve such a task and requires deep probing into finding links between explanation facts, question and its answer. To this end, we devised an ILP that can infer such links and score and rank a chain of explanation facts with the regression model. With the current system in place, we plan to generate first order logic based semantic graph structures of question, answer and explanation facts and use the alignment scores between them instead of direct phrasal entailment scores between constituents in the ILP model. We are also exploring leveraging information from more semantic resources like ConceptNet(Speer et al., 2016) and Framenet(Baker et al., 1998) instead of only WordNet based entailment scoring and ILP parameter tuning for improving regression ranking scores.

References

Tobias Achterberg. 2009. Scip: solving constraint integer programs. *Mathematical Programming Computation*, 1(1):1–41.

Collin F Baker, Charles J Fillmore, and John B Lowe. 1998. The berkeley framenet project. In *36th Annual Meeting of the Association for Computational Linguistics and 17th International Conference on Computational Linguistics, Volume 1*, pages 86–90.

Peter Clark, Oren Etzioni, Tushar Khot, Ashish Sabharwal, Oyvind Tafjord, Peter D Turney, and Daniel Khashabi. 2016. Combining retrieval, statistics, and inference to answer elementary science questions. In *AAAI*, pages 2580–2586. Citeseer.

Peter Clark, Isaac Cowhey, Oren Etzioni, Tushar Khot, Ashish Sabharwal, Carissa Schoenick, and Oyvind Tafjord. 2018. Think you have solved question answering? try arc, the ai2 reasoning challenge. *arXiv preprint arXiv:1803.05457*.

Rajarshi Das, Ameya Godbole, Manzil Zaheer, Shehzaad Dhuliawala, and Andrew McCallum. 2019. Chains-of-reasoning at textgraphs 2019 shared task: Reasoning over chains of facts for explainable multi-hop inference. In *Proceedings of the Thirteenth Workshop on Graph-Based Methods for Natural Language Processing (TextGraphs-13)*, pages 101–117.

Peter Jansen and Dmitry Ustalov. 2020. TextGraphs 2020 Shared Task on Multi-Hop Inference for Explanation Regeneration. In *Proceedings of the Graph-based Methods for Natural Language Processing (TextGraphs)*. Association for Computational Linguistics.

Daniel Khashabi, Tushar Khot, Ashish Sabharwal, Peter Clark, Oren Etzioni, and Dan Roth. 2016. Question answering via integer programming over semi-structured knowledge. *arXiv preprint arXiv:1604.06076*.

Daniel Khashabi, Tushar Khot, Ashish Sabharwal, and Dan Roth. 2019. Question answering as global reasoning over semantic abstractions. *arXiv preprint arXiv:1906.03672*.

Tushar Khot, Ashish Sabharwal, and Peter Clark. 2017. Answering complex questions using open information extraction. *arXiv preprint arXiv:1704.05572*.

Rada Mihalcea and Paul Tarau. 2004. Textrank: Bringing order into text. In *Proceedings of the 2004 conference on empirical methods in natural language processing*, pages 404–411.

Todor Mihaylov, Peter Clark, Tushar Khot, and Ashish Sabharwal. 2018. Can a suit of armor conduct electricity? a new dataset for open book question answering. *arXiv preprint arXiv:1809.02789*.

Robyn Speer, Joshua Chin, and Catherine Havasi. 2016. Conceptnet 5.5: An open multilingual graph of general knowledge. *arXiv preprint arXiv:1612.03975*.

Alon Talmor and Jonathan Berant. 2018. The web as a knowledge-base for answering complex questions. *arXiv preprint arXiv:1803.06643*.

Alon Talmor, Jonathan Herzig, Nicholas Lourie, and Jonathan Berant. 2018. Commonsenseqa: A question answering challenge targeting commonsense knowledge. *arXiv preprint arXiv:1811.00937*.

Johannes Welbl, Pontus Stenetorp, and Sebastian Riedel. 2018. Constructing datasets for multi-hop reading comprehension across documents. *Transactions of the Association for Computational Linguistics*, 6:287–302.

Thomas Wolf, Lysandre Debut, Victor Sanh, Julien Chaumond, Clement Delangue, Anthony Moi, Pierric Cistac, Tim Rault, Rémi Louf, Morgan Funtowicz, Joe Davison, Sam Shleifer, Patrick von Platen, Clara Ma, Yacine Jernite, Julien Plu, Canwen Xu, Teven Le Scao, Sylvain Gugger, Mariama Drame, Quentin Lhoest, and Alexander M. Rush. 2019. Huggingface's transformers: State-of-the-art natural language processing. *ArXiv*, abs/1910.03771.

Zhengnan Xie, Sebastian Thiem, Jaycie Martin, Elizabeth Wainwright, Steven Marmorstein, and Peter Jansen. 2020. Worldtree v2: A corpus of science-domain structured explanations and inference patterns supporting multi-hop inference. In *Proceedings of The 12th Language Resources and Evaluation Conference*, pages 5456–5473.

Red Dragon AI at TextGraphs 2020 Shared Task:
LIT : LSTM-Interleaved Transformer for Multi-Hop
Explanation Ranking

Yew Ken Chia
Red Dragon AI
Singapore
ken@reddragon.ai

Sam Witteveen
Red Dragon AI
Singapore
sam@reddragon.ai

Martin Andrews
Red Dragon AI
Singapore
martin@reddragon.ai

Abstract

Explainable question answering for science questions is a challenging task that requires multi-hop inference over a large set of fact sentences. To counter the limitations of methods that view each query-document pair in isolation, we propose the LSTM-Interleaved Transformer which incorporates cross-document interactions for improved multi-hop ranking. The LIT architecture can leverage prior ranking positions in the re-ranking setting. Our model is competitive on the current leaderboard for the TextGraphs 2020 shared task, achieving a test-set MAP of 0.5607, and would have gained third place had we submitted before the competition deadline. Our code implementation is made available at https://github.com/mdda/worldtree_corpus/tree/textgraphs_2020

1 Introduction

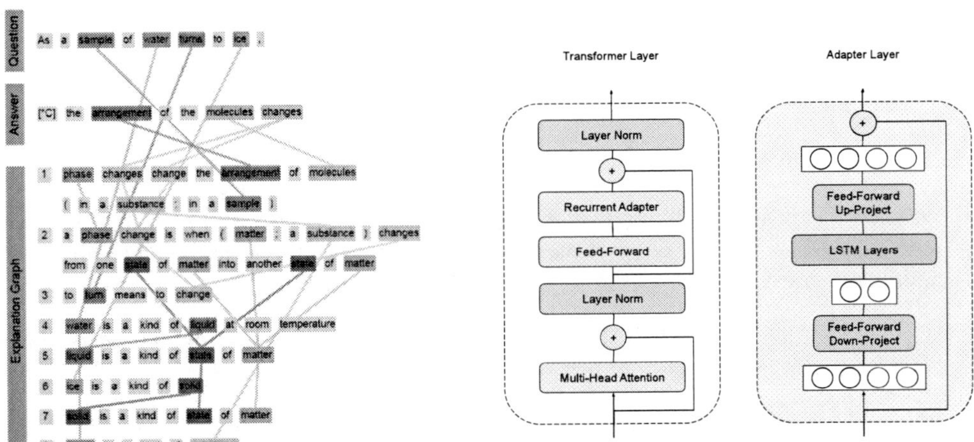

Figure 1: Example of a single question and ground-truth explanation facts in WorldTree V2 dataset.

Figure 2: Proposed LIT architecture

Complex question answering often requires reasoning over many evidence documents, which is known as multi-hop inference. Existing datasets such as Wikihop (Welbl et al., 2018), OpenBookQA (Mihaylov et al., 2018), QASC (Khot et al., 2020), are limited due to artificial questions and short aggregation, requiring less than 3 facts. In comparison, TextGraphs (Jansen and Ustalov, 2020) uses WorldTree V2 (Xie et al., 2020) which is the largest available dataset that requires combining an average of 6 and up to 16 facts in order to generate an explanation for complex science questions. The dataset contains 5k questions that require knowledge in core science as well as common sense. Figure 1 shows

This work is licensed under a Creative Commons Attribution 4.0 International License. License details: http://creativecommons.org/licenses/by/4.0/.

Proceedings of the Graph-based Methods for Natural Language Processing (TextGraphs), pages 115–120
Barcelona, Spain (Online), December 13, 2020

an example question from the WorldTree dataset. The evaluation for this dataset is framed as a ranking objective over a large set of 9k science facts, and models are scored based on the MAP metric over the predicted rank ordering. Multi-hop inference encounters significant noise or "distraction" documents in the process and this challenge is known as semantic drift (Fried et al., 2015). Compared to WorldTree V1 (Jansen et al., 2018), WorldTree V2 has more examples but is more challenging as the larger pool of science facts presents a greater risk of semantic drift.

Neural information retrieval models such as DPR (Karpukhin et al., 2020), RAG (Lewis et al., 2020), and ColBERT (Khattab and Zaharia, 2020) that assume query-document independence use a language model to generate sentence representations for the query and document separately. The advantage of this late-interaction approach is efficient inference as the sentence representations can be computed beforehand and optimized lookup methods such as FAISS (Johnson et al., 2017) exist for this purpose. However, the late-interaction compromises on deeper semantic understanding possible with language models. Early-interaction approaches such as TFR-BERT (Han et al., 2020) instead concatenate the query and document before generating a unified sentence representation. This approach is more computationally expensive but is attractive for re-ranking over a limited number of documents. However, the previous approaches consider each query-document pair in isolation. This forgoes any cross-document interaction which can leverage additional knowledge sources or benefit the ranking objective. Other work (Pasumarthi et al., 2019; Pobrotyn et al., 2020; Sun and Duh, 2020) facilitate cross-document interactions through self-attention mechanisms. However, the cross-document interaction is only applied after the feature extraction step and cannot leverage the language understanding potential in earlier language model layers.

The most straightforward loss for the document ranking objective is Binary Crossentropy where each document is ranked according to the binary classification probability of being within the gold explanation set. However, there have been recent progress in differentiable losses to optimize directly for the ranking objective (Wang et al., 2018; Revaud et al., 2019; Engilberge et al., 2019). In this work, we also compare the benefits of each loss for multi-hop ranking.

The main contributions of this work are:

1. We show that conventional information retrieval-based methods are still a strong baseline and propose I-BM25, an iterative retrieval method that improves inference speed and recall by emulating multi-hop retrieval.

2. We propose a hierarchical LSTM-interleaved transformer (LIT) architecture that maximizes early cross-document interactions for improved multi-hop re-ranking.

3. We provide empirical comparisons of training with different loss functions and show that Binary Crossentropy loss is simple yet may outperform differentiable ranking losses.

2 Models

Three different system architectures are described here, with overall schemes illustrated in Figure 3 for comparison.

2.1 Iterative BM25 Retrieval

Chia et al (2019) showed that conventional information retrieval methods can be a strong baseline when modified to suit the multi-hop inference objective. However, this method is limited due to computationally expensive inference and sensitivity to noise and semantic drift. We propose an iterative retrieval method 'I-BM25' that performs inference in a fraction of the time and reduces semantic drift, resulting in a even stronger baseline retrieval method. For preprocessing, we use spaCy (Honnibal and Montani, 2017) for tokenization, lemmatization and stopword removal. Compared to Chia et al (2019) which

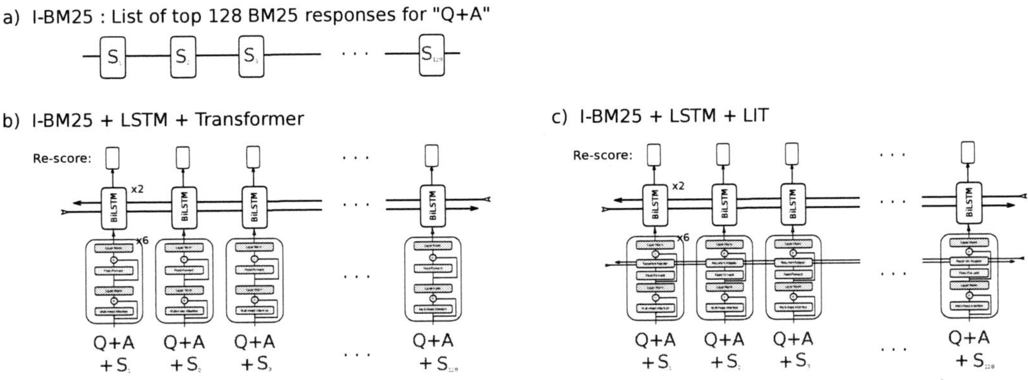

Figure 3: Overview of 3 architectures

processes each new candidate one at a time, I-BM25 processes 2^n candidates in the n-th iteration. The algorithm is as follows:

1. Sparse document vectors are pre-computed for all questions and explanation candidates.

2. For each question, the closest n explanation candidates by cosine proximity are selected and their vectors are aggregated by a max operation. The aggregated vector is down-scaled and used to update the query vector through a max operation.

3. The previous step is repeated for increasing values of n until there are no candidate explanations remaining.

2.2 LSTM-After Transformer for Re-Ranking

BERT is a pre-trained language model that is widely adapted and fine-tuned for many downstream NLP tasks. Due to computational constraints, we use DistilBERT (Sanh et al., 2020) which has 40% fewer parameters and comparable performance. In sequence-level tasks such as text classification, a [CLS] token is a special token inserted at the front of the sequence. The latent representation of the token is passed to a feed-forward network for prediction. We append an LSTM (Hochreiter and Schmidhuber, 1997) module with 2 layers that operate on the [CLS] vectors of the last layer of BERT (similar in principle to McCann et al (2018)). This hierarchical structure allows the transformer to perform cross-document reasoning and knowledge reference. The LSTM layers enable the model to be rank-aware when used in the re-ranking setting. For re-ranking, the top 128 predictions from I-BM25 are passed to the LSTM-After Transformer which performs binary classification for each document.

2.3 LSTM-Interleaved Transformer for Re-Ranking

TextGraphs is a challenging task which requires complex multi-hop reasoning, but information retrieval methods are surprisingly strong baselines. To enhance cross-document interaction and leverage language representations in earlier transformer layers, we interleave adapters (Houlsby et al., 2019) into the architecture which are recurrent instead of merely feed-forward. The LSTM-adapter modules in Figure 2 operate on the latent representation at the [CLS] position of each document *at each layer* of the transformer. After each transformer layer, the [CLS] latent representations for each input document are first down-projected, passed to the LSTM layers and finally up-projected and fed into the next transformer layer. Compared to (Houlsby et al., 2019), the LIT architecture is fully trainable and makes the transformer architecture more expressive by enabling cross-document reasoning which was previously not possible. Apart from LSTM, we also tested GCN (Kipf and Welling, 2017) and Self-Attention (Parikh et al., 2016) layers but had limited success in achieving competitive performance from them.

3   Experiments

Model	Dev MAP	Test MAP
BM25	0.4615	
Iterative BM25 (Chia et al., 2019)	0.4704	
I-BM25	0.4861	0.4745
I-BM25 + LSTM + Transformer	0.5470	0.5294
I-BM25 + LIT	0.5680	0.5607

Table 1: Main score comparison on WorldTree V2 dataset

Table 1 shows that I-BM25 is a strong information retrieval method that can be a drop-in replacement for previous information retrieval methods. The results also show the advantage of the LIT architecture in interleaving LSTM layers between transformer layers, rather than after the last transformer layer.

Loss Function	Dev MAP
LambdaLoss	0.4970
APLoss	0.5187
Binary Crossentropy	0.5680

Table 2: Loss function comparison on WorldTree V2 dataset

The results of optimization using 3 different loss objectives are shown in Table 2. Surprisingly, the direct ranking-loss oriented objectives were less effective in reducing the final evaluation MAP score, which is potentially due to the bucketisation approximation used in the APLoss calculations not being appropriately pre-scaled in our experiments. In this case, the training may require different hyper-parameters to converge optimally. Another potential explanation is that these ranking losses may be sub-optimal (when used as a training objective) when many documents have very similar underlying scores which is the case here.

3.1   Notes

Further to our experience last year, we included preprocessing steps to isolate the branching 'combo' statements (which essentially contain OR clauses between different noun phrases, for instance). This step remains in our codebase, but we did not exploit it fully, since a full treatment would require the isolation of which 'combo branch' is taken by each gold statement in the training set.

4   Discussion

Other architectures that we explored included Graph neural network (GNN) methods, however we had insufficient time to tune these for the multi-hop explanation task herein. Surprisingly, our simple LSTM methods (which can be viewed as a linear graph that performs message-passing along the list of results ordered by the I-BM25 method) already provided a competitive method. We estimate that next year's competition will require the use of graph-based methods, due to their greater expressive power.

5   Conclusion

The LIT architecture is a simple yet powerful adaptation of the Transformer architecture to learn better cross-document interactions for multi-hop ranking. The structure can be easily integrated with any transformer language model to enable cross-referencing of knowledge statements and improved ranking performance. For example, LIT can be a drop-in encoder for other multi-hop question answering datasets such as HotPotQA (Yang et al., 2018). When applied to the challenging WorldTree V2 dataset, LIT achieves competitive performance with current state-of-the-art models despite a smaller footprint. We envision that this architecture can be beneficial to many NLP tasks which require multi-hop reasoning over documents.

References

Yew Ken Chia, Sam Witteveen, and Martin Andrews. 2019. Red dragon AI at TextGraphs 2019 shared task: Language model assisted explanation generation. In *Proceedings of the Thirteenth Workshop on Graph-Based Methods for Natural Language Processing (TextGraphs-13)*, pages 85–89, Hong Kong, November. Association for Computational Linguistics.

Martin Engilberge, Louis Chevallier, Patrick Pérez, and Matthieu Cord. 2019. Sodeep: a sorting deep net to learn ranking loss surrogates. In *Proceedings of the IEEE Conference on Computer Vision and Pattern Recognition*, pages 10792–10801.

Daniel Fried, Peter Jansen, Gustave Hahn-Powell, Mihai Surdeanu, and Peter Clark. 2015. Higher-order lexical semantic models for non-factoid answer reranking. *Transactions of the Association for Computational Linguistics*, 3:197–210.

Shuguang Han, Xuanhui Wang, Mike Bendersky, and Marc Najork. 2020. Learning-to-rank with bert in tf-ranking. *arXiv preprint arXiv:2004.08476*.

Sepp Hochreiter and Jürgen Schmidhuber. 1997. Long short-term memory. *Neural Computation*, 9(8):1735–1780.

Matthew Honnibal and Ines Montani. 2017. spaCy 2: Natural language understanding with Bloom embeddings, convolutional neural networks and incremental parsing. To appear.

Neil Houlsby, Andrei Giurgiu, Stanislaw Jastrzebski, Bruna Morrone, Quentin de Laroussilhe, Andrea Gesmundo, Mona Attariyan, and Sylvain Gelly. 2019. Parameter-efficient transfer learning for nlp. In *ICML*.

Peter Jansen and Dmitry Ustalov. 2020. TextGraphs 2020 Shared Task on Multi-Hop Inference for Explanation Regeneration. In *Proceedings of the Graph-based Methods for Natural Language Processing (TextGraphs)*. Association for Computational Linguistics.

Peter Jansen, Elizabeth Wainwright, Steven Marmorstein, and Clayton Morrison. 2018. WorldTree: A Corpus of Explanation Graphs for Elementary Science Questions supporting Multi-hop Inference. In Nicoletta Calzolari (Conference chair), Khalid Choukri, Christopher Cieri, Thierry Declerck, Sara Goggi, Koiti Hasida, Hitoshi Isahara, Bente Maegaard, Joseph Mariani, Hélène Mazo, Asuncion Moreno, Jan Odijk, Stelios Piperidis, and Takenobu Tokunaga, editors, *Proceedings of the Eleventh International Conference on Language Resources and Evaluation (LREC 2018)*, Miyazaki, Japan, May 7-12, 2018. European Language Resources Association (ELRA).

Jeff Johnson, Matthijs Douze, and Hervé Jégou. 2017. Billion-scale similarity search with gpus. *arXiv preprint arXiv:1702.08734*.

Vladimir Karpukhin, Barlas Oğuz, Sewon Min, Ledell Wu, Sergey Edunov, Danqi Chen, and Wen-tau Yih. 2020. Dense passage retrieval for open-domain question answering. *arXiv preprint arXiv:2004.04906*.

Omar Khattab and Matei Zaharia. 2020. Colbert: Efficient and effective passage search via contextualized late interaction over bert. *arXiv preprint arXiv:2004.12832*.

Tushar Khot, Peter Clark, Michal Guerquin, Peter Jansen, and Ashish Sabharwal. 2020. Qasc: A dataset for question answering via sentence composition. In *AAAI*, pages 8082–8090.

Thomas Kipf and M. Welling. 2017. Semi-supervised classification with graph convolutional networks. *ArXiv*, abs/1609.02907.

Patrick Lewis, Ethan Perez, Aleksandara Piktus, Fabio Petroni, Vladimir Karpukhin, Naman Goyal, Heinrich Küttler, Mike Lewis, Wen-tau Yih, Tim Rocktäschel, et al. 2020. Retrieval-augmented generation for knowledge-intensive nlp tasks. *arXiv preprint arXiv:2005.11401*.

Bryan McCann, Nitish Shirish Keskar, Caiming Xiong, and Richard Socher. 2018. The natural language decathlon: Multitask learning as question answering.

Todor Mihaylov, Peter Clark, Tushar Khot, and Ashish Sabharwal. 2018. Can a suit of armor conduct electricity? a new dataset for open book question answering. In *EMNLP*.

Ankur P. Parikh, Oscar Täckström, Dipanjan Das, and Jakob Uszkoreit. 2016. A decomposable attention model for natural language inference. *ArXiv*, abs/1606.01933.

Rama Kumar Pasumarthi, Xuanhui Wang, Michael Bendersky, and Marc Najork. 2019. Self-attentive document interaction networks for permutation equivariant ranking.

Przemysław Pobrotyn, Tomasz Bartczak, Mikołaj Synowiec, Radosław Białobrzeski, and Jarosław Bojar. 2020. Context-aware learning to rank with self-attention. *arXiv preprint arXiv:2005.10084.*

Jerome Revaud, Jon Almazán, Rafael S Rezende, and Cesar Roberto de Souza. 2019. Learning with average precision: Training image retrieval with a listwise loss. In *Proceedings of the IEEE International Conference on Computer Vision*, pages 5107–5116.

Victor Sanh, Lysandre Debut, Julien Chaumond, and Thomas Wolf. 2020. Distilbert, a distilled version of bert: smaller, faster, cheaper and lighter.

Shuo Sun and Kevin Duh. 2020. Modeling document interactions for learning to rank with regularized self-attention. *arXiv preprint arXiv:2005.03932.*

Xuanhui Wang, Cheng Li, Nadav Golbandi, Michael Bendersky, and Marc Najork. 2018. The lambdaloss framework for ranking metric optimization. In *Proceedings of the 27th ACM International Conference on Information and Knowledge Management*, pages 1313–1322.

Johannes Welbl, Pontus Stenetorp, and Sebastian Riedel. 2018. Constructing datasets for multi-hop reading comprehension across documents. *Transactions of the Association for Computational Linguistics*, 6:287–302.

Zhengnan Xie, Sebastian Thiem, Jaycie Martin, Elizabeth Wainwright, Steven Marmorstein, and Peter Jansen. 2020. WorldTree v2: A corpus of science-domain structured explanations and inference patterns supporting multi-hop inference. In *Proceedings of the 12th Language Resources and Evaluation Conference*, pages 5456–5473, Marseille, France, May. European Language Resources Association.

Z. Yang, Peng Qi, Saizheng Zhang, Yoshua Bengio, William W. Cohen, R. Salakhutdinov, and Christopher D. Manning. 2018. Hotpotqa: A dataset for diverse, explainable multi-hop question answering. *ArXiv*, abs/1809.09600.

Association for Computational Linguistics
209 N. Eighth Street
Stroudsburg, Pennsylvania 18360

ISBN 978-1-7138-2840-2